Twentieth-Century American Fashion

Dress, Body, Culture

Series Editor: **Joanne B. Eicher**, *Regents' Professor, University of Minnesota*

Advisory Board:
Ruth Barnes, *Ashmolean Museum, University of Oxford*
Helen Callaway, *CCCRW, University of Oxford*
James Hall, *University of Illinois at Chicago*
Beatrice Medicine, *California State University, Northridge*
Ted Polhemus, *Curator, "Street Style" Exhibition, Victoria and Albert Museum*
Griselda Pollock, *University of Leeds*
Valerie Steele, *The Museum at the Fashion Institute of Technology*
Lou Taylor, *University of Brighton*
John Wright, *University of Minnesota*

Books in this provocative series seek to articulate the connections between culture and dress which is defined here in its broadest possible sense as any modification or supplement to the body. Interdisciplinary in approach, the series highlights the dialogue between identity and dress, cosmetics, coiffure and body alternations as manifested in practices as varied as plastic surgery, tattooing, and ritual scarification. The series aims, in particular, to analyze the meaning of dress in relation to popular culture and gender issues and includes works grounded in anthropology, sociology, history, art history, literature, and folklore.

ISSN: 1360-466X

Previously published in the Series

Helen Bradley Foster, *"New Raiments of Self": African American Clothing in the Antebellum South*
Claudine Griggs, *S/he: Changing Sex and Changing Clothes*
Michaele Thurgood Haynes, *Dressing Up Debutantes: Pageantry and Glitz in Texas*
Anne Brydon and Sandra Niessen, *Consuming Fashion: Adorning the Transnational Body*
Dani Cavallaro and Alexandra Warwick, *Fashioning the Frame: Boundaries, Dress and the Body*
Judith Perani and Norma H. Wolff, *Cloth, Dress and Art Patronage in Africa*
Linda B. Arthur, *Religion, Dress and the Body*
Paul Jobling, *Fashion Spreads: Word and Image in Fashion Photography*
Fadwa El Guindi, *Veil: Modesty, Privacy and Resistance*
Thomas S. Abler, *Hinterland Warriors and Military Dress: European Empires and Exotic Uniforms*
Linda Welters, *Folk Dress in Europe and Anatolia: Beliefs about Protection and Fertility*
Kim K.P. Johnson and Sharron J. Lennon, *Appearance and Power*
Barbara Burman, *The Culture of Sewing*
Annette Lynch, *Dress, Gender and Cultural Change*
Antonia Young, *Women Who Become Men*
David Muggleton, *Inside Subculture: The Postmodern Meaning of Style*
Nicola White, *Reconstructing Italian Fashion: America and the Development of the Italian Fashion Industry*
Brian J. McVeigh, *Wearing Ideology: The Uniformity of Self-Presentation in Japan*
Shaun Cole, *Don We Now Our Gay Apparel: Gay Men's Dress in the Twentieth Century*
Kate Ince, *Orlan: Millennial Female*
Nicola White and Ian Griffiths, *The Fashion Business: Theory, Practice, Image*
Ali Guy, Eileen Green and Maura Banim, *Through the Wardrobe: Women's Relationships with their Clothes*
Linda B. Arthur, *Undressing Religion: Commitment and Conversion from a Cross-Cultural Perspective*
William J.F. Keenan, *Dressed to Impress: Looking the Part*
Joanne Entwistle and Elizabeth Wilson, *Body Dressing*
Leigh Summers, *Bound to Please: A History of the Victorian Corset*
Paul Hodkinson, *Goth: Identity, Style and Subculture*
Michael Carter, *Fashion Classics from Carlyle to Barthes*
Sandra Niessen, Ann Marie Leshkowich and Carla Jones, *Re-Orienting Fashion: The Globalization of Asian Dress*
Kim K. P. Johnson, Susan J.Torntore and Joanne B. Eicher, *Fashion Foundations: Early Writings on Fashion and Dress*
Helen Bradley Foster and Donald Clay Johnson, *Wedding Dress Across Cultures*
Eugenia Paulicelli, *Fashion under Fascism: Beyond the Black Shirt*
Charlotte Suthrell, *Unzipping Gender: Sex, Cross-Dressing and Culture*
Yuniya Kawamura, *The Japanese Revolution in Paris Fashion*
Ruth Barcan, *Nudity: A Cultural Anatomy*
Samantha Holland, *Alternative Femininities: Body, Age and Identity*
Alexandra Palmer and Hazel Clark, *Old Clothes, New Looks: Second Hand Fashion*
Yuniya Kawamura, *Fashion-ology: An Introduction to Fashion Studies*
Regina Root, *The Latin American Fashion Reader*

DRESS, BODY CULTURE

Twentieth-Century American Fashion

Edited by
Linda Welters and
Patricia A. Cunningham

Oxford • New York

English edition
First published in 2005 by
Berg
Editorial offices:
First Floor, Angel Court, 81 St Clements Street, Oxford OX4 1AW, UK
175 Fifth Avenue, New York, NY 10010, USA

Paperback edition reprinted 2006, 2007

Berg is the imprint of Oxford International Publishers Ltd.

Library of Congress Cataloging-in-Publication Data
Twentieth-century American fashion / edited by Linda Welters and
Patricia A. Cunningham.
    p. cm. — (Dress, body, culture)
  Includes bibliographical references and index.
  ISBN 1-84520-072-1 (cloth) — ISBN 1-84520-073-X (pbk.)
1.   Clothing and dress — United States — History — 20th century. 2.
Fashion — United States — History — 20th century. 3.   Popular culture —
United States — History — 20th century. I. Welters, Linda. II.
Cunningham, Patricia A. III. Series.

GT615.T94 2005
391′.00973′0904 — dc22   2004030880

British Library Cataloguing-in-Publication Data
A catalogue record for this book is available from the British Library.

ISBN-13 978 1 84520 072 5 (Cloth)
        978 1 84520 073 2 (Paper)

ISBN-10 1 84520 072 1 (Cloth)
        1 84520 073 X (Paper)

Typeset by Avocet Typeset, Chilton, Aylesbury, Bucks
Printed in the United Kingdom by Biddles Ltd, King's Lynn.

www.bergpublishers.com

Contents

Contents

Figures

Acknowledgments

This book is the result of true teamwork. The editors are grateful to the contributors who accepted our invitation to write chapters for this volume on American fashion. They responded to our suggestions promptly and gracefully.

We also extend appreciation to friends, relatives and colleagues who offered advice, expertise and encouragement. Particular appreciation is extended to Craig Hassler, Dana Sargent Nemeth, Art Mead, Margaret Ordoñez, James Welters, and Whitney Blausen. Their insights helped shape the final manuscript. To the members of graduate thesis committees from which some of the authors benefited, we say thanks.

The authors are indebted to the museums, historical societies and libraries that allowed Berg to publish photographs of objects in their collections, as well as to individuals who supplied one-of-a-kind images. The Bettmann-Corbis archive graciously provided images for two of the chapters, and to them we are doubly grateful.

Notes on Contributors

Suzanne Baldaia is an Associate Professor at Johnson & Wales University in Providence, Rhode Island. Her research interests are in the historic, socio-cultural, and aesthetic aspects of dress.

Sandra Stansbery Buckland is Associate Professor at the University of Akron. She completed her PhD at the Ohio State University.

Robin Chandler is a visual artist, a sociologist, a published author on arts and culture, and a senior faculty member in the Department of African American Studies at Northeastern University in Boston. She is a director of the Hip-hop Tutorial Project, a Fulbright Scholar, and a National Science Foundation grant recipient.

Nuri Chandler-Smith is a Harvard M.Ed., a development associate at Artists for Humanity, and Executive Director of Blackout Boston, a spoken word poetry collective.

Patricia A. Cunningham, PhD, is a historian of dress. She is on the faculty at the Ohio State University. A recent publication is *Reforming Women's Fashion: Politics, Health and Art* (Kent State University Press, 2003).

Susan L. Hannel is an Assistant Professor in the Department of Textiles, Fashion Merchandising and Design at the University of Rhode Island. She earned her PhD at the Ohio State University.

Rebecca J. Kelly is textile conservator at the Preservation Society of Newport County in Newport, Rhode Island. She has a BA in Art History and an MS in Textiles, Fashion Merchandising and Design from the University of Rhode Island. Her thesis investigated costume in the paintings of Elizabeth Vigée Le Brun.

Amy Lund is a handweaver. She completed a master's thesis at the University of Rhode Island. Formerly she was an assistant curator of textiles at the Allentown Art Museum.

Heather Mangine completed her PhD in Clothing and Textiles from the Ohio State University in 2005. Her area of interest is color science.

Andrew Reilly received his PhD in Clothing and Textiles from the Ohio State University in 2004. He is an Assistant Professor at Northern Illinois University.

Deborah Saville is a master's degree candidate at the University of Rhode Island. She was most recently employed in the Department of Costume and Textiles at the Museum of Art, Rhode Island School of Design.

Patricia Campbell Warner is a Professor of Theater at the University of Massachusetts-Amherst. She has written extensively on fashion and sports.

Linda Welters is Professor of Textiles, Fashion Merchandising and Design at the University of Rhode Island. She has published on archaeological textiles, the material culture of New England, and European folk dress. She edits *Dress*, the scholarly journal of the Costume Society of America.

The Americanization of Fashion

Linda Welters and Patricia A. Cunningham

For much of its history, the United States has looked largely to England and France for fashion leadership. It took many cultural changes including an Industrial Revolution, several wars, and the development of movies, television, and popular music to create a unique 'American' style. While general histories of twentieth-century fashion touch on developments in the United States and Canada, their focus is on fashion as it occurred in Europe (Baudot 1999; Ewing 1992; Lehnert 2000; Mendes and de la Haye 1999). This collection of essays brings together recent work on the history of twentieth-century fashion in the United States. While there are many ideas that influenced the Americanization of fashion besides the ones featured in this book, this collection highlights leading elements in American culture.

Previous studies regarding the development of distinctly American dress, such as *Dress and Popular Culture* (Cunningham and Lab 1991) and *Dress in American Culture* (Cunningham and Lab 1993), offer views of American style during earlier time periods and consider the relationship of fashion to popular culture and media. Both of these books offer students and scholars useful and unique interpretations of fashion in America. Yet, few fashion history texts focus on the 'Americanization' of dress during the twentieth century. This volume attempts to solve that problem by bringing together the research of a number of scholars who have studied phenomena unique to American life during this time. As a group, these chapters offer interpretations of American fashion that reveal how issues of class, race, gender, politics, war, business, art, literary movements, music, cinema and television affected fashion in the twentieth century, and in turn how fashion expressed American ideals, attitudes and social change.

As noted by Kidwell and Christman in *Suiting Everyone* (1974) and Cunningham and Lab in *Dress in American Culture* (1993), the

Americanization of fashion began long before the dawn of the twentieth century. Americans in the early years of the Republic often sought to distinguish themselves by revealing their belief in democracy and liberty through their clothing. As the nineteenth century progressed, America's aspiration for decent clothing for everyone was realized through advances in mass manufacturing. America excelled at producing vast quantities of basic fabrics such as calico and denim that could be made into serviceable clothing for the country's expanding population. The fashion industry grew with increasing numbers of manufacturers, mail order companies, retail outlets, and print sources for fashion news. By the 1890s half of the male population wore ready-made suits. Although women's clothing did not become truly ready-made until the twentieth century, many articles of dress were mass produced. Women's reform movements promoted the need for less restrictive, more comfortable and reasonable dress styles which materialized with the so-called 'Gibson Girls' of the 1890s, who wore simple skirts and blouses. From these beginnings came the reputation of American dressing being synonymous with well-made basic styles. Later, American designers like Claire McCardell, Norman Norell, and Bonnie Cashin became known for simple, practical clothes that fit the active lifestyle of American women (Milbank 1989).

The general change in American culture from an agrarian society to one based on manufacturing, retailing and commerce affected everyone. The result was the development of an economy that became dependent on consumerism. Periodically in America's history, Americans have expended much effort to display their wealth through personal appearance. This book begins and ends with the notion of conspicuous consumption. During the Gilded Age, the nation's social elite dressed in expensive, custom-made clothing to distinguish themselves from the growing middle class. The 1990s saw hip-hop moguls spending large amounts of money on jewelry, clothes, cars and entertainment.

The development of a consumer economy sometimes met with resistance as revealed in the emergence of subcultures in pockets of America. In rejecting the status quo that supported the consumer economy, these subcultures created their own look to signify their separateness. Elements of these subcultural fashions often merged with mainstream fashion. For instance, the Greenwich Village bohemians discussed in Chapter 3 eventually influenced young women in other parts of the country to bob their hair and shorten their skirts. Today, America's voracious appetite for consumer goods has created a market for fashion products that manufacturers around the globe seek to enter.

Concomitant with consumerism is the creation of influential shopping venues. In the mid nineteenth century, the department store developed in America, England and France. In the United States, leading department stores became powerful interpreters of what it meant to be fashionable. Department stores, as well as specialty stores, were critical disseminators of fashion all across the country where customers relied on them to provide clothes that met the latest standards for style. Mention of department stores is made in almost every chapter of this book. The authors discuss shopping at Altman's, Lord & Taylor and Filene's Basement. But more importantly, they reveal the influence of these stores in creating a desire for fashion; for example, Bonwit Teller made the Greenwich Village 'bohemian' look available in its store, and Macy's provided its customers with 50,000 copies of Joan Crawford's *Letty Lynton* dress. Furthermore, the authors bring to light the Onondaga Silk Company's collaboration with department stores to market their 'American Artist Print Series' and Dorothy Shaver's promotion of the 'American look' at Lord & Taylor (Webber-Hanchett 2003).

Also important to the development of American style is the presentation of fashion in print sources by American publishers. *Godey's Lady's Book*, published in Philadelphia from 1830 to 1898, informed generations of American women about the latest styles from Paris. Its editor, Sarah Josepha Hale, dispensed advice to American women to dress within the family's financial means, and to be practical about clothing choices. The American penchant for simple, practical styles continued into the twentieth century, although *Godey's* and its competitors fell out of favor. In their place came the glossy fashion magazine. *Vogue*, published by Condé Nast, and *Harper's Bazaar*, from the Hearst Corporation, became the leading fashion magazines for consumers. Over the years, their powerful editors – Edna Woolman Chase, Carmel Snow, Diana Vreeland, and Anna Wintour – helped shape American notions of fashionability and, in conjunction with department stores, they fueled consumer desire. Chapter 9 illustrates how *Harper's Bazaar* used the space race between the US and the Soviet Union to promote fashion in a modern, up-to-the-minute manner.

Although Americans were leaders in the production of factory-made clothing, they looked to Europe for design inspiration. American manufacturers had developed a highly efficient system of copying the best that Europe had to offer in just a few weeks' time. Paul Poiret, the originator of the tunic dresses so popular in the years before the First World War, was shocked to see how quickly his styles were copied by American manufacturers without payment of royalties (Troy 2003). There were, however, a few exceptions to the domination of Paris such as New York's Jessie

Franklin Turner whose tea gowns were highly sought after by fashionable women (Coleman 1998) and MDC Crawford's 1916 'Designed in America' campaign (Whitley 1998). (Crawford was art editor at *Women's Wear*, the precursor to the influential American trade paper *Women's Wear Daily*.)

In Chapter 6, Sandra Buckland shows how the German occupation of Paris during the Second World War forced American manufacturers to look within US borders for capable designers. By 1947, as discussed in Chapter 7, the Onondaga Silk Company was able to collaborate with American fashion designers to create dresses for the 'American Artist Print Series.' Many American designer names and brand names became household words during the second half of the twentieth century: for example, 'Calvin's' meant jeans designed by Calvin Klein while 'Levi's' indicated jeans manufactured by the Levi Strauss Company of San Francisco. By the year 2000, numerous American designers were internationally recognized for their creativity (e.g., Oscar de la Renta, Marc Jacobs) while manufacturers of branded merchandise were known for quality fabrics and construction (e.g., Ralph Lauren's Polo line).

Fashion is connected to American politics in a variety of ways. As the fashion industry grew, it became a vital part of the economy. Politicians, such as New York City's mayor Fiorello LaGuardia, saw how much fashion brought in to the city coffers; he helped grow the domestic fashion industry during the Second World War as discussed in Chapter 6. In the 1970s, women adapted suit styles worn by businessmen in an attempt to break barriers in the workplace and become equally employed. In the 1990s, hip-hop fashion moguls turned the established fashion industry on its ear when they founded their own companies. For instance, FUBU (For Us By Us) is a highly successful manufacturer of men's and women's casual wear that was founded by four African Americans in Queens, New York in 1992.

Class is an important aspect of American life; it affects and is affected by fashion. The United States, often described as a melting pot, is in reality comprised of many ethnic and racial groups. Since appearance is used to signify identity, fashion becomes an important tool to say who you are in America. American society is described as an open-class society. It is easier to cross class lines in the United States than in older European societies with their long histories of aristocracy. Class is often equated with wealth in the US. Chapter 2 offers a look at how wealthy Americans, both old-money families and newly wealthy industrialists, lived and dressed during the Gilded Age. Americans see wealth (and class) as obtainable through education and hard work. Thus, in the 1970s Americans observed the importance of professional business attire to 'getting ahead' and followed the advice dispensed by John Molloy in his 'dress for success' books as seen in Chapter 10.

Race is another component of American fashion. African Americans, Native Americans, Mexicans, Cubans and other Latinos inspired many styles in the twentieth century. Such styles often emanated from the music or entertainment world. As Hannel discusses in Chapter 4, the style of Josephine Baker took Paris by storm in the 1920s. Dizzy Gillespie, the famous bebopper, popularized berets, goatees and horn-rimmed glasses among jazz aficionados as seen in Chapter 8. Perhaps most influential of all is the hip-hop style adopted by scores of American youth both in the US and abroad, a style that developed out of African American/Latino music.

Fashion is often thought of as a feminine preoccupation. This book, like many others, addresses women's fashion more than men's fashion. With its rapid changes, women's fashion seems better able to visualize the shifts in social and cultural norms. Nevertheless, four chapters in this book focus on men's styles in America: the beat look discussed in Chapter 8, the 'dress for success' movement in Chapter 10, the casual elegance of the two male leads in *Miami Vice* in Chapter 11, and the hip-hop styles in Chapter 12.

Art and literary movements, considered to be 'high culture,' inspired fashion as noted in Chapters 3, 7, 8 and 9. Like fashion design, American arts and letters suffered from an inferiority complex in the shadow of Europe. Writers and intellectuals who congregated in Greenwich Village before the onset of the First World War created their own style to signify their left-wing leanings. America's belief in itself as a nation of creators is seen in the adaptation of paintings from American realists for textiles by Onondaga in the 1940s. Similarly, writers of the beat generation developed free-flowing methods of writing poetry and prose that helped define the complexities of American life in the 1950s and create an awareness of anti-establishment values that spawned the hippie culture a decade later. Photographers, such as Richard Avedon, shaped artistic interpretations of fashion for readers of top American fashion magazines as discussed in Chapter 9.

Popular culture – movies, television, music – is a vital part of the American scene, and increasingly influences culture around the world. Jazz, the uniquely American musical form that was born in New Orleans around 1900, inspired the Jazz Age fashions and fabrics discussed by Hannel in Chapter 3. Styles worn by jazz musicians in the 1940s and 1950s – zoot suits, goatees, black glasses and berets – were appropriated by fans, eventually morphing into the beat look of the late 1950s save for the zoot suit. Hollywood movies have been a major source of style in the US since Theda

Bara strutted her vamp look as *Cleopatra* in 1917. Warner shows just how influential the movies could be on sports styles in Chapter 5. In Chapter 11, Cunningham et al. focus on MTV, *Miami Vice*, and *Dynasty* to illustrate the powerful influence of American television on fashion during the 1980s.

Casual and sporty looks are another feature associated with Americans. Griswold Lorillard is credited with wearing the first tuxedo, or dinner jacket, instead of more formal tails to the 1886 Autumn Ball in Tuxedo Park, New York (Constantino 1997). This was the beginning of a long history of firsts for wearing informal dress when rules of etiquette and custom would have opposed it. Americans love sports, both team sports such as baseball, football, and basketball and the individual sports of tennis, golf, and cycling. American manufacturers succeeded in creating attractive sport clothes early in the twentieth century. Schiaparelli and Dior both acknowledged American supremacy in sportswear. The stars who wore sport clothes on the silver screen helped show Americans how to imitate the California casual lifestyle by wearing these looks. American fashion became increasingly casual and sporty as the century progressed, in part because of the middle-class suburban lifestyle that first surfaced in the 1950s. In the 1990s, wearing a sports jersey and a baseball cap was the ultimate in style for hip-hoppers.

Not only do fashion histories tend to simplify and generalize what people wore in specific time periods, but they often focus only on the middle class or those who wore high fashion. The bias has been toward the urban or more sophisticated American. The reader should not be surprised to realize that the clothing worn by the bohemians of Greenwich Village, as noted in Chapter 3, was not the choice of most American men and women during the early decades of the twentieth century. Yet, the bohemians' dress is important because it was a precursor of the bobbed hair and knee-length skirts to come in the 1920s. Several of the chapters address the styles and looks emanating from working-class youth. For example, the black garb of the beats trickled up to haute couture, as seen in Yves St. Laurent's 'Beat' Collection.

All of the above aspects of American fashion are featured in the chapters that follow. While the editors have chosen to organize the chapters chronologically by decade they do so only for the sake of convenience. Readers should not believe that fashion suddenly changed at the beginning of each decade, for nothing could be farther from the truth. For instance, the hip-hop fashions so popular in the 1990s continue to be worn in the new millennium as depicted on the back cover.

Thus, the chapters together show the reader how Americans developed their own quintessential style that featured practical, well-made ready-to-wear looks. These looks were inspired by American life, particularly sports, but also music, movies, and television. The importance of subcultures in creating new styles that represented changing values is underscored in several chapters. These changes are reflected in the 'bricolage of fashion' that began to appear in the 1960s (Craik 1994).

Dress historians, students and instructors will find this book useful when seeking to flesh out an understanding of basic dress history. Each chapter commences with the editors' introductory comments on the relationship of the chapter topic to general fashion at the time. The chapters will provide supplemental readings for general histories of fashion that merely touch on the twentieth century, or provide additional points of view for a twentieth-century fashion text. Additionally, the book offers a forum for discussion and thought about American fashion and its function in American life and culture in the past, present and future.

While there were many influences on American dress during the twentieth century, the ones chosen for these essays tell a compelling story. The authors gleaned evidence for these essays from a variety of sources ranging from personal diaries to popular music. Popular culture sources include magazines, newspapers, advice books, movies, television, music videos, as well as literature and scholarly journals. These essays offer provocative thoughts about the development of a distinctive American style in fashion, and how American fashion shifted from being dependent on European style to influencing the world.

References

Baudot, F. (1999), *Fashion: The Twentieth Century*, New York: Universe.

Coleman, A. (1998), 'Jessie Franklin Turner: A Flight Path for Early Modern American Fashion,' *Dress* 25: 58–64.

Constantino, M. (1997), *Men's Fashion in the Twentieth Century*, New York: Costume and Fashion Press.

Craik, J. (1994), *The Face of Fashion: Cultural Studies in Fashion*, London: Routledge.

Cunningham, P.A. and S.V. Lab (1991), *Dress and Popular Culture*, Bowling Green, OH: Bowling Green State University Popular Press.

—— (1993), *Dress in American Culture*, Bowling Green, OH: Bowling Green State University Popular Press.

Ewing, E. (1992), *History of Twentieth Century Fashion*, 3rd ed., Lanham, MD: Barnes and Noble.

Kidwell, C.B. and M.C. Christman (1974), *Suiting Everyone: The Democratization of Clothing in America*, Washington, DC: Smithsonian Institution Press.

Lehnert, G. (2000), *A History of Fashion in the 20th Century*, Cologne, Germany: Könemann.

Mendes, V. and A. de la Haye (1999), *20th Century Fashion*, London: Thames and Hudson.

Milbank, C.R. (1989), *New York Fashion: The Evolution of American Style*, New York: Harry N. Abrams.

Troy, N. (2003). *Couture Culture: A Study in Modern Art and Fashion*, Cambridge, MA: The MIT Press.

Webber-Hanchett, T. (2003), 'Dorothy Shaver: Promoter of "The American Look"' *Dress 30*: 80–90.

Whitley, L.D. (1998), 'Morris De Camp Crawford and the "Designed in America" Campaign, 1916–1922,' in *Creating Textiles: Makers, Methods and Markets. Proceedings of the Sixth Biennial Symposium of the Textile Society of America.*

2

Fashion in the Gilded Age: A Profile of Newport's King Family

Rebecca J. Kelly

Editors' Introduction: By the turn of the twentieth century Americans had seen tremendous growth through industrialization. While this progress aided the development of a substantial middle class, there were still large numbers of European immigrants toiling to achieve the American dream. Great poverty existed in urban areas. Yet immigrants participated in fashion when they could; it was a means to 'become' American. Fashion in dress was still very much influenced by Paris, so much so that wealthy Americans frequently sailed to Europe to partake in the social scene as well as shop for French couture. Wealthy American families had developed a taste for luxury that propelled them to acquire beautiful homes and clothing, but also collections of art and a desire to support cultural institutions. Yet, as pointed out by Rebecca Kelly in this chapter, the changing lifestyles of the offspring of these wealthy families caused them to shift their values to become more frugal and egalitarian. Kelly relates the story of the Kings, an 'old money' family that had owned a summer home in fashionable Newport, Rhode Island since 1863. The mother, Ella King, had her clothes custom-made in Europe. Her daughter, Gwendolen, had been brought up to wear Paris couture; yet after she married she shopped in department stores. Gwendolen represents the 'new woman' who was not satisfied to be just a society matron. She promoted alternative education and played on a women's basketball team. The King family exemplifies the changes taking place in America, even at the upper levels of society.

The Gilded Age has typically been defined by the decadent and lavish standard of living enjoyed by America's most wealthy and influential families. Fantastic tales of how the Vanderbilts and Astors lived their lives and spent their fortunes are legendary. The Gilded Age in America lasted from 1870 to 1914. According to Alexis Gregory, there had never been a time of such 'extravagance and splendor' or 'a moment so golden with opportunity' for those who could 'seize the day' and become astonishingly 'rich and powerful'. The successful opportunists, the *nouveau riche*, built palatial houses and bought masterpieces to fill them. They traveled in high style, dressed fashionably and acquired expensive jewels (Gregory 1993: 10).

The lifestyle enjoyed by the wealthiest Americans during this period has often been explained within the parameters of Thorstein Veblen's economic theories. *The Theory of the Leisure Class*, published in 1899, first found popularity in literary circles where Veblen was celebrated as a satirist. *The Theory of the Leisure Class* is now perhaps best known for its cutting commentary on upper-class frivolity. Veblen's major catch phrases, 'conspicuous consumption,' 'conspicuous waste' and 'conspicuous leisure' have become synonymous with the spending habits and lifestyle enjoyed by America's social elite during the Gilded Age (Veblen 2001).

On the surface, the 'Old New York Society' and the newly wealthy industrialists who spent their summers in the fashionable seaside resort of Newport, Rhode Island appeared to be the ultimate perpetrators of behavior and spending as described by Veblen. Days in Newport, for the wealthy, were spent on extravagant yachts, or in stylish carriages. Women promenaded along the fashionable Bellevue Avenue bedecked in finely made European couture fashions. Extravagant dinner parties, balls and a host of theatrical events occupied summer evenings. According to Veblen, the wealthy engaged in such social rituals because they understood that their participation was pertinent to maintaining good social standing.

Veblen further claims that clothing expenditures at all social levels are driven by the need for a respectable appearance rather than by the more basic need of protection. Gilded Age fashion is often used as a prime example of Veblen's theory of conspicuous consumption because the women of the leisure class wore elaborate clothing in the latest mode to showcase their status and reflect the pecuniary strength of their husbands or families. The impracticality and fragility of many fashionable outfits from 1870 to 1914 implied that the wearer had unlimited financial resources to spend on clothing. Everything about the fashionable women of this period, from their tightly corseted silhouettes to the delicate heels of their shoes, signified a life of 'conspicuous leisure.'

The Theory of the Leisure Class was published at the very apex of the Gilded Age, and is theoretically accurate rather than historically reflective of the period. In reality, the sensational antics and acts of 'conspicuous consumption' that are now so often cited as proof of Veblen's theory, were really enjoyed by very few, perhaps only the very wealthiest and most eccentric of the leisure class. Thus, examples of *everyday* living rather than occasional outlandish acts should be used to interpret Gilded Age dress and lifestyle.

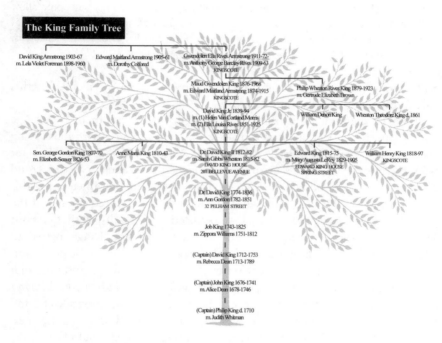

Figure 2.1 Genealogy of the King family. Compiled by the PNSC Curatorial Department. Courtesy of the Preservation Society of Newport County.

The complexities and sartorial transitions of the age can be seen through a lens focused on the King family of Newport. (See genealogy in Figure 2.1.) A large group of extant letters, scrapbooks, photographs, financial ledgers, clothing and textiles in the collection of the Preservation Society of Newport County carefully chronicle the lives of the King family, and give scholars an intimate and personal look into the lives of one family during the Gilded Age. The juxtaposition of the older Ella King's sartorial tastes with those of her daughter, Gwendolen King Armstrong, enriched the narrative, and offers the perspective of different generations of women who lived through this period. Mrs King held fast to her Victorian tastes, while her daughter adopted new modern ideas about dress and social activities.

Gwendolen's changing aesthetic puts her in the company of young women such as those described by dress historian Patricia Cunningham:

> In the second half of the nineteenth century and early twentieth century it was no longer enough to *look* modern by adopting the latest fashion; many women now wanted to *be* modern. These women desired simple, healthful, practical clothing that would allow them to be active participants in the public, professional, and economic arenas of society, but fashion and its accompanying rules for behavior were tenacious. (Cunningham 2003: 1)

King family documents allow us to see how Gwendolen navigated this sartorially tenacious period of history.

To begin, the King family must be placed in context with their Gilded Age contemporaries. Social arbiter Ward McAllister is credited with developing the 'Society Four Hundred' with Mrs. Astor (née Caroline Webster Schermerhorn): the ballroom of the Astor's Fifth Avenue mansion could comfortably accommodate 400 guests, thus setting the parameters for this list (Patterson 2000: 71). Although the Kings never appeared on any of the published Four Hundred lists, they coexisted successfully with the Four Hundred set during their summers in Newport. The Kings better fit McAllister's description of another level of Society, the old established families: 'Behind what I call the smart set in Society there always stood the old, solid, substantial and respected people. Families who held great social power as far back as the birth of this country who were looked up at by society, and who always could, when they so wished, come forward and exercise their power' (Patterson 2000: 89). The Kings occupied this respected place in the complex social matrix that was Society during the Gilded Age in which the newly wealthy mixed with older, established families.

The Kings were highly regarded in Newport. Their genealogy extended back to colonial America. David King Jr, Ella's husband, was the son of Dr David King II, a respected second-generation physician. The family saw an influx of wealth during the 1850s as Dr King's brothers ventured eastward and found success in the China trade. Their nephew, David King Jr, hoping to secure his own fortune, set out for China aboard the *Surprise* in 1859. He spent the next fourteen years in China working first at Wetmore, Williams & Company and later Russell & Company. In 1874, at the age of thirty-six, David King Jr, left China having earned not just a fortune, but also an adventurous and worldly spirit.[1]

Figure 2.2 Wedding portrait of Ella Louisa Rives King, 1875. Courtesy of the Preservation Society of Newport County.

In 1875 David King Jr married Ella Louisa Rives, an accomplished equestrian and linguist from an equally respected family from Virginia (Figure 2.2). The Kings had two children: Maud Gwendolen (always referred to as Gwendolen) born in 1876, and Philip Wheaton King born in 1879 (Ferguson 1977: 19). David and Ella's esteemed family histories coupled with their China trade wealth easily earned them a respected place amongst the leisure class during the Gilded Age.

The following summation of the King's lifestyle is drawn from David King Jr's diaries dated 1880–93. His diaries accurately reflect a refined and unpretentious upper-class family life. The diaries lend insight into Ella's activities and clothing choices, and reveal Gwendolen's childhood and adolescent experiences. The information in the diaries serves as the comparative basis from which to consider the clothing choices and attitudes of both Ella and Gwendolen in later years of the Gilded Age, 1900–15.

The King family, who had antiquarian tendencies, preserved many facets of Newport's history. The Kings owned fine Chinese export porcelains and paintings, rare books, eighteenth-century American furniture, silver and an array of decorative objects, many of which are still in place at Kingscote, their home in Newport (Figure 2.3). The house came into the King family in 1863. In 1876 David and Ella began the first of several renovations by adding additional living space to accommodate increases in household staff. The most notable change to the house came in 1880 when architect Stanford White was contracted to alter the layout and design of the dining area. He created an Arts and Crafts interior for the Kings, which remains one of the most exceptional interiors of its type extant in the United States today.[2] The new dining room could host small dinner parties and be cleared to serve as a ballroom to accommodate the

Figure 2.3 Kingscote, Newport, Rhode Island, *c.* 1882. Courtesy of the Preservation Society of Newport County.

formal evening entertainments that had become fashionable in Newport (Ferguson 1977: 22).

In 1882, David King Jr built a townhouse at 1228 Connecticut Avenue, Washington, DC, and it became the family's winter residence. It is difficult to surmise exactly what David King's responsibilities in Washington were, since he did not consistently hold an elected or appointed position. Yet, both he and Ella were familiar with the workings of American politics from their familial connections to affairs of state. David's uncle, George Gordon King, was a Rhode Island delegate to the House of Representatives from 1849 to 1853 (Russell 1934: 7). Ella's grandfather, William Cabell Rivers of Virginia, served in the senate from 1832 to 1845. He also served as Minister to France in the years prior to and just after his time in Congress (Ferguson 1977: 19).

The diaries suggest that the Kings were highly respected residents of Washington, DC, They were occasionally entertained at the White House. The Kings were often in the company of various visiting dignitaries. They developed a particularly close bond with M. de Reuterskoild, the Swedish Minister to the US, and his family, whom they entertained in Newport during the late summer of 1887. On November 13, 1888, David King Jr was officially appointed assistant commissioner to the Paris Exposition of 1889 by President Harrison.

Although the Kings had regularly spent time in Paris during the later winter or early spring, the family greeted this appointment to the 1889 Exposition with enthusiasm. Like many of their contemporaries, the Kings divided the year into allotments of time spent in fashionable urban areas with sojourns to stylish resorts and short-term stays at the country retreats of extended family and friends. When Mr and Mrs King traveled, as deemed necessary by social and diplomatic obligations, the children were often left in the charge of a nurse, and later tutors; family and friends always surrounded them. When in Europe, the Kings established a household in Paris. Mr and Mrs King used their 'home base' apartment as a starting point for their extended travels to Rome, London, Monte Carlo, parts of Spain and even Constantinople. The Kings returned to Newport to spend the summer at Kingscote.

David King's leisurely interests went beyond politics and travel, for he was an experienced sportsman. A wide variety of outdoor activities caught his interest ranging from fox shooting and salmon fishing, to the more 'conspicuous leisure' activities of coaching (carriage driving) and yachting. Many more leisure activities such as lawn tennis and beach outings with the children are also mentioned.

The whirl of social activity outlined in David King's diaries suggests that Ella King would have needed an extensive wardrobe in order to be appropriately attired for her diverse social obligations. These included attending weddings, balls, dinners and private receptions and paying calls, all of which were taken very seriously by Gilded Age women (Patterson 2000: 57). Scholars have noted that: 'For the women of the summer colony, the seasonal return to Newport was no idle vacation. Newport was a stop on the social circuit where intricate rituals and a demanding social calendar were maintained at great financial and often psychological costs' (Snydacker et al. 1989: 102).

An August 1907 article in *Cosmopolitan* suggests that women could spend up to $38,000 annually outfitting themselves for the aforementioned variety of occasions. An estimated $8,000 would be spent on opera and ball gowns with another $5,000 allotted for dinner gowns and furs. Casual clothing for riding, motoring and walking are listed, with about $3,000 a year spent on each of these less formal toilettes. Women also needed a full range of accessories including fans, handbags, hosiery, shoes, slippers and handkerchiefs.

Although incomplete, the King's extant financial records indicate that Ella did not spend quite such exorbitant sums. However, clothing she left behind indicates that she, like the wealthiest of her contemporaries, sought the opulent creations of Parisian couturiers to fulfill her sartorial needs. David King's dairies indicate that while on the family's annual holidays in Europe, Ella purchased a wide variety of couture fashions and custom-made sportswear.

Historians credit the Englishman Charles Fredrick Worth with founding the couture industry in Paris during the late 1850s. His clients were invited to his showroom to view various gowns modeled in an elaborate salon-like setting. Worth designed pieces that were interchangeable: a bodice to which several different sleeve styles could be added and which could then be matched to a few different skirts. Having gowns partially constructed allowed his seamstresses to work speedily. He claimed that, 'We can finish a costume in twenty-four hours. French ladies have ordered a dress in the morning and danced in it that night' (De Marly 1980: 49). This system was different from the older *couture à façon* system of dressmaking where client and dressmaker worked together to produce a custom creation (Coleman 1989: 32). The House of Worth was well known for its use of opulent textiles and trimmings, which were said to appeal particularly to American clients.

According to an 1896 edition of the *Paris Herald*, the houses of Worth, Doucet, Paquin, Redfern, Felix, Rouff and E. Raudnitz were listed as the 'Great Dressmakers of Paris' (Dorsey 1986: 137). Early photographs of Ella suggest that she had an appreciation for such finely made, fashionable clothes. Figure 2.2 depicts her elegant satin wedding gown covered with orange blossoms. Other photographs show her in stylish riding and after-noon costumes. Numerous 1880s and 1890s gowns, one by Worth and three by Maison Doucet, were found at Kingscote. These were presumably Ella's. Other Parisian-made gowns by P. Barroin and an 1880s walking costume by Wallès were also found. Little is known about the dressmakers Barroin and Wallès, yet their work is similar in quality to that of Worth or Doucet in both materials and construction. David King's diary of 1889 documents a partial payment of $600 to the House of Worth (July 1, 1889). The diary also includes expenditures for lace and jewelry while the Kings traveled in Europe (April 11, 1887). Ella's own accounts further document shopping in Europe; her letters mention Maison Rouff and various shops where she purchased hats, gloves, corsets, hair combs, night-gowns and other accessories.

As early as 1887, eleven-year-old Gwendolen began to show interest in her mother's wardrobe. On December 23, 1887, she wrote wistfully: 'How lovely your new dresses must be, according to Grandmamma's account' (King Family Archives). Gwendolen's childhood correspondence is filled with reflective comments such as this. She was already anxious to join in the shopping rituals enjoyed by her mother, grandmother and aunts.

By the 1890s Gwendolen left her childhood behind and took her place as a young society woman. She viewed herself as a serious and fashionable young lady. She had distinct ideas about what types of clothing she wanted. At this time Gwendolen began to communicate often with her mother about clothing. Her emerging clever, witty and tenacious personality is evident in the following:

> I like white summer dresses very much and am very glad you got a Roman sash for me . . . I learned that there is a tailor in London who makes nice grey linen riding habits very cheaply. Don't you think it would be nice for me to have one next summer? . . . Please tell me when I'm going to Paris. I trust it will be soon. My green dress is going to rags and it won't last much longer . . . Dear Mamma how much I miss you. Why did you not take me with you? The children are well and go out whenever it does not actu-ally rain. Now good bye from your very loving daughter Gwendolen . . . we are well but not happy. (King Family Archives)

Gwendolen's letter, penned at age fourteen, indicates that she was well aware of shopping trends in Europe. When looking for a smart ball gown or dress, Paris was where women chose to shop. Yet, a finely tailored riding habit could be made in London, which rivaled Paris in the production of tailored clothing and sportswear.

During this period Gwendolen wrote of clothing often and expressed strong opinions. On April 8, 1890, she wrote, 'In the afternoon, I went out with Aunt Con and she bought me a sun hat but I do not like it as it is the same sort as the market women wear' (King Family Archives). She also prepared to attend what seems to have been one of her first cotillions for which her aunt helped her choose a dress and took her for fittings. In a letter dated March 15, 1890 she provided her mother with a detailed description:

> My dress is very pretty, the dress is lined with taffeta and there is a front of very pretty *mousseline de soie*, and a sash of white moiré, the sleeves are very full and plain and are buttoned from the elbow downwards. I wore a brown ribbon in my hair and Aunt Con gave me a pair of gloves. I put on the lovely clover leaf bracelet you gave me. And Franklin Roosevelt[3] gave me a very nice bouquet of yellow daffodils and a sprig of asparagus tied with a white ribbon, which I wore in my sash. (King Family Archives)

Gwendolen also seemed acutely aware of the fact that clothing could serve as an indicator of status. She commented to her mother on February 5, 1892 after attending an art exhibition in Washington, DC: 'There were many lovely pictures though I think that people who came to show their clothes must have been disappointed as they could not be seen in such a crowd!' Later in that same letter she noted that she did not let a stretch of bad weather get her down as she exclaimed that it was 'a good chance forthwith of showing off my new waterproof!' (King Family Archives).

It was clear by 1892, when Gwendolen turned sixteen, that she accepted her duties as a young Society woman. At this time she was anticipating her own coming-out party, and represented her family at various social functions. On February 21, 1892, she wrote of viewing the trousseau of American heiress Mattie Mitchel.

> My Dear Mamma I received during Lunch today a card from Miss Mitchel asking me to come and see her presents. We went and they are splendid all her lingerie is shown off too. The presents are in a room next to the drawing room. I suppose you saw the list of her gifts in the [Paris] Herald but there are loads that are not down . . . The Duke gives her two carriages besides the lace and jewels. She is radiant and so excited! (King Family Archives)

A few weeks later she commented on the wedding in her own journalistic style. Mattie Mitchel's marriage to the Duke de la Roche-Foucauld was one of many arranged matches between young, wealthy American heiresses and titled Europeans. One of the best known was that of Consuelo Vanderbilt and the 9th Duke of Marlborough, which took place in New York in 1895. (Consuelo's family owned Newport's Marble House.) Gwendolen wrote on

February 28, 1892 of Miss Mitchel's wedding in Paris which she attended while her parents were in Constantinople.

> We went yesterday to Mattie Mitchel's wedding; oh what a lovely bride she made! You have read all about it in the [Paris] Herald no doubt but it can give you no idea of the beauty of the spectacle. The long dark church with beautiful stained glass windows was filled with greatest of France and the richest of Americans. Suddenly the big doors are thrown open the organ begins to play and the procession walks up the aisle. Mattie was as white as her dress but looked so beautiful. After the services we went to the sacristy and I kissed the Duchess de la Roche-Foucauld. Her Duke looks very nice and very happy. (King Family Archives)

The Kings' annual routine of social activity – residing at their home in Washington, DC, from October to late winter, traveling to Europe, then returning to the United States in time to go to Newport for the summer season (June to early October) – remained unchanged until March 8, 1894 when David King died of complications following an appendectomy. David King's death came as a great shock to his many friends and, of course, his immediate family. The loss of her husband and confidant greatly affected Ella. She retreated to Paris with her children, Gwendolen and Philip, for a two-year period of mourning.

Ella, not wanting to delay Gwendolen's coming out, emerged from mourning in 1896 and returned to Kingscote where she hosted a cotillion for Gwendolen. An account of the cotillion in the August 26, l896 *Newport Mercury* reads:

> Mrs. King gave a dance last night in honor of her daughter. An addition was built to the piazza, and this was enclosed with red bunting and decorated and lighted by Landers. A tent was also put up, the grounds were illuminated, and a Hungarian band furnished music. Mrs. King in black tulle trimmed with jet, received with her daughter, in white tulle and pink roses.

The account goes on to speak of the lavish flowers and favors.

Dresses found at Kingscote closely match the descriptions given in the press accounts. (Ella's dress has a P. Barroin label, while Gwen's has Raudnitz and Co., Huet and Chéruit Srs label.) The combination of the press account and extant garments are telling of the preferred taste of each of the King women. After her husband's death, Ella wore almost exclusively black clothing. A February 8, 1900 edition of *Vogue* advised: 'A widow mourning to be in the best of taste should avoid for the first year approaching fanciful modes ... Widows who have reached middle life seldom return to gay color.'

Figure 2.4 Gwendolen King, 1899. The photograph, taken in Paris, has been airbrushed to aid in creating the fashionable hourglass silhouette. Courtesy of the Preservation Society of Newport County.

Edward Maitland Armstrong, son of artist David Maitland Armstrong, proposed to Gwendolen King in 1899. The Armstrongs were an established New York family. Although Ella had much respect for the Armstrong family, she had reservations about the match, possibly because of Edward's hearing loss due to injuries sustained during the Spanish–American War, or because of his rumored shy and somewhat melancholy temperament. However, by the winter of 1900 Ella permitted Gwendolen to accept Mr Armstrong's proposal and mother and daughter headed off to Paris to prepare her trousseau (Ferguson 1977: 27). Figure 2.4 is a photograph of Gwendolen taken in a Paris studio around the time of her engagement.

Although King family documents give insight into Ella's clothing choices and suggest her preference for custom-made and couture clothing, it was really the discovery of her daughter Gwendolen's trousseau and later correspondence between mother and daughter that solidified this sartorial story. Most of the clothing found at Kingscote was worn by Gwendolen and dates from 1901 to 1910.

Lovingly packed and wrapped in tissue paper, dozens of pairs of kid opera gloves, monogrammed handkerchiefs, finely embroidered and monogrammed nightgowns, petticoats and corset covers, all of which were part of Gwendolen's trousseau, were found at Kingscote by the Preservation Society. In addition to these standard trousseau items, Gwendolen purchased several complete ensembles at the house of Raudnitz and Co., Huet and Chéruit Srs, a group of dressmakers who had become partners by the 1901 shopping season. Little is known about the operation of this fashion house. While Huet remains a mystery, the house was certainly a collaborative effort of the older established couturier Ernest Raudnitz with the emerging Madeleine Chéruit. Valerie Steele writes: 'Mme Chéruit is now a rather shadowy figure . . . Stylish and attractive, she was her own best mannequin . . . She apparently received her training in the 1880s at Raudnitz' (1991: 207).

Gwendolen chose this house over those of Worth and Doucet, which seemed to be favored by her mother. The ensembles from the house of Raudnitz and Co., Huet and Chéruit Srs although not extraordinary in cut, are light, airy, and beautifully constructed of fine fabrics. They also exude a sense of youthfulness and simplicity, possibly Chéruit's influence, and the lure for Gwendolen. Gwendolen's wedding gown of a similar aesthetic is documented only in photographs (see Figure 2.5) and the following press account in the *Newport Mercury* dated September 12, 1901:

Miss Gwendolin [*sic*] King, daughter of Mrs. David King, was married at noon at Trinity Church to Mr. Edward Maitland Armstrong of New York. The church was well filled, the admission being only by card, and a large crowd congregated at all the entrances. Rev. Henry Morgan Stone, the rector, officiated. The bride was given away by her mother . . . The chimes were rung as the bride and groom left the church to enter their carriage. The bride wore a plain satin gown trimmed with white mousseline de soie and carried a bouquet of lilies of the valley and white orchids, trimmed with lace. The veil of lace was the one worn by her mother on her wedding day. The gift of Mrs. King to the bride was a diamond crescent, and her aunt Mrs. Edward King gave her a diamond brooch, the diamonds being unusually large and brilliant.

Figure 2.5 Wedding party at the marriage of Edward Maitland Armstrong and Gwendolen King, Newport, Rhode Island, September 12, 1901. Courtesy of the Preservation Society of Newport County.

Saved also were all the response cards; thus a very accurate guest list could be determined. The list of close family and friends is peppered with the names of well-known members of Society. Mrs Cornelius Vanderbilt replied for herself and her youngest daughter, Gladys, that they would be unable to attend, while Mrs. Astor accepted.

After their marriage, the couple went to Europe on their honeymoon. In the honeymoon photographs Gwendolen wore the clothing that she had purchased in the months prior to her marriage. Gwendolen was photographed wearing a formal evening dress by Raudnitz and Co., Huet and Chéruit Srs (Figure 2.6). Some of the depicted jewelry may be the wedding gifts from her mother and aunt.

Gwendolen's trousseau also included outfits for casual afternoon activities, which she often enjoyed. One ensemble by Raudnitz and Co., Huet and Chéruit Srs is a tailor-made suit of beige summer-weight silk faille with embroidered collar and cuffs. Gwendolen was photographed wearing a similar tailor-made ensemble when she was out promenading with friends in Cannes in the winter of 1901. A tailor-made was considered appropriate for many casual day activities from promenading to yachting.

Figure 2.6 Portrait of Gwendolen King, 1902. This is her first portrait as a married
woman. The dress, which belonged to her trousseau, is in collections
of the Preservation Society of Newport County. The dress was made
by Raudnitz and Co., Huet & Chéruit Srs of Paris. Courtesy of the
Preservation Society of Newport County.

Gwendolen also had several riding habits dating from this period, two of
which were found at Kingscote. One is a summer-weight linen habit
purchased in Newport, and made by Nardi of New York and Newport. The
other is a London-made gray wool habit. Numerous photographs show her

Figure 2.7 Gwendolen King Armstrong on her honeymoon outside Rome, Italy, 1901. Courtesy of the Preservation Society of Newport County.

in riding habits. In Rome an amateur photographer caught Gwendolen on horseback wearing her London-made ensemble (Figure 2.7).

During this period, although choosing styles according to her own taste, such as the youthful designs of Raudnitz and Co., Huet and Chéruit Srs, Gwendolen was still much influenced by her mother. As we have seen, she followed the prescribed Gilded Age tradition for young women of the leisure class. Her trousseau was made up of finely crafted European couture clothing and lingerie. Even her casual clothing and sportswear were custom fit in London or Paris.

After her marriage, as Gwendolen settled into quiet married life, her clothing styles began to change. She and her husband settled in Babylon, a region of Long Island in what is now Suffolk County. With the arrival of her two boys, David in 1903 and Edward in 1905, Gwendolen became occupied with domestic duties and the running of her household (Figure 2.8). There are many letters from the early years of Gwendolen's marriage, as mother and daughter wrote at least once a week, if not more often. Gwendolen was dependent on her mother's wise advice when it came to family and financial issues, but socially she became more independent. Gwendolen cultivated her own circle of friends and forged a strong bond with her in-laws. In Babylon she often dashed off to New York City on the train to visit friends and do

Figure 2.8 Gwendolen King Armstrong with her children, *c.* 1905. Courtesy of the
Preservation Society of Newport County.

some shopping. In her letters Gwendolen often mentioned buying a number
of ready-made accessories and shirtwaists at department stores such as Lord
and Taylor, Wannamaker's, Dutton's and Altman's.

After her marriage, Gwendolen no longer traveled annually to Europe.
However, her mother supplemented Gwendolen's wardrobe with fine
European accessories and lingerie. Mrs. King continued to make regular
crossings to visit friends and pass the long winter months. While in Europe
she purchased many items for her daughter. Ella ordered accessories to be

shipped to Gwendolen. On February 20, 1912, Ella wrote: 'I am glad to hear that you like the blouse and coat; have you the collars too? I gave them to your Aunt G. to take to you. I hope you have the hats and blue veil by this time. I wrote to Mme Bertraud to send the chemises de nuit . . . and corsets.' She continued:

> Your two hats will go by steamer of this week 30 April, and I do hope all will reach you safely . . . I hope you'll like them. The bonnet is intended to protect your hair from dust and to protect far enough in front to support the veil so that it won't rub your nose or front hair. Your nightgowns will be ready about the middle of May, and will be sent to whatever address you send me. (King Family Archives)

While Gwendolen no doubt greatly appreciated her mother's gifts, she also clearly enjoyed making her own clothing choices when shopping in New York, and even when buying a second-hand gown from a friend. On November 8, 1911, she wrote:

> I have just decided to buy a tea gown from Pauline Wagstaff! The way of it is this. It was sent over to Elsie Vanderbilt from Paris, she did not think it becoming and sent it as a present to Pauline. Pauline found it – too small and unbecoming and offered it to Una for $25. – She was going to take it and have it made into an evening dress but as I liked it *tel que* she let me take it! So I thought I might as well as it is such a bargain and just what I wanted and you can bring me something else instead! It is pale blue alternately stripes of lace and blue liberty satin and lined with blue chiffon – very full under the lace, it has a 'V' neck and a high girdle and the back and train is all of lace. I hope you think I was wise to take it as it is really very pretty and must have cost a great deal more. (King Family Archives)

As much as this might be indicative of change in financial circumstances for Gwendolen, it is also reflective of larger societal changes. The Armstrongs did not have the abundant financial resources of their parents. Edward Maitland Armstrong was employed as a landscape architect in the early years of their marriage and later made some poor financial investments (Jones 1999: 241). It seems that Gwendolen appreciated the accessories and fashions that her mother sent from Europe, yet she was also quite happy shopping in New York, and not shy about snatching up a Parisian-made bargain when it came her way. A February 15, 1900 edition of *Vogue* magazine advises:

> SMART FASHIONS FOR LIMITED INCOMES – It has now an entirely new significance to what it was in the time of our mothers. This has come to be a season of a thousand and one distractions. We are rushing from this to that, and our days are cut up into

attending this subscription course, that recitation, this lecture, that morning concert. We have our club meetings, expositions of pictures, auction sales, organ recitals, and club receptions. All day and everyday . . . Next morning we rise and repeat the same experiences. Time was when only women of fashion led lives approaching these lines but this is a fair example of the average town woman's life which is lived moreover under the obligation of small expenditures.

The column 'Smart Fashions for Limited Incomes' appeared in the 1900 and 1901 editions of *Vogue* and addressed both the financial and time restrictions placed on the new modern 'woman about town.' The articles recommended shopping for ready-made accessories and shirtwaists, and remaking last season's models in order to keep up with the changing fashions when resources were limited. Gwendolen's letters indicate that she adopted much of this advice.

Gwendolen was involved in a variety of local activities. She was instrumental in setting up a primary school in Babylon, which her boys attended. She organized skating parties and joined a ladies' basketball league. She was an active member of a sewing group that merged with the local Red Cross at the outbreak of the First World War to provide bandages and dressings for troops overseas.

Gwendolen was comfortable managing her young modern family. The family spent the majority of each year in Babylon with short vacations to Newport and the Armstrong family retreats in North Hatley, Quebec in the summer and Flemings Island, Florida during the winter. During this period Gwendolen appeared in dozens of family snapshots in casual and simple clothing. In his memoirs, Gwendolen's brother-in-law, Hamilton Armstrong, writes of the clothing worn by the girls at the North Hatley camp:

> If I describe how the girls' dressed-middy blouses, wide pleated serge skirts, black stockings, hair tied with bows – they will sound like a basketball team from a reformatory. I can only say that to us they were beautiful. Even when camping the bathing costumes were more decorous than decorative . . . The girls were completely covered in black or navy blue . . . Frilly sleeves extend almost to the elbows. The bloomers were not visible, except by mischance, for the skirts covered them to below the knees. The bloomers joined long black cotton stockings. Unlike less emancipated creatures at Bailey's Beach in Newport, however, they did not wear black gloves or straw hats in the water. (1963: 95–6)

Photographs dating from 1907 depict Gwendolen fishing in Florida wearing a shirtwaist and skirt (see Figure 2.9). She canoed in North Hatley wearing shirtwaists and dark serge skirts, and picnicked in a very casual, 'no frills' linen tailor-made. Other snapshots reveal her preference for lightweight

Figure 2.9 Edward and Gwendolen Armstrong on Fleming Island, Florida, *c.* 1907. Courtesy of the Preservation Society of Newport County.

lawn dresses embellished with cutwork for yachting and lawn parties.

These snapshots reveal a Gwendolen different from the couture-clad young woman pictured in the formal studio shots that chronicled her early life. Are we seeing a new, modern version of Gwendolen, or just one not previously caught so readily on film? Had she completely cast away all her couture-made ball gowns? While difficult to surmise exactly, Gwendolen's change in financial circumstances, the influence of her free-spirited, artistic in-laws and larger societal changes are probably all responsible for her changing tastes. Casual entertaining seemed to be the trend for the ladies of Babylon. Yet, Ella certainly did her best to ensure that Gwendolen's wardrobe was supplemented with Parisian-made accessories.

Dress historian Madelyn Shaw described the changing American aesthetic affecting Gwendolen's generation: 'Between 1900 and 1950, the ways in which American women of all social and economic levels thought about and acquired their clothing changed considerably. Any pretense to true high fashion in the early twentieth century required the purchase of a custom made and custom fitted wardrobe from Paris couturiers or from American importers and reproducers of Paris models' (2000: 105). By 1950 America was certainly a different place for women than it had been during the years of the Gilded Age. However, many of the changes that came to fruition after the First World War had actually seeped into the culture and found acceptance by the turn of the twentieth century. Upper-class American women, as we have seen in the case of Gwendolen King Armstrong, set aside what had been the social duties of their mothers and became involved in a variety of social, political, charitable and educational organizations. Gwendolen's correspondence is very different from her father's journals. Like her father, Gwendolen writes with candor, wit and humor; yet, she gives us a glimpse into what was a rapidly changing American society. Gwendolen's writings reveal a bustling, busy, less constrained social life. This view of Gwendolen is further supported by the fact that some of her trousseau shows little wear. Dozens of pairs of opera-length gloves appear unused, suggesting that Gwendolen prepared a trousseau for an intended social life that all too quickly became old-fashioned.

The world of Gwendolen's adulthood had rapidly changed and the grand traditions of her upper-class upbringing were falling by the wayside. The balls and parties of the early years of the Gilded Age became passé. Gwendolen seemed happy to wear the ready-made, stylish and neat clothing adopted by her middle-class contemporaries. This clothing allowed her to travel easily about town and participate in a wide variety of social and sporting activities. Although Gwendolen's clothing styles had changed to accommodate her more modern lifestyle, clothing and shopping still occupied a great deal of her time and thought. It is apparent that Gwendolen considered the acquisition of a new hat or dress newsworthy. She forlornly closed a letter written to her mother on March 10, 1914 with this thought: 'Well I have no news, not even new clothes' (King Family Archives).

Ella, on the other hand, maintained a preference for European-made couture fashions and viewed American department stores and the assortment of ready-made goods available by the early twentieth century as beneath her. She continued to buy European-made clothing as it was indicative of her upper-class status, as well as a complement to her reserved temperament and comfort with the Victorian conceptions of modesty and propriety. She wrote to Gwendolen on April 4, 1916:

> So I went to Altman's about baby's hat; the choice is exceedingly small when you eliminate pink & blue . . . however I sent one white straw. I will try at Best tomorrow, but fear I won't find anything prettier; a black straw with marguerites would be pretty, but would have to be made . . . I got another hat for Baby – a little more dressy, much more expensive, and a very good straw. I had the little flowers added and I hope you will like it. And

also the Altman hat well enough for the spring. It seems impossible to get hats that are pretty and simple and they say so few are coming from Europe. Anyway I don't think you ought to tire yourself in these horrific shops – such crowds. (King Family Archives)

She wrote later: 'I have a hat for you, which I hope you will rather like . . . if the shape suits you I think it's a hat you can wear a great deal. I daresay one can get nice ready made clothes, but I have never had any, and have shopped so little in New York that I really know nothing about it' (King Family Archives).

As the Gilded Age came to a close, the King women were faced with yet another tragic and unexpected death. Gwendolen was widowed in 1915. She stayed on living in New York for a year or two, and eventually came to live year-round at Kingscote. As Gwendolen's life changed after the death of her husband, the world was forever changed by the war going on in Europe. The two women's correspondence diminished because they were together much of the time. The letters in the winter of 1915 are insightful, as Gwendolen settled her husband's estate in New York. Ella wrote many thoughtful and comforting letters. The letters are also filled with anecdotes intended to lift Gwendolen's spirits. In a letter dated February 19, 1915 Ella wrote: 'The family has heard a rumor that [cousin] Millie has cut her hair off short and are nearly wild with the news' (King Family Archives).

By the teens and twenties fashions were significantly simpler in cut and construction than their Gilded Age counterparts. There are relatively few snapshots of Ella King, who shied away from casual informal dress. Ella lived until 1925 and throughout her lifetime preferred the look and refinement of what was quickly becoming a bygone age. Gwendolen, who grew up enjoying a privileged childhood, quickly moved into a more modern world as a young married woman. Gwendolen's lighthearted personality, athleticism and wide social circle no doubt allowed her to make a simple and harmonious transition to modernity. As Gwendolen left the confines of her life in cosmopolitan New York, Washington, DC, and Paris, and posh seaside resorts of Newport and the French Riviera, she found a simpler lifestyle, with a wider range of accepted activities, in Babylon. She adapted her wardrobe and shopping habits accordingly. The various formal gowns that made up her trousseau were replaced with simple shirtwaists and skirts, as well as tea gowns and casual sporting costumes which were appropriate for the activities that now occupied many modern women of the leisure class.

The personal letters and journals of the King family show that the Gilded Age was a complex multilayered and transitory period of American history that provided a bridge from the Victorian world to the new Modern era.

By 1900, young women of the leisure class were no longer satisfied with dressing in the same constrained formality of women a generation earlier. The minor and somewhat subtle dress modifications of the Gilded Age were pivotal in preparing women for the sweeping fashion changes to come during the post First World War era. By 1914, the introduction of various new clothing styles forever blurred previously established sartorial indicators of socio-economic class.

Notes

1. David King Jr's letters from China are in the collection of the Newport Historical Society; his daybooks/diaries are at the Newport Preservation Society.
2. By contrast, the grandiose 'cottages' commissioned by Cornelius Vanderbilt (The Breakers) and William K. Vanderbilt (Marble House) were completed in the 1890s.
3. She probably is referring to the future president of the United States. The Roosevelts moved in the same social circles as the Kings.

References

Armstrong, H.F. (1963), *Those Days*, New York: Harper & Row Publishers.

Coleman, E.A. (1989), *The Opulent Era: Fashions of Worth, Doucet and Pingat*, New York: Thames and Hudson and The Brooklyn Museum.

Cunningham, P.A. (2003), *Reforming Women's Fashion, 1850–1920: Politics, Health and Art*, Kent, OH: The Kent State University Press.

De Marly, D. (1980), *Worth: Father of Haute Couture*, New York: Holmes & Meier Publishers, Inc.

Dorsey, H. (1986), *The Belle Epoque in the Paris Herald*, London: Thames and Hudson.

Ferguson, J.W. (1977), *Kingscote: Newport Cottage Orne*, Newport, RI: Preservation Society of Newport County.

Gregory, A. (1993), *Families of Fortune: Life in the Gilded Age*, New York: Rizzoli International Publications.

Jones, R.O. (1999), D. *Maitland Armstrong: American Stained Glass Master*, Tallahassee, FL: Sentry Press.

Patterson, J.E. (2000), *The First Four Hundred: Mrs. Astor's New York in the Gilded Age*, New York: Rizzoli International Publications.

Russell, E.K. (1934), *Journal and Letters of Edward King 1835–1844*, New York: Privately printed.

Shaw, M. (2000), 'American Fashion: The Tirocchi Sisters in Context,' in S. Hay (ed.), *Fashion Art and the Tirocchi Dressmakers' Shop, 1915–1940*, Providence,

RI: Museum of Art, Rhode Island School of Design, pp. 105–30.

Snydacker, D. Jr., M. Christiansen, D. Walker and E. Caldwell (1989). 'The Business of Leisure: The Gilded Age in Newport,' *Newport History* 62: 97–126.

Steele, V. (1991), *Women of Fashion: Twentieth Century Designers*, New York: Rizzoli International Publications.

Veblen, T. (2001), *The Theory of the Leisure Class*, New York: The Modern Library.

Vogue, 1990–02.

Archives

Diaries of David King Jr, Preservation Society of Newport County.

King Family Archives, Preservation Society of Newport County.

King Family Papers, Newport Historical Society.

3

Dress and Culture in Greenwich Village

Deborah Saville

Editors' Introduction: When the Gilded Age ended on the eve of the First World War, some Americans expressed dissatisfaction with the conventional life. Intellectuals in Greenwich Village in New York City began to practice alternative lifestyles based on radical feminism and new psychological thought. As discussed by Deborah Saville, their style, identifiable as American bohemian, signified their ideological leanings. Young Greenwich Village women's style included artists' smocks, peasant blouses, sandals and bobbed hair. While most women did not yet customarily wear these avant garde styles, the emerging mainstream look of the period did have a shorter skirt and looser silhouette. The bohemians' artistic tendencies may be related to designers and artists within modern design movements who presented new, uncorseted garments at exhibitions throughout Europe. Liberty of London and designers such as Paul Poiret and Mariano Fortuny became well-known creators of comfortable, exotic gowns. These efforts created a trend for more comfortable, if not exotic, clothing. Therefore it is not surprising to learn that clothing manufacturers soon adapted village styles and offered them to the American public. Saville argues that these Greenwich Village bohemians were precursors to the free-living flappers who appeared all over America in the 1920s.

Women's mainstream fashion in the early twentieth century changed from an S-curved corseted silhouette at the turn of the century to the straight, slim, short-skirted look of the flapper in the 1920s. This change in fashion occurred not simply from the expected influence of European designers – Poiret, Chanel, Lucile – or from the necessities of the First World War that put women in comfortable work clothes. Rather, the change involved social and artistic movements at a grass-roots level.

The study of dress in Greenwich Village, a small area below 14th Street in lower Manhattan, shows that distinct clothing styles developed from 1910 to 1923 that influenced American fashion. The bohemians in the Village experimented with dress in a highly politicized, cultural and artistic environment permeated with feminist, socialist and Freudian thought. The study of this subculture reveals how cultural meanings of fashion change and the process by which these changes took place. Indeed, it can be argued that Greenwich Village dress and behavioral trends in the 1910s originated some of the fashion and social norms typically associated with the flappers of the 1920s.

A confluence of cultural and political factors in Greenwich Village in the 1910s generated a bohemian enclave where alternative lifestyles and trends flourished. The development of Greenwich Village as 'America's Bohemia' was due largely to its geography and history. In contrast to the orderly grid of uptown Manhattan, the tangled web of Greenwich Village streets allowed the area to retain its quaint atmosphere well into the twentieth century. Its small artist colony blossomed circa 1910 as landlords and real estate agents transformed the once-fashionable homes and stables of the Knickerbocker aristocracy around Washington Square into artist's studios and small, affordable rented rooms (Watson 1991).

Attracted by the cheap rents and pleasant surroundings, artists and intellectuals moved in, creating a vibrant bohemian subculture during the period 1912–18. The initial group, who were engaged in radical politics, included feminists, writers, publishers, theatrical troupes, artisans and educators. As developers simultaneously sought to market the charm of the Village's developing art community, 'shops dealing in antiques, hand-wrought jewelry, and peasant wear moved into the locality' (Ware 1935: 94–5).

Joseph Freeman, the editor of the *Liberator*, described this middle-class rebellion of feminists and male intellectuals:

> Whatever individual differences the [Greenwich] Villagers had, their common bond was a hatred for the environment from which they came. They did not want to attend the Methodist church, the synagogue, the confessional; to enter business or the professions, to settle down to marriage and babies. They were . . . young people in their early twenties who wanted to love, to create beauty, to have friendships, to talk, all without the crushing responsibilities which they had escaped. (1938: 233)

Personal liberation from convention became political for these highly ideological radicals as they sought to revolutionize society through their avant-garde lifestyle.

This bohemian group wrote and thought about the time in which they lived, leaving extensive evidence that serves as a record of their lives. Several bohemians wrote memoirs and fictional accounts of their experiences. Others documented their observations and philosophy in poetry and art. Residents published articles in Greenwich Village periodicals, socialist publications and newspapers; vice investigator reports reflect the activities within the community. They kept scrapbooks and memorabilia of the Provincetown Players, as well as letters, diaries, and feminist club notes. Visual records of their lives appeared in magazine articles. These as well as photographs and other artifacts remain in private and public collections in the United States. All of these provided a plethora of documentary evidence to investigate this bohemian era.

In this chapter, I will provide background on the cultural climate in Greenwich Village from 1910 to 1923, trace the fashion and appearance of bohemians in the Village, and finally interpret the meaning of their dress both within the Village milieu and for the larger culture. Furthermore, I will examine how bohemian dress influenced the fashions worn by 1920s flappers.

The Cultural Climate of Greenwich Village

Greenwich Village became a center for feminism, radical politics, examination of Freudian psychology, and experimentation with new social mores. Village inhabitants were committed to freedom and equality. Social life in the Village supported the liberal ideals of the new bohemians. They discussed and presented ideas in salons and clubs, and through theatrical performances. Bohemian ideas began to filter into the mainstream culture by the middle of the 1910s.

Understanding the transformations within the women's movement is critical to an examination of the cultural changes, including dress, that took place in Greenwich Village in the 1910s. The women's movement split into factions. The genteel National American Woman Suffrage Association (NAWSA) split from the more confrontational and militant Congressional Union (later called the National Women's Party [NWP]). The emerging feminists of the NWP were, for the most part, of a younger generation whose educational, social and political connections no longer confined them to the domestic sphere. Despite the split, the movement's forcefulness led to a national suffrage amendment in 1920.

During the 1910s, feminists in Greenwich Village engaged in personal history talks at their women's special interest discussion groups, becoming even more aware that feminist work entailed a change in psychological consciousness beyond suffrage and legal equality (Anthony 1915: 231; Wittenstein 1998). The radical feminists of the NWP argued that birth control, motherhood endowment and notions of heterosexual liberation would transform the inequities found in the workplace, politics and home.

Greenwich Village radicals viewed sexuality as a free speech issue. Feminists theorized that claiming the freedom to take and dismiss lovers and engage in meaningful dialogue with men would provide a chance to make the household a democracy rather than a patriarchy, and in turn democratize the culture. They aimed for full expression of the individual by going beyond conventional gendered behavior. Marie Jenny Howe stated that it was critical for females to be more than their 'little female selves' and to develop their 'big, whole human selves' at a meeting of feminists at the Cooper Union (*New York Times*, February 21, 1914: 18).

Intrigued with working-class mores, Greenwich Village artists and intellectuals 'learned of new sexual possibilities not only from the "highbrow" writings of the sexologists but also from the "lowbrow" behavior of their less intellectual neighbors' (Meyerowitz 1993: 51). Choice and personal independence without regard for middle-class societal expectation informed the 'free' heterosexual unions.

Freudian theory was first used to explore socialistic forms of liberation (e.g., how to improve society). As leftist politics collapsed under an increasingly skittish conservative political climate, the bohemian fad for psychoanalysis instead became the method for resolving personal problems and adapting oneself to society (e.g., how to improve oneself). Psychoanalysis fit well with doctrines that stressed self-realization through personal expression.

The vogue for Freudian psychology justified the radical repudiation of artistic and sexual inhibitions and further provided the basis for the ideology of 'free love' in Greenwich Village. A sizable exodus of middle-class young adults from midwestern and north-eastern states descended upon Greenwich Village by 1914. Freudian psychology was a hot topic for them: 'Everyone at that time who knew about psychoanalysis was a sort of missionary on the subject, and nobody could be around Greenwich Village without hearing a lot about it' (Dell 1969: 294).

Villagers learned of new ideas and the latest movements through social venues – at clubs, eating houses, bars and theater groups. Ideologies were generated through talk, plays, politics and sexual experimentation, particularly as bohemians negotiated notions of liberation. This psychological transformation involved intellectualizing ideas about sexual mores. Former Villagers credit feminist high school teacher Henrietta Rodman as the original driving spirit behind bohemian Greenwich Village.

In 1913, Rodman organized Greenwich Village's Liberal Club, a coffee house where intellectuals and bohemians convened to discuss current topics including politics, Eastern religions, artistic expression and sexuality. Carl Jung was a guest lecturer. Club members staged plays, often satires on romantic themes in their own lives. Through the Liberal Club, an adjacent book shop and a restaurant (named Polly's), Rodman's coterie – her friends from social settlement houses, socialist journalists, 'students and professors' – became acquainted with newly-arriving bohemians and 'artist folk' in the Village (Dell 1926: 20).

Another such club was Heterodoxy, a luncheon club for 'unorthodox women' that met in Greenwich Village from 1912 to 1940. Comparable to a women's support group, the participants – professionals and a smattering of female labor leaders – included heterosexuals, lesbians, married and single women.

The wealthy art patron and activist Mabel Dodge hosted a salon from 1913 to 1915 which brought together 'Socialists, Trade-Unionists, Anarchists, Suffragists, Poets . . . Psychoanalysts . . . Birth Controlists, Newspapermen, Artists, Modern-Artists . . .' for an unprecedented 'coalition politics of the left' (Luhan 1936: 83; Stansell 2000: 118). The salon was held weekly in her Village home.

Probably the best known of the Village-based clubs was the Provincetown Players theater group. In the summer of 1916, while vacationing in Provincetown, Massachusetts, a group of Villagers staged several personal plays including Susan Glaspell's *Suppressed Desires*, a spoof on the psychoanalysis craze, and those of the neophyte playwright Eugene O'Neill. Frustrated with commercial theater in New York, the group started their own experimental theater in Greenwich Village from which the genre of American realism developed (Watson 1991: 213–22).

Bohemian Ideas Go Mainstream

Beginning in the 1910s, Freudian concepts filtered through Greenwich Village into mainstream culture, continuing throughout the 1920s. Articles written by Greenwich Village intellectuals for popular magazines and plays provided a basic understanding of psychoanalysis for the public while linking its more faddish aspects to Village culture. Pop psychology in the Village – the parlor games of dream analysis and the radical practices of 'free-love' and birth control – was linked to Freudian doctrine in the popular press which tended to exaggerate sexual content, neglecting the political aspects of these practices.

These ideas filled the pages of the skillfully edited Greenwich Village political magazine, the *Masses*, published from 1912 to 1917. Renderings of bohemian females in 'pagan' paraphernalia on its covers, and the proliferation of advertisements for books related to psychology and women's sexuality, reflected the attitudes towards sexuality gaining currency around the later 1910s.

As more Americans learned about Greenwich Village through popular magazines and newspapers, they became intrigued with the liberal ideas and lifestyles of the bohemians. It was not long before enterprising marketers began to 'sell' the Village. The notions of greater personal freedom and expression were exciting and attractive to the public. The revolution in manners and morals sought by the intelligentsia did not evolve as they had envisioned. But some loosening of old restraints resulted (even if only in a commercialized, cheapened form) as the wider culture picked up on the bohemian idea of greater personal freedom and expression. Madison Avenue and Hollywood used the Village ethos to generate a new ideology based on 'sex appeal' and personal gratification (Cowley 1934: 64).

Poet Malcolm Cowley described how marketers employed the middle-class bohemian revolt in the 1920s to sell products: 'Prohibition [and "prosperity"] surrounded the new customs with illicit glamour ... Freudian psychology provided a philosophical justification and made it unfashionable to be repressed ... American business was quick to use the bohemian ideal and exploit the new markets for cigarettes and cosmetics. Wherever one turned the Greenwich Village ideas were making their way' (1934: 62–4). An ethos of personal satisfaction via psychology, sex and self-expression spread though the culture. Cowley explained that 'conversations ran from mother fixations to birth control while they smoked cigarettes (1934: 62–4). As he observed, the Village revolt of the 1910s gave form to the social revolution of the 1920s, thereby setting a precedent for cultural alternatives to a Protestant work ethic that delayed gratification.

Dress in Greenwich Village 1910–23

In 1910, American women wore shirtwaists with flared black skirts, tailor-mades, lingerie dresses, Poiret-inspired tunic dresses and hobble skirts. Most women wore corsets. The 'spiritual haven' found in Greenwich Village allowed the new youth culture to develop their ideologies in conjunction with new modes of behavior, socialization and dress (Scherman 1964: 60). By 1914, feminist dress was clearly evident. The

Masses illustrated rebellious women smoking cigarettes in loose-fitting tunic dresses with bobbed hair held in place by headbands to accompany articles on controversial feminist causes.

Women in the Village who considered themselves bohemians wore clothing that separated them from the mainstream. They first donned loose tunics that they either designed themselves, or purchased from purveyors of 'artistic' or 'reform' dress. Later, the artist's smock became almost a uniform. Clothing that incorporated artistic surface design techniques, such as embroidery or batik, also found favor among Villagers as did bobbed hair and sandals. Village styles may be divided into three phases: 1910–15, 1915–20, and 1920–23.

1910–15

Cultural revolutionaries – designers, artists and dancers, such as Isadora Duncan – influenced attitudes about the body and dress from the early years of the twentieth century. These women of Greenwich Village adopted aesthetic and couture fashion in relation to their developing views of the body. By 1912, the fashion of modern women in Greenwich Village indicated knowledge of avant-garde and couture designs and the assimilation of such designs into their own wardrobes.

Accounts describing women in 'classical dress' and 'floating tunic[s] of [their] own design' reflect exposure to 'artistic' dress and the work of Poiret and Fortuny (Van Vechten 1922: 129). Classical designs that were conducive to movement and aesthetic interpretation may have been more prevalent in the Village repertoire than Poiret's more narrow and restrictive empire designs. The interest in Fortuny's designs is evidenced in several sources including one memoir that described 'the uniform of the New Freedom . . . bobbed hair, cigarettes, sandals, batik blouses and Fortuni [*sic*] gowns' (Freeman 1938: 230).

Graphic artist Clara Tice embodied the new Greenwich Village style. Photographs of Tice reflect her awareness of forward-thinking designers, including Fortuny. For a *Vanity Fair* 1915 photo shoot, Tice wore a revealing avant-garde ensemble with no corset – sleeveless, low décolleté, straps off the shoulder tied in large bows (Figure 3.1). Described by a Dada publication as the 'artist of undressing par excellence' (*Rogue* 1915), Tice set and personified radical Greenwich Village style trends throughout the 1910s and 1920s, including her hair which she claimed to have bobbed in 1914 before the popular dancer Irene Castle (Tice 1921).

Henrietta Rodman is credited by several Villagers with inspiring fashion change in the early period. Rodman worked as an English teacher in some

Figure 3.1 Clara Tice, *Vanity Fair* 5(1), September 1915: 60.

of New York's best girls' schools. In her social life she 'wore sandals and a loose-flowing gown exactly like a meal sack . . . And her hair was bobbed in a day when bobbed hair, far from being the fashion, brought street notoriety to its possessor' (Kemp 1926: 85–6).

Greenwich Village's Liberal Club, Polly's, and the offices of the *Masses* served as the political and social epicenter in the first days of radical Greenwich Village. The Village took on a 'new character' when the literary and artist crowd and the social settlement crowd began to mix (Dell 1969: 247). In 1913–14, one Village poet recalled meeting Peggy Baird, an artist who wore 'Russian blouses,' and was the 'first girl [he] had seen with bobbed hair' at the Liberal Club (Johns 1937: 218).

Villagers distinguished between reform dress and artistic dress; the latter included long robes of silk and Chinese sandals. But evidence points to a confluence of feminist ideals and aesthetics associated with artists. Although the '[V]illage sacks' (Van Vechten 1922: 134), the crude brown or gray linen tunics worn by Rodman and her feminist following, were highly political, artistic trends in dress (e.g., peasant embroideries) met the needs of radical feminist politics. The dress worn by feminist actress Ida Rauh (Figure 3.2) is similar to descriptions of the dress of women artists involved with alternative education in 1913. Years earlier Rauh had 'renounced so hotly all the frills and luxuries of bourgeois life' and adopted an 'informal garment, a simple, self-made, unobtrusively becoming garment' for indoor wear (Eastman 1948: 266–7). Like Rauh, Montessori teachers wore 'voluminous dress[es] of silk . . . clothes that [gave] the body freedom of motion' (Kemp 1926: 199, 222).

Rodman's peasant dresses and embroidered garments were a style viewed by contemporaries as feminist garb. Malcolm Cowley observed the omnipresence of Rodman and her feminist contingency as they continued to affect Village dress around 1918:

> The women had evolved a regional costume, then widely cartooned in the magazines: hair cut in a Dutch bob, hat carried in the hand, a smock of some bright fabric (often embroidered Russian linen), a skirt rather shorter than the fashion of the day, gray cotton stockings and sandals. With heels set firmly on the ground and abdomens protruding a little – since they wore no corsets and dieting hadn't become popular – they had a look of unexampled solidity. (1934: 70)

Village memoirs and news stories of the period attest to the influence of the early artist colony on radical fashion and ideology. Nina Wilcox Putnam, a writer and Heterodoxy member, claimed credit for a self-designed, 'one-piece' style (Putnam 1930: 236), noting that her artist friends approved 'because of its beauty – never as a reform measure' (Tarbell 1913: 36). Putnam's loosely fitting kimono-style dress, photographed in the New York periodical *American Magazine* in May 1913, shocked the public, especially when worn without a corset and with colored Moroccan sandals. Putnam likely drew inspiration from the 'artist-folk' in Greenwich Village for her dress design. She was a member of a Greenwich Village-based social and artist's club around 1910–12 prior to

Figure 3.2 Ida Rauh, *c.* 1916. Schlesinger Library, Radcliffe Institute for Advanced Study, Harvard University.

the relocation of the Liberal Club to the Village and to her becoming a member of Heterodoxy.

Denizens of Mabel Dodge's Greenwich Village salon distinguished between emancipated dress and artistic dress that included batiks, floating tunics and Fortuny fashions – 'a purple velvet dress with long tight sleeves ending in points which reached her knuckles.' One woman who was

'dressed with some attempt at stylization . . . [wore] a robe of batik, irides-
cent in the shades of the black opal, with a belt of moonstones set in
copper, and huge ear-rings fashioned of human hair. On her feet were
copper-coloured sandals.' Bobbed-hair girls wore '[V]illage sacks' (Van
Vechten 1922: 129, 134, 142–3). Batik artists had been working at their
craft for a few years, creating a market in Manhattan by 1912 (Lillethun
2002: 142).

One fictional account, set in the years 1913–15, described a Montessori
school teacher 'noted as almost the sole member among the group [of femi-
nists] who advocated dress-reform, who possessed any proper understanding of the aesthetics of dress . . . The first thing I noted about her, this
tall handsome rather than beautiful woman – was how well her clinging
gown fitted her slim, elegant body.' Reminiscent of Fortuny styles, the dress
was described as 'medieval . . . caught . . . by a depending rope, silken-
tasseled' (Kemp 1926: 199–200).

The newly inspired dress practices of wearing rolled hose and going
without a corset, advocated by Putnam in 1913, also appeared in Harry
Kemp's autobiographical novel in which he described artists' fashion in the
Village. Kemp's character, who engages in a brief romantic interlude with
a woman artist he previously observed meditating (apparently Buddhist
style), 'felt only a brassiere' under her 'long robe of silk' and also noted the
'lemon-colored hose to the knee' (Kemp 1926: 223–5).

Changes in group-related activity also influenced Villagers to adopt
casual, less restrictive clothing. Heterosexual dialogue, eating and
drinking, and dancing took the place of activities that involved social
decorum and propriety such as church-going and chaperoned dances.
Exposure to working-class segments of the population influenced social
rules. Villagers ventured uptown to dance halls to observe new dance
forms and, while shocked at first, subsequently found themselves
'tugging and joggling over the floor in the thick of the sweaty, head-
bobbing mob' (Kemp 1926: 141). Women at Village dances wore simple
dress including comfortable, calf-length skirts, jumpers, and tunic tops,
with low sandal-type shoes. Women even danced by themselves. Through
experimentation in socialization, radicals set a liberal tone for the
evolving Village culture.

Dress trends set in feminist Greenwich Village during the 1910–15
period evolved into ubiquitous Greenwich Village fashions in the later
years of the decade: 'sack' dresses worn with socks and sandals, loose
flowing artistic dresses, smocks, peasant blouses and batik garments.

1915–20

As rents tripled around Washington Square, America's Bohemia spread to Sheridan Square beginning in 1915. The Village became a tourist attraction and a haven for uptown visitors. With the advent of tearooms, the Village provided business opportunities for single women who ran successful restaurants, hat and batik shops, and tour guide companies.

Photographs of tearoom hostesses, restaurant proprietors, Village guides, and shop managers all provide evidence of Village dress forms that became popularized through commercialization in the tearoom phase of Greenwich Village from 1915 to 1920. Artistic Village fashions in the tearoom/bohemian phase, however, derived from earlier feminist and artists' fashions. Caftan-style and simple smock dresses worn by tearoom hostesses originated with women on the scene in Greenwich Village, such as restaurant owner Polly Holladay, who 'in the early days . . . usually wore long, unbelted sack-like dresses' (Conklin 1958).

Tour guide Adele Kennedy wore a casual, calf-length skirt, smock, and sandals with no stockings to conduct tours, according to a report in the (first) Sunday *New York Times* in October 1918. Personal dress and modern textile designs of leading textile artists like Ilonka Karasz helped to promote bohemian art trends to the tourist market and Village clientele (Saville 2003).

Greenwich Village shops sold smocks, sacks, and Russian blouses. Simple tie-dyed, caftan-style sack dresses and hand-printed tunic blouses sold in several Village shops around 1918. Flambeau Weavers' Shop sold authentic peasant fashions from 1916 on. M.D.C. Crawford, art editor for *Women's Wear*, promoted artistic dress from Greenwich Village boutiques to textile manufacturers and retailers. Sketches of Russian blouses designed for the department store Wanamaker's demonstrate the intermediary stage of adapting original styles of subcultural dress for a larger, more mainstream market. Retailers jumped on the market potential in Greenwich Village fashions. On April 11, 1917 Bonwit Teller advertised in *Women's Wear* 'Greenwich Village Art In Bonwit Teller Costumes.' These were negligee dresses and fashionable peasant smocks. By 1916, Florence Gough, owner of The Paint-Box Gallery, specialized in sportswear, including trendy hand-dyed tunic tops, scarves, and floppy hats. Anna Alice Chapin, author of a guidebook, declared, 'Do you think all the artistic costume-creating is done in the Rue de la Paix? Try the Village!' (1917: 253).

Jessie Tarbox Beals, a photojournalist, sold souvenir picture postcards through a gallery and tearoom she managed from 1917. A photograph of Beals at the time of her gallery opening (Figure 3.3) reflects changes in

Figure 3.3 Jessie Tarbox Beals at The Village Art Gallery. Museum of the City of New York, 95.127.19.

Greenwich Village fashion from perhaps just a few years earlier. Beals, a shrewd businesswoman in her forties, likely saw the need to be stylish and bohemian in her dress. She wore a tunic blouse, a novel adaptation of peasant dress with a beaded design on the front. Her large beaded sash is another trend seen among Village women, worn either belted or around the neck. Similar dress items found in several shops, especially items that could be mass manufactured in home industries, suggest increasing commercialization. Beal's tunic and belt are trendy rather than highly artistic or indigenous and demonstrate how women in the Village evolved idiosyncratic fashions.

The smock was the dress item most associated with Greenwich Village. A protest garment, the comfortable, inexpensive smock signified ideological arguments surrounding sexuality and capitalist-oriented social norms, particularly for radical women in the first part of the 1910s. As the Village commercialized in the bohemian/tearoom years, Alice Chapin, author of a 1917 guidebook titled *Greenwich Village*, noted, 'the crowd is younger, poorer, more strikingly bizarre – immeasurably more interesting' and identified Village girls 'in smocks of "artistic" shades – bilious yellow-green, or magenta-tending violet' (212). Newly arriving young women quickly became a part of the bohemian scene by donning this wardrobe staple. The new-found popularity of the Village within a youth culture drew criticism from some conservatives who complained about the 'pseudobohemians' who try to prove their status by 'the garments that they wear – Hazel bobs her hair short and favors a loose smock' (Cobb 1917: n.p.). Greenwich Village dress prompted ambivalence within the culture.

1920–23

By the early 1920s, variations of styles first seen in the Village trickled across to the larger culture. Fashionable hem lengths rose to below the knee in late 1920. This knee length prevailed in the Village and among groups including retail workers and working-class women, college and high school girls, through the first half of the 1920s, despite the best efforts of the fashion industry to drop hem lengths to the ankles (Milbank 1989; 'Battle of the skirts', *The Outlook*, October 18, 1922). On June 11, 1921, the highly respected Greenwich Village artist Clara Tice depicted herself and her friends wearing knee-length dresses and rolled hose in an illustration for the *St. Louis Star*. Tice defended the fashion in a July 2, 1921 *Star* interview – 'I think short dresses and rolled stockings are ideal for women and girls.'

Other renderings, including one in a 1922 Greenwich Village community magazine called the *Quill*, suggest that short pleated and fringed skirts, rolled stockings, and jaunty hats worn over one eye were the defining fashions among Greenwich Village young women. These trends among others, including open coats and long scarves, brightly hued woolen stockings, and 'Betty Beads,' are described by commentators of the same period as the fashion among high school girls (Hall 1922: 771–80). The cover of the July 27, 1922 issue of *Life* magazine depicts a college-age woman with an open knee-length coat, long scarf, white stockings, flat oxford shoes, cropped

hair and soft cloche hat. Variations of such garb can be found in renderings in many Greenwich Village periodicals and photographs from 1918 to
1923. (See Saville 2003.)

Cultural Meanings of Bohemian Dress

In this section, cultural meanings of bohemian dress are explored at length.
Dress is interpreted within the context of the social and cultural dynamics
of the Village. As personal, social and political change occurred, personal
and cultural identity evolved into that generally associated with the culture
of the 1920s. Dress is analyzed from its inception as political expression to
its trajectory as a pretentious expression of a growing commercialized and
socially trendy culture and finally to its adoption by the wider youth
culture. Decisions to change one's dress and hair were part of the social
experimentation prevalent in the Village. Dress, and other aspects of the
culture, expressed aversion to outdated standards.

As we have seen, dress in Greenwich Village differed from mainstream
fashion for cultural reasons, yet in the end it influenced the larger culture.
As the culture explored various schools of thought, bohemians created and
assimilated new approaches to the body. Small groups of artists wore
peasant dress, batiks and Fortuny designs in the first half of the 1910s.
These and other feminist fashions including bobbed hair and sandals were
worn and used to express the changing dynamics of the community.

The political objective of artists/bohemians and political radicals – a
more equal and harmonizing society – was expressed through paradigms
that included their activities, philosophies and dress. Feminists demonstrated their repudiation of standards related to sex, gender, and socialization politically and intellectually, in terms of dress. Rodman's 'mealsack'
dress, brown socks, and sandals subverted any notion of traditional standards related to the female sex. By doing as she wished in her personal life
while continuing to battle for teachers' rights, Rodman made political
statements about the capabilities of women. Rodman lived a very unconventional life for 1913 and yet influenced important legislation.

Rodman's so-called Group 'in a real sense invented Greenwich Village as
a sanctuary for bohemian life off the job' (Richwine 1968: 150). Rodman's
feminist garb, bobbed hair and public cigarette smoking set a precedent for
not following conventional rules and for having a comfortable environment in which to relax and live one's ideals. Polly Holladay's smocks and
unbelted sack dresses likewise expressed her anarchist tendencies and
disinterest in a lifestyle compounded with standards.

The confluence of feminist sexual politics and art as philosophy can be viewed through the lens of dress. Feminists redefined political and social paradigms for modern women. In the new modernism, art provided the justification for revolution and liberty. Art and sex were philosophies unto themselves, the expression of which would lead to personal and spiritual fulfillment, and ultimately social balance. Nina Wilcox Putnam was careful to stress the aesthetic qualities and revolutionary nature of her 'one-piece' dress and sandals. An updated feminist ideology was part of Putnam's 'revolt': 'I had abandoned all the nonsensical claptrap of dress with which women unconsciously symbolized their bondage' (Putnam 1930: 237). Feminists viewed artistic expression in dress and sex as one more way in which to refute gender norms and negate the perennial matronly stereotype of old-wave feminists. Putnam related the new ideal through her dress: 'I was . . . not unbeautiful, for these new clothes were full of color . . . no corset is necessary with this form of garment' Tarbell 1913: 34).

Accounts often portray Henrietta Rodman and young feminist 'Village girls' wearing sacks, batik dresses and bobbed hair. They are often distinguished from seemingly more cultured women in fashionable robes and footwear. Such differences probably demonstrate degrees of financial means and aesthetic savvy as well as personal social expression.

Dress signified free speech in early radical Greenwich Village. Dress as heterosexual liberation was very much about finding ways to arrive at equality, a new orientation to the world. Just as sexuality was a philosophy unto itself and sexual expression without social rules was considered to be a right of women, dress signified personal freedom. The women of Heterodoxy who engaged in personal disclosure viewed the experience as integral to changes in their consciousness. Many discussed their lives in terms of 'before and after Heterodoxy' and some alluded to the changes in their physical appearance. A 1920 scrapbook dedicated to the originator of the club is representative of how these women viewed their dress as an extension of personal development. The 'Heterodoxy to Marie' photo album included photos of women in their Gibson Girl personae around 1900 and their very different appearance in 1920 with bobbed hair and large artistic earrings (Irwin Papers).

Mabel Dodge, who used her salon as a vehicle for free speech, and introduced psychoanalysis in a social forum in 1913, remarked of the new psychology: 'it was thought to be just as queer as all other attempts people were making to achieve some kind of social adaptation' (Luhan 1936: 142). Dodge's comment, eclectic venue, and the variety of dress found there constitute cultural indicators of the period. People longed for social and personal change; the salon became a hub for sharing ideas and social experimentation. Avant-garde artist and reputed playwright Djuna Barnes' first years in Greenwich Village, when she attended the Dodge salon, 'seemed to her some years later to be a kind of transitional phase in her life when she stood poised between her old manner and a new personality that was about to unfold' (Field 1985: 48). Barnes' self-portraits of the later 1910s depict a bohemian appearance.

The rebellious climate of Greenwich Village permeated the culture and found expression in dress. Brenda Ueland, an aspiring writer and sister of a settlement house supervisor, proudly related her encounters with the revolutionary John Reed. Ueland bobbed her hair, wore a tam-o'-shanter, and took up smoking shortly after her arrival in Greenwich Village from Minnesota. Such symbols of freedom and chic were simple enough to do quickly and on a limited budget. An element of daring (being a 'little tough') achieved by this dress allowed young women to be a part of the rebellion and excitement in Greenwich Village. Ueland, in her book *Me*, contrasts short-haired Village girls who were dashing, bold, and modern in their views and appearance with Myrtle, a plain uptown conventional girl (1983: 130).

Exposure to trends in downtown Manhattan and exchanges of information among young women of various groups and classes inspired young women to change their appearance. Brenda Ueland, while still in the Midwest, first learned of the new trends in hair through a 1913 visit from her bobbed-hair factory worker friend who resided in a settlement house in New York. Students exposed to Henrietta Rodman (in her English classes) cut their hair.

Dodge intermittently sought psychoanalysis during her years in Greenwich Village and circa 1913–16 discussed with her analyst her desire to cut her hair short. Mabel recalled, 'I confided to him my curious hankering to cut off my hair. No women cut their hair in those days . . . Yes, for a long time, now, I had wanted to cut my hair off, and I knew I'd be doing it one of these days.' Dodge bobbed her hair upon relocating to New Mexico in 1917–18 (Luhan 1936: 444).

During a nationwide speaking tour in 1919, Louise Bryant had her hair bobbed in a straight, glossy cut referred to by one newspaper as a 'George Sand' haircut (Dearborn 1996: 113). Bryant, who covered the Russian Revolution with her famous journalist husband, John Reed, created an exotic look, particularly with the use of make-up, that expressed her new-found sense of independence and vitality.

Feminist philosophies about sexuality and the body – largely derived from Swedish feminist ideology – translated into fashionable pagan notions in bohemian Greenwich Village towards the second half of the 1910s. Serious radical sexuality grounded in ideology had a freewheeling edge found among the drinking and theater crowd who socialized at popular spots like the Hell Hole. Radicals used psychology to explain their behavior to themselves and others. In reality liberation was well under way by virtue of the eclectic mix of men and women from all walks of life in the Village. Single, independent women casually interacted with men at favorite hangouts, drank, smoked, took lovers, and wore tight sweaters and chic berets. The 'loose draperies that fell off the shoulders' (Werner, 1958–1960) of one restaurant owner, a member of the Provincetown Players theater crowd, had a grass-roots panache that became part of the trendy, exotic look, viewed by original Villagers as pretentious.

Stereotypical and outlandish bohemian dress was strongly lampooned in Greenwich Village publications. Cartoons depicted 'Radicals': women in hand-printed dresses and striped rolled socks with long cigarette holders and overdone artistic jewelry, and men in baggy and striped suits, and Villagers reading Freud (*Quill*, April 1923).

But Villagers believed themselves to be distinct in their attitudes and dress from the more frivolous uptown Broadway culture. Bohemians did not wear lingerie dresses popular in the later 1910s. Radicals' ideals, however, became construed within the commercial Village culture. One vice reporter observed Villagers at a Pagan Rout costume ball: 'All are close students of sex psychology and read every book on sex that can be found' (Reports of the Committee of Fourteen, 1916/17). Political ideas surrounding sexuality and personal ideology developed into faddish paradigms of sexuality commonly discussed at recreational venues such as dances.

Hobohemia, a play set and staged in 1919, reflected the trends in Village pop culture: modern art on the walls, batik dress, bobbed hair, a vamp look in make-up, women smoking, interest in primitive art and esoteric religions, and alternative forms of dress for both men and women. The main female character clearly appeared to emulate serious Village artists like Clara Tice, whose exotic persona New York newspapers and magazines captured (Saville 2003). One Village author stated 'The brooding and oddities of bohemia led to poses, theatricalism, pretense' (Freeman 1938: 247).

In her 1920 play, *Chains of Dew*, Pulitzer prize playwright Susan Glaspell captured the notion of creating identity through dress: 'You are starting anew. You can be anything you like – according to the kind of bob you have.' While Glaspell satirized the pretense of Greenwich Village, she also emphasized the bohemian view of dress as a cultural indicator. One

Figure 3.4 Edna St. Vincent Millay, *c.* 1920. Library of Congress. Courtesy of the
Edna St. Vincent Millay Society.

character explained 'The people I know don't wear clothes – that is – not
what you would call clothes. They wear ideas.'

Edna St. Vincent Millay transformed herself from a precocious and
provincial young woman into the embodiment of liberated sexuality and
personal independence through her poetry, attitudes, and dress developed
while living in Greenwich Village. Millay represented through her poetry a
bold and brash idealism for young women in the 1920s. In one *c.* 1920
photograph (Figure 3.4), Millay expressed her bohemianism through

artistic dress that included a peasant blouse, a scrimshaw necklace, and bobbed hair. Not keen on social movements such as psychoanalysis but rather driven to subvert outworn familial and social boundaries, Millay epitomized the adventure and spontaneous spirit of the 1920s (Epstein 2001).

Movements such as psychoanalysis that had a profound influence on the art and writing of such bohemians as Eugene O'Neill, did not in and of themselves change people or dress. Most people (including Villagers) were only superficially aware of the meaning of Freudian theory. The subject and its paradigms, however, were an important component of the mutable ideology that shaped the evolving bohemian culture through the 1910s and in the 1920s, eventually impacting the larger culture.

Dress signified changes in cultural mores, not only through the expression of dress in Greenwich Village, but through what dress represented to the wider culture. Pop psychology in the Village that included the parlor game of dream analysis infiltrated the wider culture through connotations to Village dress. *Vanity Fair*, in December 1916, satirically captured the Greenwich Village artist/poet who has 'renounced hair dressers, given up stays, and entered a smock for life. She inhabits Washington Square and lives on . . . the Freudian theory of dreams' (76).

Dress in the Village transcended conventional norms. Techniques in textile crafts were used to manufacture artistic dress styles for the popular market, often with hemlines and silhouettes of mainstream dress. But many dress trends unique to the Village did not follow popular lengths or silhouettes. Exotic garb, such as batik caftans, artistic dress, tunics and peasant blouses, were often designed and cut according to ethnic models or aesthetic dress. Shorter skirts and rolled stockings popular towards 1920–2 were worn within the bohemian culture prior to their adoption in the dominant culture. Mainstream women learned of bobbed hair to a large extent through references to Village women. Thus, the dress of the 1920s flapper period followed a course set by the dress and culture of the 1910s.

Changes in fashion and social mores through the 1920s are related to various social and cultural factors specific to that era. Feminist historians contend that the flapper iconography towards the mid 1920s manifested itself in response to the feminist movement. The late 1910s and early 1920s bohemian literature portrays the victimization of the emotionally available bohemian male archetype by the suddenly polarized bitter feminist. Simmons (1993: 17–42) suggests that the continuation of feminist paradigms into the 1920s was a threat to the very basis of culture. The adolescent and less threatening flapper replaced the bohemian feminist as the cultural archetype.

Social accounts portray adolescent girls in middle-class neighborhoods dressing and acting in the same nonchalant manner as 'flappers' and bohemians in the Village in 1922. Village fashions such as scarves, hats without brims pulled over the eyes, and bobbed hair are condescendingly described in conservative commentary of the period. By the early 1920s, Village girls wore knee-length skirts with socks and sandals, a variation of the feminist garb initiated in 1913. Bohemian Greenwich Village supported and widened the parameters for acceptable dress and behavior in the 1920s.

Conclusion

Dress in Greenwich Village of the 1910s was imbued with cultural signifi-cance. Feminist ideology combined with art and social movements resulting in far-reaching cultural change. Dress and philosophy in the Village were shaped through experimentation with political and psycho-logical models that stressed free speech and social and sexual equality. Feminists adopted artistic dress while shaping their sexual paradigms and philosophies. Peasant dress of simpler societies, aesthetic dress styles and emancipated garb, including uncorseted sack dresses and sandals and socks, expressed the liberated ethos of the Village.

As Greenwich Village commercialized, political and artistic dress devel-oped into faddish dress. Artistic robes, tie-dyed caftans, tunics and smocks and peasant blouses became chic styles worn by tearoom hostesses and tour guides, and sold widely in bohemian shops. Smocks and bobbed hair became the means by which an increasingly young population assimilated into the community. The idea of the body as a shrine and expressing oneself through art, dance, movement, and sensuality facilitated the use of scarves, beads, robes, cropped hair and cosmetics. Exotic themes in dress and culture occurred in conjunction with fashionable views on sexuality and psychology.

The traditional image of the flapper evolved over a period of time. However, several elements of dress and behavior associated with the American flappers stemmed from reforms first seen in Greenwich Village. Bobbed hair, loose-fitting dresses with short skirts, rolled hose, beaded necklaces and slouchy hats with brims pulled down on the forehead were the hallmarks of bohemian dress in Greenwich Village prior to the roaring twenties.

Acknowledgment

Research was funded by the Stella Blum Research Grant (2000), awarded annually by the Costume Society of America in support of original student research on North American dress.

References

Anthony, K. (1915), *Feminism in Germany and Scandinavia*, New York: Henry Holt. 'The Battle of the Skirts' (1922), *Outlook*, 18 July: 275–6.

Chapin, A.A. (1917), *Greenwich Village*, New York: Dodd, Mead and Co.

Cobb, I.S. (1917), 'Twixt the Bluff and the Sound: Improbable People of an Impossible Land,' *Saturday Evening Post*, July 28.

Conklin, P.B. (1958), Interview by Louis Scheaffer, The Scheaffer-O'Neill Collection, Charles E. Shain Library, Connecticut College.

Cowley, M. (1934), *Exile's Return: A Literary Odyssey of the 1920s*, New York: Viking Press.

Dearborn, M.V. (1996), *Queen of Bohemia, The Life of Louise Bryant*, New York: Houghton Mifflin Co.

Dell, F. (1926), *Love in Greenwich Village*, New York: George H. Doran Company.

—— (1969). *Homecoming*, Port Washington, NY: Kennikat Press.

Eastman, M. (1948), *Enjoyment of Living*, New York: Harper & Brothers.

Epstein, D.M. (2001), *What Lips My Lips Have Kissed: The Loves and Love Poems of Edna St. Vincent Millay*, New York: Henry Holt.

Field, A. (1985), *Djuna: The Formidable Miss Barnes*, Austin: University of Texas Press.

Freeman, J. (1938), *An American Testament: A Narrative of Rebels and Romantics*, London: Victor Gollancz Ltd.

Glaspell, S. (1920), 'Claims of Dew,' unpublished play, February 21, Washington, DC: Library of Congress.

Hall, G.S. (1922), 'Flapper Americana novissma,' *Atlantic Monthly* 129, June: 771–80.

Johns, O. (1937), *Time of our Lives; The Story of My Father and Myself*, New York: Stackpole.

Kemp, H. (1926), *More Miles: An Autobiographical Novel*, New York: Boni and Liveright.

Lillethun, A.G. (2002), 'Batik in America: Javanese to Javanese, 1893 to 1937,' Ph.D dissertation, The Ohio State University.

—— (2003), 'Javanese influence on American Ladies Fashion in the Early 20th Century,' Paper presented at the annual national symposium of the Costume Society of America, Charleston, SC.

Luhan, M.D. (1936), *Movers and Shakers. Vol. 3 of Intimate Memories*, Albuquerque: University of New Mexico Press.

Madame Rogue (1915), 'Philosophical Fashions: The Importance of Being Dressed,' *Rogue*, July 15.

Meyerowitz, J. (1993), 'Sexual Geography and Gender Economy: The Furnished Room Districts of Chicago, 1890–1930,' in Barbara Melosh (ed.), *Gender and American History Since 1890*, London: Routledge.

Milbank, C.R. (1989), *New York Fashion: The Evolution of American Style*, New York: Harry N. Abrams.

Putnam, N.W. (1930), *Laughing Through*, New York: Sears Publishing Company.

Reports of the Committee of Fourteen, Office for the Suppression of Vice, New York City, The Greenwich Village Dances at Webster Hall 1916/17, Manuscripts and Archives Division, New York Public Library, New York City.

Richwine, K. (1968), 'The Liberal Club: Bohemia and the Resurgence in Greenwich Village, 1912–1918,' Unpublished Ph.D. dissertation, University of Pennsylvania.

Saville, D. (2003), 'Freud, Flappers and Bohemians: The Influence of Modern Psychological Thought and Social Ideology on Dress, 1910–1923,' *Dress* 30: 63–79.

Scherman, B.K. (1964), *Girl from Fitchburg*, New York: Random House.

Simmons, C. (1993), 'Modern Sexuality and the Myth of Victorian Repression,' in Barbara Melosh (ed.), *Gender and American History Since 1890*, London: Routledge.

Stansell, C. (2000), *American Moderns: Bohemian New York and the Creation of a New Century*, New York: Henry Holt.

Tarbell, I. (1913), 'Nina Wilcox Putnam: Woman Who Has Unset the Tyranny of Feministic Fashion,' *American Magazine*, May: 34–6.

Tice, C. (1921), Interview in 'Greenwich Village "Queen" here decries beauty that is purchased,' *St. Louis Star*, June 9.

Ueland, B. (1983), *Me*, St. Paul: The Schubert Club.

Van Vechten, C. (1922), *Peter Whiffle; His Life and Works*, New York: Alfred A. Knopf.

Ware, C. (1935), *Greenwich Village, 1920–1930: A Comment on American Civilization in the Post-War Years*, New York: Harper & Row Publishers.

Watson, S. (1991), *Strange Bedfellows: The First American Avant-Garde*, New York: Abbeville Press.

Werner, H.H. (n.d.), Interview by Louis Scheaffer, The Scheaffer-O'Neill Collection, Charles E. Shain Library, Connecticut College.

Wittenstein, K. (1998), 'The Feminist Use of Psychoanalysis: Beatrice M: Hinkle and the Foreshadowing of Modern Feminism in the United States,' *Journal of Women's History* 10, summer: 38–63.

Archives

Billy Rose Theater Special Collections, New York Public Library for the Performing Arts, New York Public Library.

Culin Archival Collection, Brooklyn Museum of Art.

Edna St. Vincent Millay Papers, Library of Congress.

Greenwich Village Follies and Provincetown Players Papers, New York Public Library for the Performing Arts, New York Public Library.

Greenwich Village Research File, Museum of the City of New York.

Guido Bruno Collection, Museum of the City of New York.

Inez Haynes Irwin Papers, Schlesinger Library, Radcliffe Institute for Advanced Study, Harvard University.

Mabel Dodge Luhan Papers, Beinecke Rare Book and Manuscript Library, Yale University.

Madeline Zabriskie Doty Papers, Smith College.

Mary Ware Dennet Papers, Schlesinger Library, Radcliffe Institute for Advanced Study, Harvard University.

M.D.C. Crawford Collection, Brooklyn Museum of Art.

Photographs of Jessie Tarbox Beals, Museum of the City of New York.

Robert F. Wagner Archives, Tamiment Library, New York University.

Scheaffer-O'Neill Collection, Charles E. Shain Library, Connecticut College.

Tessim Zorach Collection, National Museum of American Art, Smithsonian Institution.

Textile Collection, National Museum of American History, Smithsonian Institution.

Theater Collection Photographs, Museum of the City of New York.

William Zorach Papers, Library of Congress.

4

The Influence of American Jazz on Fashion

Susan L. Hannel

Editors' Introduction: The efforts to provide more sensible dress for women finally came to fruition in the 1920s, as seen in Chapter 3. Many factors help explain the change in women's dress from highly structured complex garments to the short, shapeless dresses that emerged in the 1920s. The change occurred, in part, with a shift from Victorian and Edwardian sensibilities to modernist concepts of functionality. Also, in America more young people were entering college and creating new lifestyles for their generation. With the emergence of better communication, airplanes and affordable automobiles, life began to move at a faster pace. Clothes reflected a changing society. Women wore simple, boyish styles that eliminated the need for boned corsets, and they bobbed their hair. The styles allowed for freedom of movement that the dress reformers of the past only dreamed of. But still, American women's fashion was mainly Paris fashion; the French label held sway in American retail establishments.

In keeping with this new age, Americans embraced a newly discovered musical form – jazz. Originating in New Orleans, jazz spread to major cities all across the United States. In New York, Chicago and other cities young men and women danced to the music of jazz. It soon had an effect on clothing styles. Our collective memories place the flapper at the center of 1920s fashion. We know the music; we know the clothes. But not every American woman was a flapper; the flapper was a young, adventurous woman who experimented with her new-found freedoms and lifestyle, and of course, swayed to the music. When the music spread to Europe, Paris in particular embraced jazz. As discussed by Susan Hannel, the American and French love of jazz dance expressed itself in dress via motifs in printed textiles, 'slave' jewelry, African hairstyles, and fringed dresses that imitated grass skirts.

When we imagine the 1920s, the picture that often comes to mind is the rail-thin 'flapper' wearing a short dress embellished with beaded fringe kicking up her heels while dancing the Charleston. The flapper wore her dress shockingly short and bared more skin than women of previous generations in Western history. The look of the flapper has become a symbol of modern America and is emblematic of women's changing roles in society. In 1920 women gained the right to vote, and many young women attended college and were making a living for themselves. Changes appeared on every front, and the emergence of a new youth culture was central. Seeking new ways to define themselves, young people quickly embraced the new music of the era, jazz, and jazz dancing. It was the latter, jazz dancing, that would set the stage for the emergence of the youthful American flapper.

Like the flapper's dress, jazz was a radical departure from the past and became a symbol of the 1920s. The music was unique and, with its African origins, its rhythms and its syncopation, many considered it exotic. Jazz musicians, invariably African Americans, were considered the 'savage' creators of this music and were themselves perceived as exotic.[1]

As jazz became increasingly popular, it permeated many elements of popular culture, including fashion. Music and fashion have always had a close relationship, so when jazz became popular in the post-war years, it is not surprising that it had an effect on fashion. Women needed new clothing to wear while dancing the new dances. The energetic nature of jazz dances like the Charleston and the Black Bottom no doubt contributed to the need for shorter evening dresses without sleeves, dresses that would allow the legs and arms to move with complete freedom, dresses with skirts, fringe and beading that would fly away from the body like the arm and leg movements required by the dances. Mounds of hair pinned to the top of the head would never stay in place during such vigorous bouncing. Shorter hair clearly was more appropriate for these dances. The popular and fashionable dancer Irene Castle had already set an example when she bobbed her hair in the teens.

The swinging, sparkling, and sometimes cacophonous fringe and jewelry of the quintessential 'flapper' were but one manifestation of the fashion for jazz music. Costumes for costume balls and the decoration of accessories also capitalized on dance themes and the vogue for jazz. Images of jazz musicians were printed onto fabrics. Geometric print patterns applied to textile surfaces also reflected the active and improvisational nature of jazz. Jazz changed the musical landscape, and then contributed to the transformation of fashion in France and the United States.

This essay illustrates the specific ways in which jazz dance influenced garment silhouettes and embellishment, as well as how the idiom of jazz music influenced the content and geometry of modern textile prints. More importantly, the essay shows how African American musicians and performers, and stereotypes about their tribal African heritage, influenced perceptions about jazz and thereby influenced jazz fashion.

History of Jazz and Jazz Dance

While jazz music and dancing seemed forward and completely novel in the early 1920s, the musical elements of jazz had developed at the turn of the century. African American amateur brass bands in New Orleans were playing early forms of the music around 1900. The diverse nature of New Orleans with its inhabitants of many races and cultures allowed musicians to borrow from multiple genres of music. By 1910 professional musicians were able to make a living playing jazz in New Orleans and all over the South. The Original Dixieland 'Jass' Band, a five-member band consisting of a trumpet, a trombone, a clarinet, a piano, and drums, is credited with bringing this style of music to New York in 1917. New Orleans jazz simultaneously gained popularity in Chicago. Jazz music grew out of syncopated ragtime piano music and blues played during the early part of the twentieth century. Both ragtime and the blues were considered African American music before Tin Pan Alley, the sheet and recorded music industry, altered them for mass audiences. Paul Whiteman popularized jazz dance, toning down its African American blues elements to make it more appealing to a wide audience (Erenberg 1981; Leonard 1962). Whiteman's type of jazz has been called 'refined' or 'commercial' jazz, and was the kind of dancing music many people in white communities enjoyed.

Jazz was not limited to American soil, for its influence was felt in Europe, particularly in France, where a critique of Western civilization by the Parisian avant-garde followed the First World War. Jazz music and Africa were at the center of that critique. The French had been aware of African art since at least 1906 when Picasso and his circle began to incorporate images based on African sculpture in their art. It took 'the dreadful, mechanical slaughter of the war [to] sharply . . . increase this fascination, for African culture seemed to embody the lush, naïve sensuality and spirituality that cold, rational Europeans had lost' (Stovall 1996: 31). As a way of finding new traditions in which to believe, the French looked to the myth of the 'noble savage,' seeing African people not as equal, but rather as innocent and uncorrupted, with a proximity to nature that rendered them superior to white Europeans (Rousseau 1984 [1755]).

The power of the connection between jazz music, black culture, and the critique of Western culture is well illustrated in the following example. For the surrealist artist Paul Lebeer, jazz was the catalyst to study African art. The primary reason for his interest in blacks was not black art or the opening of the Sudan in Africa, but jazz. He attended his first black jazz concert in Paris when he was a very young man at the end of the First World War. In that period he also began to write about modern art. In his account of how jazz brought him to African art, Lebeer explains that one of the main elements of surrealism was an extremely violent critique of Western civilization that in turn elevated other civilizations. Though African art was not as closely related to surrealism as Oceanic art, it was more desirable for its creativity and remained part of the surrealist critique (Leiris 1967).

Though jazz became popular during the First World War, the raucous, unorthodox jazz music of the 1920s, like the interest in African Art, eventually came to represent a critique of French life and a rejection of traditional values (Blake 1999; Stovall 1996: 37). Jazz reflected this change for two reasons. First, it sounded like nothing ever before created and thus nourished the desire for a break with the war-torn past. Second, most people playing jazz in Paris were African Americans. The French saw all blacks as primitive and exotic; it was unimportant to them that black people came from many parts of Africa and the New World. The result of this ignorance and stereotyping was that jazz music became the music of the 'noble savage' and fit into the vogue for blacks and black arts as symbols of an uncorrupted past in the history of the human race. In fact, the Parisian demand for black jazz musicians was so intense during the 1920s that white jazz musicians had trouble competing for jobs (Stovall 1996: 38; Archer-Straw 2000).

As the 1920s commenced, France began to look with interest to America's jazz and skyscrapers, not only as a way of reacting against the past, but also as a way of becoming modern. In fact, Americans travelling to France in 1922 were astounded 'to discover that the very things they have come abroad to get away from – the machines, the advertisements, the elevators and the jazz – have begun to fascinate the French' (Wilson 1922: 49). The couturier Paul Poiret observed in 1927, 'At the present moment we in France are slaves to the American influence' (Poiret 1927: 32). Poiret also believed the French popularity of cigarettes and pajama pants came from America.

Until this time European popular music and concert music existed in separate spheres as low and high musical art. Phillipe Soupault, in his 1930 essay, 'The American Influence in France,' stated that along with American cinema and poetry, jazz music had had a strong effect on the French: 'What remains profoundly true is that this music worked its way in and struck violently those whom the cinema had already awakened to the American influence' (19–20). He believed that jazz had exposed the French to the 'close relationship between art and life' in American culture (20), and encouraged a new mingling of forms in highly stratified France.

The popularity of jazz music in France led many French fashion magazines to include articles about jazz musical events occurring in Paris. There were also obtuse references to jazz music, as seen in a 1922 illustration titled 'Le Jazzoflute,' where a woman wearing a De Beer evening dress plays a slide flute in front of a wind-up phonograph (*Gazette du Bon Ton* 1922). The demand for jazz music in Paris during the 1920s brought many African American musicians and performers to the city, and consequently articles about African American performers began to appear in the pages of French fashion magazines (Stovall 1996). Photographs of performers in costume and descriptions of their doings outside the music halls gave the French public information about the jazz and music hall scene. These descriptions reflected contemporary stereotypes of blacks. In 1923, *Vogue Paris* included a photo of the African American performer Florence Mills, in costume, noting that she evoked 'warm earth and long nights' ('Florence Mills' 1923: 35). Suggesting Africa with references to warm earth, tom-toms, and jungle rains was frequently a part of these descriptions. It seems that to be of African descent, whether truly African or African American, was to be forever attached to the geography and climate of Africa. Linking jazz music to the jungle and its inhabitants was fairly typical for the period. The artist Charles Lepape demonstrated this tendency when he designed a picture rug in knotted wool, *c.* 1928, called *La Jungle,* depicting three black musicians: one on a guitar, one on a saxophone and one on a washboard (*Art of Textiles* 1989: Plate 223).

African American performers were also part of the French social pages and mentioned in the accounts of social events around Paris. In the summer of 1926 the French magazines *Femina* and *Le Figaro* sponsored a fundraiser showcasing French fashion called 'Le grande nuit de Paris.' The magazines later featured portraits and photos of several African Americans who attended the fundraiser. 'Midnight in New York' was one of many entertainment skits that were staged that night: 'This very modern tableau was composed for the pleasure of our eyes . . . and our ears . . . To the rhythm of a jazz band disrupting everything, this [evocation] created an amusing exhibition of the dances currently in vogue, among others a Charleston performed by two superb blacks' ('Grand Nuit' 1926).

Of course the Paris-based American dancer and singer Josephine Baker made it into the fashion pages. She modeled couture, and advertised

Bakerfix hair pomade. Despite the economic control and racial bias of whites, Baker was the master of her image. By manipulating her onstage image to coincide with European and American expectations of the exotic, she made millions. She used her scanty costumes, make-up and jungle stage settings, as well as 'conventions of the burlesque to create a *danse sauvage* that played with the paradigm of the black exotic in the context of white colonialism' (Martin 1995: 311). By playing the less evolved, less civilized black woman, Baker allowed her audiences to feel superior and in control while at the same time providing a vicarious sexual experience forbidden in everyday life.

While Josephine Baker had much more of an impact on the French than she did on Americans, news about her accomplishments in Europe was enthusiastically reported in the United States. Information about Josephine Baker in popular magazines like *Vanity Fair* was so upbeat and flattering as to be almost fawning ('Dark Star in Paris' 1934: 34, 74). By 1934, she was seen as one of the two most famous Americans in Europe. (Woodrow Wilson was the other.) Despite the positive review of Baker's successes, language describing her was often couched in racial stereotypes associating blacks with the jungle and childlike qualities. In her private life she dressed casually 'like a comfortable child' (74). She was the 'Pennsylvania Negress' with the 'superb slim jungle torso' and 'erotic rhythm' (34). The reader was never permitted to forget that Baker was a black American, though it was mentioned that she was more the product of the Champs Élysées in Paris than of New York's Broadway.

American fashion magazines also featured jazz themes, especially in advertisements. An advertisement appealing to 'The Sophisticated Smoker' depicted exuberant dancers etched into a French-made cigarette case illustrating 'youth, joy and jazz' ('For the Sophisticated Smoker' 1929: 118). Another ad for shoes took advantage of the jazz craze by trumpeting: 'Shoes that Jazz to the Jubilant Sax' ('Shoes that Jazz' 1927: 56). The extreme reach of jazz themes is well illustrated with the design for a sampler, a traditional textile art form used to teach young women needle skills, that included a dancing couple and black musicians, presumably playing jazz ('Dear Me!' 1928: 64).

As Harlem became one of the centers of jazz music, American fashion magazines pointed to its importance to New York nightlife, covering the popular nightclubs and the celebrities who performed there, all the while perpetuating the same stereotypes and rhetoric found in French magazines. By 1931 *Vogue* reported that 'Every one [*sic*] can go to Harlem – and everyone does. You might almost say it was part of an American education to see the dusky high lights of Harlem' ('Came the Dawn' 1931: 120). It was a 'hot-spot' (Shaw 1931: 73), and the 'Mecca of foreign visitors and jaded New Yorkers' ('Came the Dawn' 1931: 43).

Harlem was perceived as a place where one could throw off the constraints of American morality. A guide to the nightlife of New York City in 1931 stated that Harlem, like Paris, 'changes people. Especially the "proper" kind, once they get into its swing' [*sic*] (Shaw 1931: 73). Travelling to Harlem to hear and dance to jazz music was one way that Americans could alleviate sexual repression. 'Jazz culture and Harlem in the 1920s represented liminal space – a continual carnival where whites [went] slumming to "let off steam"' (Martin 1995: 318; Edwards 2001: 155).

Jazz symbolized cultural change, and the interest in Harlem and jazz rhythms, that 'peculiarly modern commodity,' was also seen as a symptom of degeneration by those who felt threatened by the changes; 'Perhaps it is a sign of the lack of virility of our modern "smart set" that the contemplation of the sensuous, tropical, and erotic savageries of the Negroes gives an exhilaration and a sense of the quickened life that even the wildest antics of Broadway fail to give' ('Came the Dawn' 1931: 120). When attending the clubs of Harlem, where the performing blacks 'know only too well the charms of their darkness,' the white audience, 'huddled in the surrounding dusk, inert from drink and lack of air . . . feel the anaemia of their own race; and the white girls glance with a sort of dull resentment at the vital contortions of their tea-colored sisters' (Mannes 1934: 94).

Jazz dances like the Charleston and the Black Bottom were popularized on Broadway and Harlem stages. The Charleston, a dance well known to African Americans in the South, had been seen in the South at least since the turn of the century (Stearns and Stearns 1994: 111–4). The Charleston is danced with the knees bent, then straightened, while the feet pivot in and out. Weight is shifted from one leg to another and the free leg is kicked out from the body at an oblique angle. The arms swing forward and back in opposition to the legs. The dance was performed in several African American shows in the early 1920s, and became a dance craze only after the 1921 musical review *Shuffle Along*, where it was danced to a melody called *Baltimore Blitz*, and James P. Johnson and Cecil Mack's 1923 version in *Runnin Wild*, a musical with African American performers that opened at the New York Colonial Theatre on 62nd street (Stearns and Stearns 1994: 111–2). The careers of both Ginger Rogers and Joan Crawford were launched by the Charleston. Rogers was even billed as 'Queen of the Charleston' (Stearns and Stearns 1994: 112). Unlike the Black Bottom, the Charleston remained popular and was revived many times. In telling the history of the Charleston for *Vanity Fair* in 1926, Eric Walrond stated that:

people like the Charleston because it satisfies an instinctive urge in them. In a measure it is for this very reason that there is interest in the primitive songs and music of the black slaves and their descendants. It certainly is the spirit preeminently responsible for the vogue of the black and brown reviews, Florence Mills, Paul Robeson, Roland Hayes, African art, the creative writings of the 'new' Negro, Countée Cullen, Harlem and the Negro cabarets. ('Charleston, Hey! Hey!' 1926: 116)

The Black Bottom, like the Charleston, was danced by African Americans in the South long before the African American pianist/composer Perry Bradford introduced it in 1919 as a dance-song available in sheet music (Stearns and Stearns 1994: 110–2). George White saw the Black Bottom in Harlem in 1924 in the stage play *Dinah* and had it adapted for his Broadway review *Scandals of 1926* after which it became an official dance craze. The Black Bottom incorporated slapping the backside with forward and backward hopping, feet stomping and pelvic gyrations, movements that were considered overly erotic for the period. The Charleston and the Black Bottom were refined by making the movements less exaggerated for the ballroom in order to suit white Americans' tastes.

Jazz Fashion

The Black Bottom and the Charleston were popular enough to influence dancing dresses, fancy dress costumes and images on textile prints. Even Poiret pointed to their influence on French fashion, predicting that 'the implacable and hypertrophic rhythms of the new dances, the blues and the Charleston, the din of unearthly instruments, and the musical idioms of exotic lands' as well as other American influences would eventually lead to increasing masculinity and severity in women's fashion (1927: 32). His design prediction for pants influenced by 'Some Future Charleston,' he described as 'a costume which is largely a matter of bracelets' (1927: 36). Stacked heavy bracelets could serve two purposes: to be an additional source of sound and to reflect an interest in things African, as in the stacks of African bracelets worn by women in the avant-garde like Nancy Cunard (Chisholm 1979). The bracelets were thus a reference to the African origins of the Charleston. Interest in pants made sense in a period where the androgyny and youthfulness of short hair, flattened chests and tubular silhouettes were in evidence. Pants would also be more modest than a skirt for a dance like the Charleston.

Jazz dance was parodied in the design costumes for fancy dress balls. In 1925 *Art-Goût-Beauté* suggested 'Miss Jazz' as an appropriate costume.

'Miss Jazz' was a long thin dress of black and silver geometric shapes worn with a tall hat similar to a wizard's hat. The sharp triangles of contrasting black and silver in the costume were as much a reflection of modern geometric design as they were of the energy and syncopation associated with jazz. Costumes based on the popular dances, the Black Bottom and the Charleston, were illustrated in January 1927, also in *Art-Goût-Beauté*. Both costumes have pants decorated with large jazz motifs. The Charleston costume has a large music note close to the hem and the Black Bottom costume has a banjo in the same place. The model wearing the Black Bottom costume also carries a 'golliwog' doll. The Oxford English Dictionary defines golliwog as 'A name invented for a black-faced grotesquely dressed (male) doll with a shock of fuzzy hair' (1989). The original golliwog character was a doll in B. Upton children's book *The Adventures of Two Dutch Dolls – and a Golliwog,* 1895. In the Black Bottom costume, the golliwog doll connects the dance to its African American origins.

Fancy dress costumes incorporating jazz themes allowed those who wore them to participate in the fashion for jazz in an environment where fantasy was allowed. The enduring nature of jazz costumes is illustrated by the two Black Bottom costumes worn to a party with the theme 'Come as a Song' on Long Island in the United States in 1939, when the dance had long since been eclipsed by other dances ('Party Given on Long Island' 1939: 86–7).

Jazz music was dance music and the popularity of dancing to jazz influenced the design of evening wear, including uneven handkerchief hems, fringe that swayed and made percussive sounds when the body moved, shiny fabrics that reflected light to the beat of that movement, and shorter hems which allowed the legs to move freely (*Robes Du Soir* 1990: 125–6). (Historic costume collections throughout the United States have significant numbers of short, beaded evening dresses from the 1920s, despite their fragility.) French couturiere J. Suzanne Talbot designed a 1927 evening dress fringed and strung with wooden beads. These elements simultaneously satisfied the desire for sound and movement while dancing the Charleston and reflected interest in primitive materials, a trend very much associated with the interest in African art and jazz music. The importance of fringe as an African influence can be seen in Figure 4.1, which depicts one of four dresses suggested for dancing by *La Gazette du Bon Ton* ('Robes a Danser' 1922: 161–4+). 'Femme Amaguilla (Afrique)' has a straight skirt covered by a voluminous, fringed overskirt. Fringe made up of small strips of fabric and exposed legs were often associated with African dress. In Figure 4.2, the cover of a 1925 composition by Richard Stevens called 'Dance of the Cannibals,' two of the dancers wear such

Figure 4.1 Fringe associated with African dress. 'Femme Amaguilla (Afrique)'
from 'Robes a Danser,' *La Gazette du Bon Ton*, May 1922: 166,
plate 38.

skirts. The skirts are remarkably similar to the 'banana' skirt worn by
Josephine Baker for her 'Danse Sauvage' in *La Revue Nègre* in Paris in
1925.

By the mid 1920s dance dresses were short and often the arms were bare,
allowing both the legs and the arms to move freely away from the body.
Exposed skin and the shortened skirt also reflected the more casual, less
formal atmosphere of the nightclub cabaret where much of the dancing

Figure 4.2 Fringed skirts on caricatures of Africans. 'Dance of the Cannibals,'
1925. Illustration by R. Ashley for sheet music cover. Composer:
Richard Stevens. Published by J. Fisher & Bro., New York.

was taking place (Erenberg 1981: 233–59). The shortness of evening
dresses for dancing most likely influenced similar trends in day dresses. A
July 1926 cover of *Life* by L.J. Holton (Figure 4.3), illustrates a woman
dancing the Charleston in a short day dress. Lest the viewer forget the
African origins of the Charleston, the background of the illustration
includes a veritable tribe of Africans, carrying their spears to heighten the
effect and wearing short, fringed skirts, in the same Charleston dance position as the female figure in front of them.

Figure 4.3 'Everything is Hot-tentotsy Now,' *Life*, July 15, 1926: cover. Illustration by L.J. Holton.

Jazz Textiles

Jazz and dance themes also made their way onto fabric prints. The 'Charleston' crepe was a textile designed by Edgar K. Frank & Co:

> the spirit of jazz has been cleverly caught and portrayed upon Canton silk and cotton crepe in its gayest and most daring of mood. The Englishman with the monacle danger-ously perched upon the edge of the tabouret is attempting to keep the drummer in time

Figure 4.4 African American playing saxophone. Silk crepe textile, *c.* 1925–30. The Museum of the Fashion Institute of Technology, ACOFA #125.

who seems to be 'running wild,' while the figures grouped around them are apparently trying to out-step one another. ('"Charleston" Crepe' 1925: 16)

A 'Jazz' print was included with the spring 1926 line of textiles called 'Americana Prints' from Stehli Silks ('Americana Prints' 1925: 1, 47). In 1928 Stehli again included a jazz-inspired print in its 'Americana' collection. 'Rhapsody,' a print inspired by George Gershwin's *Rhapsody in Blue* and designed by John Held Jr, was covered with figures of white men playing assorted instruments in a jazz band ('Characteristic New Spring Weaves and Prints' 1928: 87; McKnight, 1999). While jazz musicians were typically white in these textile prints, one extant silk textile of unknown provenance in the Textile Collection of The Museum of the Fashion Institute of Technology illustrates a black man in a tall hat playing what appears to be a saxophone (Figure 4.4).

John Held Jr, credited with creating the exquisite image of the flapper and her 'sheik,' did many covers for *Life* and illustrations for *Vanity Fair* and the *New Yorker*. Held was so influential that the society he caricatured began to imitate his satires; 'Of him it can be truly said: he set the style for the era: clothing, coiffure, manners, figures of speech and, most important of all, a youthful exuberance and all encompassing impudence' (Merkin 1968 n.p.).

Textiles were also influenced by the sounds of jazz, not just the images of jazz. Patterns in textiles reflected the wildly rhythmic and spontaneous qualities of jazz while also paying homage to the geometric, mechanized world of the 1920s. The Charleston inspired two such textile patterns. The painter and textile designer, Sonia Delaunay, sketched a garment and textile pattern called 'Charleston' in 1925 (Damase 1991: 105). The textile pattern has rows of small black triangles which emphasize visual rhythm through strong contrast of color and sharp edges. Their geometric shape is reiterated in the silhouette of the dress, two triangles turned so that their points join at the waistline, forming an hourglass shape. The angularity of the dress silhouette, like the textile motifs, reflects the jerky, angular movements of the Charleston.

An afternoon dress from 1927 by the couture house Philippe et Gaston, also titled 'Charleston,' has long strips of fabric applied down the length of the back of the dress, creating a visual beat from strip to strip ('Charleston Dress' 1927: 23). The strips fall away from the body of the skirt at the hem and then loop upward again and reattach to the skirt as they wrap toward the front. The loosely hanging strips of fabric provide extra swing and movement to the dress, reiterating the idea of movement found in its namesake, the Charleston dance.

Orienting Jazz Fashion

The introduction of jazz fashion into mainstream fashion may have been assisted by the tendency to link jazz themes with Orientalist themes already present in fashionable dress. Orientalist print motifs and garment silhouettes had been a strong influence for many years before the influence of jazz.

The term Orientalism arose in the late eighteenth century when it was associated with British policy in India, including the study of Indian culture in order to facilitate the administration of Britain's colonies. Orientalism also described a specific kind of exoticism in types of painting begun by the French and developed in other European countries early in the nineteenth century which used Middle Eastern and North African subjects (MacKenzie 1995: xiii, 2–3). It has since been used to describe the influence of the East on patterns, textiles, ceramics, furniture, and building styles. In the past twenty-five years Edward Said's interpretation of Orientalism has had much influence (Said 1978). Said argued that Oriental studies reflected 'intellectual and technical dominance and a means to the extension of political, military, and economic supremacy' by the West over the East, particularly the Middle East (MacKenzie 1995: xii). This more negative interpretation of Orientalism has come to dominate scholarly work on Orientalism, particularly in literary criticism.

Richard Martin and Harold Koda, in analyzing Orientalism in dress, noted: 'the Orientalist objective in Western dress was to cull from the various Easts that spellbinding foreignness for the purposes of rendering Western dress richer and more exotic' (1994: 12). Orientalism in dress was appealing because it was an alternative to Western dress. Jazz fashion was also an alternative to the dress that came before it and had the potential to enrich Western dress and textile design. The difference lay in the racial anxiety caused by associations with African American dance and music. To link the art of African Americans, people from the West African diaspora, to an Orient that included North Africa, Egypt and the Middle East, was to render them more exotic and less radical.

An example of associating jazz with an exotic East is found in a 1927 advertisement for William H. Davidow Sons Co.'s scarves and belts ('Wm. H. Davidow' 1927: 164). The accessories were decorated with Held's flappers playing jazz instruments. The advertisement also showed a woman in a desert oasis environment, as if in the Sahara in North Africa, wearing a coat or sweater with one of these Held jazz illustrations on the back. During the 1920s people were more familiar with North Africa than sub-Saharan Africa. Placing the coat and its jazz image in North Africa situated the coat in a recognizable African landscape. The desert oasis context also instructed the reader on the appropriate context for the garment: a sunny, resort-like locale with palm trees. An advertisement for Club Alabam in New York City features an illustration of a black man in tails wearing a turban and dancing in a landscape with a palm tree, again presumably North Africa ('Club Alabam' 1925: 30). The advertisement combines the American South (Alabama), African Americans (the dark face with the exaggerated white lips was a standard 'blackface' depiction of American blacks), and another North African landscape.

Jazz was linked to the Middle East when the term 'sheik' was to describe the white man dancing to jazz with his flappers depicted by John Held. 'John Held Jr drew the jazz-flapper and her sheik best . . . The lad was apple-headed, his hair buttered tight down, he wore bell-bottomed trousers, a raccoon coat, drove a Stutz Bearcat and played or danced to jazz a lot' (Longstreet 1956: 95). The term meant a 'type of a strong, romantic lover; a lady-killer,' and came into use after Hollywood adapted E.M. Hull's novel *The Sheik* (1919) for the 1921 film *The Sheikh* starring

Rudolph Valentino. Many young girls during the era eventually came to call their boyfriends 'my sheik' (Longstreet 1956: 95).

The title 'Jazz Cleopatra,' given to Josephine Baker is yet another way jazz was associated with the Middle East (Rose 1989). The title linked jazz and Baker, an African American of West African descent, to Egypt – considered at the time to be the Orient and not a part of Africa – while also identifying her as the queen of jazz. The connection between jazz and Orientalism was also seen in the popularity of 'slave' jewelry. Slave collars were a fairly innocuous way for fashionable women to incorporate exotic African themes into their modern look. Interest in slave collars as jewelry may have originated with the metal collars seen on eighteenth-century Venetian ceramic figurines of black slaves called 'Blackamoors.' An eighteenth-century Venetian Blackamoor torch-bearer sculpted in wood was described as having a slave collar 'in bright gilt' ('Blackamoor' 1926: 57). The twentieth-century slave collar jewelry could be made up of from one to many bands of solid metal that hung stiffly around the neck or tightly against the neck. The earliest French examples appear around 1925. The artist Jean Dunand, considered at the time to be an expert in colonial art (Howard 1931), painted several portraits of women in this kind of collar, including the hat designer Madame Agnès (Marcilhac 1991). Dunand eventually created his own version of the collar in lacquer and silver (Marcilhac 1991: plate 76). A 1927 illustration of one of Madame Agnès's Congo-inspired hats showed a model wearing a slave collar (de Meyer 1927: 71). The combination of African headdress and slave collar was a double reference to Africa.

In February of 1926 the slave collar in the United States was called a 'Charlot Necklet' because one was seen in *Charlot's Revue*, a yearly musical review that began in London and then moved to Broadway in New York. The collar was 'a ring of fourteen-karat gold, as plain as an old-fashioned wedding-ring, worn about the throat like a slave collar of long ago' ('Charlot Necklet' 1926: 53). The slave/Charlot necklet was popular enough to be on a *Vogue* cover by July of the same year.

The term 'slave' was also applied to bracelets. 'Slaves of fashion' in 1926 wore these bracelets and necklets ('Slaves of Fashion' 1926: 38). The slave bracelet was usually a series of rectangular links, sometimes connected with enamel links in red, green and black ('New Gold Jewellery' 1926: 85). The model wearing the 'Charlot necklet' above wore this style of slave bracelet. Slave bracelets were so widespread by December of 1926 that *Vogue* reported 'they had an exaggerated and much cheapened popularity' that could be alleviated by the Van Cleef and Arpels versions covered with diamonds, emeralds or rubies ('French Chic' 1926: 61). Such bracelets were often worn in multiples, a practice which had its detractors. A 1938 tongue-in-cheek 'psychiatric' analysis about the meaning of stacking numerous bracelets concluded that: 'one or two bracelets, you'll be relieved to know, are considered normal enough, but piling them on in quantities is likely to show an eagerness to be chained and enslaved, a regression to savagery, possibly even a bit of heinous masochism' ('Psychiatry Analyzes the Fashions' 1938: 68–9). Although meant to be humorous, the passage clearly links stacked bracelets to primitive cultures, but specifically Africa because of the references to slavery and savagery.

In 1926 *Vogue* illustrated a turbaned African whipping two bareheaded African slaves. In reference to the source of slave bracelets *Vogue* stated matter-of-factly, 'whatever their origin, slave bracelets like those shown just below are too intrinsically chic to be omitted' ('French Chic' 1926: 61). The African slaver in this illustration wears a turban on his head and is therefore associated with Orientalist or Middle Eastern depictions of slavery. The Orientalist connection to slave collars and bracelets is also seen in an advertisement for non-alcoholic Vermouth ('The Sultan's Secret' 1927: 159), where the sultan's woman wears a series of metal coils around her neck and wrist. Even her torso and ankles seem to be bound by the same accessory. The neck coils are related to the multiple coils seen as a slave collar on the July 1926 cover of *Vogue*. The images in the advertisement illustrate how easily the style for slave collars was transferred between Oriental and African-inspired fashion.

The process of associating jazz motifs and performers to North Africa and the Middle East makes sense in a culture comfortable with Oriental motifs but not so comfortable with African-derived and inspired motifs. Jazz and its performers were linked to Orientalist themes like slavery, the desert, and sheiks because Orientalism was already a very important part of fashionable dress and linking jazz and Orientalism was a way to make jazz more accessible, more exotic, and perhaps a little less radical.

Conclusion

Jazz-influenced fashion during the 1920s was an exciting amalgam of garments, accessories, and textiles. It included clothing designed for dancing to jazz music, as well as textiles that either illustrated jazz musicians or incorporated motifs with the visual rhythms of jazz syncopation and improvisation. Jazz influence extended also to fancy dress costumes that parodied the popular jazz dances like the Charleston and the Black Bottom.

Jazz fashion had two significant components, the recognition of the African American origins of jazz, and the competing desire to cloak and ameliorate those origins in comfortable Orientalist contexts and language. Underlying all of jazz fashion are the origins of African American music itself. References to the origins of jazz appear again and again in depictions and descriptions of jazz fashion. When clothing and textile designers connected African American art forms like jazz music and dance to fashion, a major shift occurred in the canon of Western dress. The new dance dresses created by these designers were shorter and more revealing than ever before. They made it easier to move to the music of jazz and they encouraged the shortening of day dresses. A flapper who wore such garments and danced the Charleston was seen as wild and untamed. The addition of fringe that swayed imitated African dress and, along with the sound it generated, contributed to perceptions about the primitive aspects of the performance and of the dance.

Jazz and jazz fashion were exciting and novel, but also produced anxiety. When slave jewelry was combined with African-inspired garments, the designer of the ensemble was recognizing the African origins of slavery and unconsciously referencing African American performers, descendents of African slaves. Anxiety produced by the radical changes associated with jazz and jazz fashion had to be tempered. Placing jazz images in recognizable African environments, or using terms like 'Jazz Cleopatra' for an African American performer, and 'sheik' for men who danced to jazz, made the changes easier to understand in a culture where Orientalist imagery and terms were already prevalent.

Note

1. 'Savage' is a word best used carefully. Writers used the word to describe jazz, African American performers, and even the 1920s decade. The term originates with the eighteenth-century French philosopher Jean-Jacques Rousseau, who invented the idea of the 'Noble Savage,' as being guided by his feelings and not his thoughts, and therefore perceived as untouched, unspoiled and innocent in his idyllic environment (Rousseau 1984 [1755]).

References

'"Americana Prints" Reflect American Themes by Six Prominent American Artists' (1925), *Women's Wear* 31(81) October 5: 1, 47.

Archer-Straw, P. (2000), *Negrophilia: Avant-Garde Paris and Black Culture in the 1920s*, London: Thames and Hudson.

The Art of Textiles (1989), London: Spink & Son Ltd.

'Blackamoor: A Novel Decoration' (1926), *Vogue*, August 1: 57.

Blake, J. (1999), *Le Tumulte Noir: Modernist Art and Popular Entertainment in Jazz-Age Paris, 1900–1930*, University Park: Penn State University Press.

'Came the Dawn' (1931), *Vogue*, February 15: 43–5, 120.

'Characteristic New Spring Weaves and Prints' (1928), *Harper's Bazaar*, February: 87.

'The "Charleston" Crepe' (1925), *Women's Wear* 31(82) October 6: 16.

'Charleston Dress by Phillipe et Gaston' (1927), *Art-Gout-Beauté*, January: 23.

'The Charlot Necklet Encircles the Mode' (1926), *Vogue*, February 15: 53.

Chisholm, A. (1979), *Nancy Cunard; A Biography*, London: Penguin Books.

'Club Alabam' (1925), *Vogue*, May 1: 30.

Damase, J. (1991), *Sonia Delaunay: Fashion and Fabrics*, New York: Harry N. Abrams.

'Dark Star in Paris: Josephine Baker, the American Primitive Who Became a European Sophisticate' (1934), *Vanity Fair*, October: 34, 74.

'Dear Me! These Modern Samplers!' (1928), *Vogue*, September 1: 64.

Edwards, J.D. (2001), 'Carl Van Vechten's Sexual Tourism in Jazz Age Harlem,' in *Exotic Journeys: Exploring the Erotics of U.S. Travel Literature, 1840–1930*, Hanover, NH: University of New Hampshire Press.

Erenberg, L.A. (1981), *Steppin' Out: New York Nightlife and the Transformation of American Culture*, 1890–1930, Chicago: University of Chicago Press.

'Florence Mills' (1923), *Vogue Paris*, December: 35.

'For the Sophisticated Smoker' (1929), *Harper's Bazaar*, March: 118.

'French Chic by Viola Paris' (1926), *Vogue*, December 1: 61.

'La Grand Nuit De Paris' (1926), *Femina*, August.

Howard, M. (1931), 'Paris Hats,' *Harper's Bazaar*, May: 86–7, 89–91, 138–40.

'Le Jazzoflute-Robe De Soir' (1922), *Gazette du Bon Ton*.

Leiris, M. (1967), '*Au-Delà D'un Regard' Entretien Sur L'art Africain Par Paul Lebeer ('Beyond a Glance' a Conversation on African Art by Paul Lebeer)*, Lausanne, Switzerland: La Bibliotheque des Arts.

Leonard, N. (1962), *Jazz and the White Americans: The Acceptance of a New Art Form*, Chicago: University of Chicago Press.

Longstreet, S. (1956), *The Real Jazz Old and New*, Baton Rouge: Louisiana State University.

MacKenzie, J.M. (1995), *Orientalism: History, Theory and the Arts*, Manchester: Manchester University Press.

Mannes, M. (1934), 'Vogue's Spot-Light on the Nightclubs,' *Vogue*, March 1: 46–7, 94.

Marcilhac, F. (1991), *Jean Dunand: His Life and Works*, New York: Harry N. Abrams.

Martin, R. and H. Koda (1994), *Orientalism: Visions of the East in Western Dress*, New York: Harry N. Abrams.

Martin, W. (1995), 'Remembering the Jungle' Josephine Baker and Modernist Parody, in E. Barkan and R. Bush (eds), *Prehistories of the Future: The Primitivist Project and the Culture of Modernism*, California: Stanford University Press, 310–25.

McKnight, L.S. (1999), 'Stehli: Innovation and Style,' in M. Boardman (ed.), *All That Jazz: Printed Fashion Silks of the '20s and '30s*, Allentown, PA: Allentown Art Museum.

Merkin, R. (1968), *The Jazz Age as Seen through the Eyes of Ralph Barton, Miguel Covarrubias, and John Held, Jr.*, Providence: Museum of Art, Rhode Island School of Design.

de Meyer, B. (1927), 'Burnt Straw and Black Ribbon,' *Harper's Bazaar*, February: 71.

'The New Gold Jewellery' (1926), *Vogue*, November 15: 85.

The Oxford English Dictionary (1989), Oxford: Oxford University Press.

'Party Given on Long Island by Charles Payson' (1939), *Harper's Bazaar*, August: 86–87.

Poiret, P. (1927), 'Will Skirts Disappear? A Thirty-Year Prophecy by the Paris Arbiter of Fashion,' *The Forum 77*, (1): 30–40.

'Psychiatry Analyzes the Fashions' (1938), *Vogue*, May 15: 68–9.

'Robes a Danser' (1922), *La Gazette du Bon Ton*, May: 161–4+.

Robes Du Soir [Eveningwear] (1990), Palais Galliera, Paris: Musée de la Mode et du Costume.

Rose, P. (1989), *Jazz Cleopatra: Josephine Baker in Her Time*, New York: Doubleday.

Rousseau, J. (1984 [1755]), *A Discourse on Inequality*, trans. by Maurice Cranston, London: Penguin Books.

Said, E.W. (1978), *Orientalism*, New York: Vintage Books.

Shaw, C.G. (1931), *Nightlife*, New York: The John Day Company.

'Shoes That Jazz to the Jubilant Sax' (1927), *Vogue*, December 1: 56.

'Slaves of Fashion Advertisement for Cohn & Rosenberger, Inc. Jewelry' (1926), *Women's Wear*, 1 April: 38.

Soupault, P. (1930), 'The American Influence in France,' trans. by B. and G. Hughes, Seattle: University of Washington Press.

Stearns, M. and J. Stearns (1994 [1964]), *Jazz Dance: The Story of American Vernacular Dance*, New York: Da Capo Press.

Stovall, T. (1996), *Paris Noir: African Americans in the City of Light*, Boston: Houghton Mifflin Company.

'Suggestions Pour Travestes' (1925), *Art-Gout-Beauté*, February: between 15 and 16.

'Suggestions Pour Travestes' (1927), *Art-Gout-Beauté*, January: between 19 and 20.

'"The Sultan's Secret"-Martini & Rossi Non Alcoholic Vermouth Advertisement' (1927), *Vogue*, December 1: 159.

Upton, B. and F. Upton (1897), *The Adventures of Two Dutch Dolls – and a Golliwog*, Boston: De Wolfe, Fiske.

Vogue, July 15, 1926: cover.

Walrond, E. (1926), 'Charleston, Hey! Hey!' *Vanity Fair*, April: 72–73, 116.

Wilson, E. Jr (1922), 'The Aesthetic Upheaval in France: The Influence of Jazz in Paris and Americanization of French Literature and Art,' *Vanity Fair*, February: 49.

'Wm. H. Davidow Sons Co. Advertisement' (1927), *Harper's Bazaar*, March: 164.

5

The Americanization of Fashion: Sportswear, the Movies and the 1930s

Patricia Campbell Warner

Editors' Introduction: The 1929 stock market crash brought an end to the roaring twenties. The short skirts of the boyish flapper gave way to a new silhouette – dresses with longer skirts and body-hugging slim shapes – that mimicked New York's newest skyscrapers, the Chrysler Building and the Empire State Building. Madeleine Vionnet's bias cut and Elsa Schiaparelli's slim silhouette, hard-edged styles dominated 1930s fashion. Yet, the 'Made in Paris' label no longer had a stranglehold on American women. This occurred, in part, because governmental limitations on importing Paris fashion during the Depression slowed the volume of Parisian imports, but also because Americans began to desire the dresses, suits, coats and sporty American styles created and promoted by New York and California designers and the movies. Indeed, in Hollywood, where the movie industry had taken root, designer Gilbert Adrian and others dressed glamorous stars in screen versions of the latest styles, including sportswear. Patricia Warner shows us how the sporty styles worn by the stars of the silver screen spread to every hamlet in America (and beyond) that had a movie theatre. Clearly they made an impression, for there was a rising interest in an American look as seen in department stores and the movies.

The American look in women's fashion emerged in the 1930s. It was influenced by the interrelationship of three major developments that came together in the United States at that time: the clothing initially designed specifically for sport but later broadened into sportswear; the new ideals of

79

beauty that were closely connected to the lithe, sporting look, created in large part for and by Hollywood movies; and the role those movies played in selling new fashion ideas and goods to the movie-going public. There is no argument that the couturiers of that period, most of whom were European, helped to create the look of the time. Many are still well known – Chanel, Vionnet, Patou, Schiaparelli, Lanvin, to name a few. But even they, like everyone else in the 1930s, paid attention to significant trends during the decade, including sports and movies (Mulvagh 1988; Ewing 1992; Seeling 2000).

The United States' reputation as a sports leader by the 1920s and 1930s owed a great deal to Hollywood and the movies which glorified, as only Hollywood can, the American penchant for playing and winning. In addition, by the 1930s, Hollywood had emerged from its unsophisticated beginnings to enter its Golden Age. In the process, it became perhaps the single greatest influence on society and culture the world had ever seen. It is how Hollywood influenced sport and its clothing, and ultimately world fashion, that this chapter addresses.

The movies fed, and ultimately shaped, not only the new social realities of the 1930s but the clothing as well. The decade provided the critical seeds that set the tone and the style for the American Century, and provided the fashion industry with the tools it used to shape the look, first of Americans, then later the rest of the world. How successful was this venture? We scarcely need ask. By now, in the early twenty-first century, the clothes of the world are undeniably American in style.

The clothes today are simple in cut and construction, functional, comfortable, relaxed, sensible and easy-care. They emerged directly from the radically simple clothing that was free of linings, understructures, confining fit and unnecessary decoration that sport and athletic activity demanded at the end of the nineteenth century. Many of these new sartorial ideas came out of higher education, which spread its influence at this time. Eventually, athletic-oriented clothing became what we now routinely call 'sportswear.' Sports lent that uncluttered, easy look to the clothing that became the hallmark of American Style. The movies showed the world what it looked like, how it was worn, and under what circumstances it was acceptable. Through Hollywood movies, we will see how the process of the Americanization of fashion worked.

Many European immigrants saw the new moving pictures as a golden opportunity to thrive in their new country. It was they who formed the fledgling studios, first in New York and New Jersey at the turn of the century, then, around 1910, in California. In 1915, they settled on the West Coast. By the 1920s, all the world had embraced their productions, had seen the young and beautiful stars wearing wonderful clothes and moving in elegant surroundings, and had even read about their favorite stars and movies in movie magazines (Fuller 1996: 133).

The early history of the movies plays directly into the long, leggy look of the 1930s. A slow progression led to that look beginning in 1912 when D.W. Griffith asked his female actors Blanche Sweet and Dorothy Bernard to bare their legs in a caveman film, *Man's Genesis*, and they refused. He gave the role instead to Mae Marsh, who had no such inhibitions (Eyman 1990). That same year, Mack Sennett formed Keystone, the film company that included not only the slapstick Keystone Kops but the Bathing Beauties. Within a year or two, Bathing Beauties figured prominently in the Keystone films, wearing modifications of the body-fitting men's swimsuits that had first shown up in the 1912 Olympics (Warner 1997). It seems clear that the movies helped delighted audiences accept the newer, barer and more daring bathing suits long before they were more generally seen on American beaches. Other clothing these Beauties wore, usually of their own choice at this time—anything from home-made to designer-crafted – was equally influential. Audiences admired the 'looks' of their favorites who were acknowledged by on-screen credit only in the 1910s. Movie magazines followed almost instantaneously with articles on the stars, their lives, and their clothing choices.

Another factor that contributed to the 1930s look was the thin, svelte, youthful body. Generally, women in that decade abandoned the girlish, pert look of the 1920s for a look based on a leaner, sleeker body that appeared to be the product of diet and exercise, one that spent leisure time actively participating in sports. That body has more or less stayed with us ever since. It was a body that both enhanced and was enhanced by beautiful clothing. The move away from womanliness as the ideal was evident as early as 1909, when Mary Pickford, lured by the better prospects films offered, had moved from the stage to film. That first year, at age sixteen, when she saw how she looked in pictures, she was horrified. 'I had no idea I was so stocky,' she admitted much later. She was 5'1" and weighed 115 pounds. From then on, during her film career, she kept her weight at ninety-five pounds (Eyman 1990; Desser and Jowett 2000).

Other actors too were appalled by their film image, realizing that the camera gives the impression of being ten pounds heavier. The young men who created the movies chose young actors, especially young women, to appeal to a youthful audience. The camera loved fresh, unlined faces, and D.W. Griffith's new close-up camera, dating from the 1910s, emphasized the need for them. Small wonder, then, that as early as 1921, a well-known artist and designer of his day, Penrhyn Stanlaws, declared that 'absolute feminine perfection' came between the ages of thirteen and seventeen. 'I would never use a model over 17,' he declared (Stanlaws 1921).

It is clear, then, that by the early 1920s the die was cast. Youth had not only 'won the Great War,' the most beautiful of them had become the models for the young, slim and fit ideal. I argue that the American (and now global) obsession with youth and thinness began here during the early years of Hollywood and the subsequent love affair with the camera. Still photography too had its place in the transformation. During the 1920s, fashion photography was just coming of age, competing almost equally with fashion illustration, which elongated bodies to an impossible proportion (Warner 1992). By the 1930s, print technology had advanced significantly, allowing fashion magazines to use photography almost exclusively. However, by that time, the public accepted without question that the fashionable body was a long, lean and elegant one, as it was in fashion illustration. Thus, as it had been earlier with film actors, so was it for photographic models: the inexorable camera eye demanded slim, lithe bodies to display the beauty ideals of the time as well as the fashions; and the thinner the body, the more elegant the hang of the clothes. Hence, the lean look of the 1930s.[1] Sports, whether active or spectator, undoubtedly were a part of that ideal.

By the 1930s, playing sports suggested leisure, money, and success in the larger sense of living well. Fashion magazines sold this concept by showing sportswomen (or elegant spectators) whose bodies were trim and young, invariably wearing expensive clothing appropriate only for the activity shown, rather than for the broader, more generic use of clothing today. Inevitably, the common sense and practicality behind the simple and comfortable new styles eventually overwhelmed the more elaborate – and limited use – couture dress that paralleled their emergence. However, though sports helped crystallize a new ideal, it was the movies that imprinted that ideal image so carefully on our consciousness and helped keep it alive into our own day. The clothes for sporting activities, however, as they shifted away from specific sports usage, were another thing entirely, as we shall see.

Just how pervasive was the impact of American movies at the time? If we consider that by 1930, between 90 and 110 million people in the United States out of a total population of 117 million went to the movies *every week*, it is not hard to accept that movies wielded considerable influence. Even in the depths of the Depression, 1932, when almost 77 per cent of all American families earned less than $2,000 an year (comparable to under $20,000 today), 60 million people attended movies weekly (Palladino 1996;

Jarvie 1970). By 1940, with the help of marketing ploys, the numbers were back up to some 80 to 90 million steady customers each week in the United States alone (Eckert 1978). As for foreign markets, in the 1920s they generated some 30 to 50 per cent of a picture's worldwide gross. At this time, Hollywood produced between 75 and 80 per cent of all movies made throughout the world, and collected nearly $200 million in film rentals out of a total annual world gross of $275 million. Nearly half of that came from English-speaking markets, primarily Great Britain. Although this number fell to only 20 per cent at the beginning of the Depression, by the middle years of the 1930s, it had recovered (Ballio 1993).

Movie producers during those years never lost sight of the tastes and demands of their typical viewer, who was, depending on the source, either a nineteen-year-old working girl waiting to get married, or the wife of the household (Eckert 1978; Thorpe 1939). Both were white. (Movie-going in the South was segregated at this time.) And, even as it is today, when young people did earn money, they tended to spend it on consumer goods and leisure activities: clothes, dancing, radio music and fun. Going to the movies was part of the fun. When adult women were the targets, they paid attention to clothes, make-up and hair styles first of all – things they could afford to copy – even if the elaborate settings and furnishings they saw were out of their bracket. They also went for romance. As Margaret Thorpe put it, 'In the movies a wife finds it quite worth while to get into a new evening frock for a *tete-à-tete* dinner at home because her husband is sure, by dessert time at least, to take her hand across the intimately small and inconvenient table and say, "Darling, you get lovelier every day"' (Thorpe 1939: 6). Thus the movies had turned into a marvelous selling tool, pitched to the most vulnerable. Commercial tie-ins abounded – everything from soft drinks to cigarettes to clothing and cars. Even more unsettling to traditional authority, as we learn from one sixteen-year-old girl in the 1930s, 'The movies [gave] some ideas about the freedom we should have' (Palladino 1996: 6). – not only the freedom to escape from the limitations of the past, but to want what was shown in the movies.

This awareness was not new, nor limited to the United States. As early as 1912, German and English manufacturers had observed the notable rise in demand for things American as their countrymen saw them in movies, and of the subsequent American imports generated by these demands. This situation continued throughout the Golden Age of the movies (Eckert 1978; Massey 2000). The irony was that the circumstances of these goods – what they stood for in American life – never really existed for the average American. The things the audiences saw, the beautiful houses with vast rooms, high ceilings and gracious stairways, the racy motor cars, the elegantly dressed men and women, the luxurious hotels, spas, resorts and clubs that spoke 'American' to the audiences who wanted them all as a result, were in fact the products of the movie makers' imaginations, the outcomes of situations created by the immigrant moguls who themselves wanted, in the most 'Gatsbyesque' way, to fit in. The life they presented in the movies, especially the opulent, leisured and moneyed life, was *their* dream, *their* vision of America, and almost never reality. But so successful were they in creating this extraordinary Movie World that audiences everywhere unquestioningly accepted it all, and were prompted in turn to demand the goods they saw on the screen.

Movie magazines helped promote the longing. In the words of James R. Quirk, editor from 1917 to 1932 of *Photoplay*, the first (1912) and leading fan magazine with a circulation of half a million a month in his time, the movies created 'perfect consumers.' *Photoplay*'s ads and articles aided and abetted the buying public. Quirk predicted with deadly accuracy that motion pictures and star endorsements would inevitably lead to unprecedented growth in a new kind of consumer culture, one fed by movie fans (Fuller 1996: 151). Then as now, the most obvious way to show admiration for your idol was to dress like her. All through the 1920s and 1930s the fashion departments of the fan magazines filled readers with breathless detail about both movie costumes and 'real' clothing through pictures and articles. They encouraged the stars to expound on their philosophy of dress, pointing out how the stars' choices could be adapted to a minimum-wage budget as easily as a comfortable one. The 'imitative fans,' as Thorpe called them (all female) ate it up (Thorpe 1939: 91). The influence of the movie magazines survived through the 1930s to emerge in the 1940s, transformed via a new style of magazine directed specifically at primary targets, teenaged girls in high school and college. The most enduring of these, a magazine called *Stardom*, began in 1942 then switched focus two years later in 1944 under its new name, *Seventeen* (Fuller 1996).

In 1930, partly to counteract the decline in retail sales from the Depression but also to exploit this hard-nosed interest in motion pictures, Bernard Waldman organized Modern Merchandising Bureau, Inc. to be the middleman between all the major movie studios and retailers in New York and across the country (Thorpe 1939; Eckert 1978; La Valley 1987). His job, he felt, was to guess which of the products appearing in forthcoming movies would capture the imaginations and hearts of the women who saw them. His ability to anticipate not only the attractiveness of the items to the American woman but their practicality as well, whether they were hats (like Garbo's Eugénie hat or Norma Shearer's Juliet cap), bags, shoes or dresses, was what drove the business. Next, he established in-store shops,

Cinema Fashions, Screen Star Styles or Cinema Modes, to sell the outfits and accessories worn by the stars. Film designers were cooperative; they not only created for the screen, they kept the average American woman in mind as well. Labels verified that the item's design was taken from a specific movie. The shops, only one in each city, located in a major department store, got a commission of the sales, and the movie productions got the publicity they wanted. Through this system, a movie could open on any given day, and, as if by magic, in the store down the street from the theater, there would be, as Charles Eckert has suggested, 'the Carole Lombard in Macy's Window' – or, even more specifically, the Joan Crawford *Letty Lynton* dress, available instantly for whoever had the money. Ironically, Waldman had a hard sell with the idea in 1930, when he began. According to Margaret Thorpe in *America at the Movies*, 'Everybody in the trade scoffed at the idea at first. They said the movies had no influence on fashion.' But a decade later, she said: 'The American public today is convinced that they have an influence on practically everything' (Thorpe 1939: 110).

To see just how this process worked, let's digress to look at that Letty Lynton dress. It provides a perfect example of the system, both in retailing the new and in borrowing trends with abandon, thereby obliterating any true design origin. Adrian designed the dress for Joan Crawford's character in the 1932 movie, and it appears in virtually every book on Hollywood costuming and glamour (Basinger 1993; Gaines and Herzog 1990; Schreier 1998). It was a white organza or organdy two-piece evening dress, with a demure high-necked, collared, slim-fitting and self-belted jacket top defining the torso and hips but flaring to a swirling hem outlined with three tiers of restrained ruffles. Its chief claim to fame, however, was its enormous short sleeves, a froth of organdy ruffles, crisp, sheer, voluminous – and unforgettable. Even as the movie appeared, the dress was on the street. Macy's claimed to have sold 50,000 copies of the dress the year the movie came out (Ballio 1993: 94). There is no doubt, then, that Adrian designed the dress and the movie sold it to the masses.

Bernard Waldman was not alone in using movie design to promote retail sales. Thorpe gives us a wonderful sports-related example. When Sonja Henie won her first Olympics in 1927 (and long before television coverage) there was little enthusiasm for figure skating. But after her move to Hollywood and the starring vehicles that showed off her grace and skill, raising her by 1938 to the third-ranking box-office star (after Shirley Temple and Clark Gable), skate sales in the United States increased 150 per cent (Thorpe 1939: 116). Men too were equally influenced by the movies. When Clark Gable took off his shirt in *It Happened One Night* (1934) and revealed his bare chest instead of the ubiquitous undershirt, the entire men's underwear industry quaked. Thorpe gives us the view from the 1930s, telling us that so sharp and breathtakingly fast was the decline after the release of the movie that 'knitwear manufacturers and garment workers unions sent delegations to the producers asking them to take out the scene' (1939: 117).

The movies further influenced audiences to lose the formality in dress that had existed before the 1930s. The heroines, often working girls with dreams of love, marriage and financial success (not necessarily in that order) began to dress more as their American sisters in the audience might. As early as 1927, Clara Bow in her greatest success, *It*, dressed casually in snug-fitting sweater and skirt (at that time, clothing for sport) when she was off work. This movie, as *Our Dancing Daughters* did in 1928, gave a whole new way of wearing sportswear. Both stars, Clara Bow and Joan Crawford in 1928, showed off their slim figures to best effect with dresses and sportswear tailored to cling to every curve. This was very different

Figure 5.1 Clark Gable and Greta Garbo in *Susan Lenox, Her Rise and Fall*, 1931. Image donated by Corbis-Bettmann.

from the couture of the late 1920s, which still maintained the straight chemise look that scarcely acknowledged the waist.

Movies offered other messages as well. From the early years of the Depression, one film that showed audiences how to vary their meager wardrobes was *Susan Lenox, Her Fall and Rise*, starring Greta Garbo (1931). In the first several scenes of the movie, Garbo wore the same outfit, a short-sleeved pullover sweater and a dark, skirted jumper cinched with a leather belt (Figure 5.1). She has, according to the storyline, no other clothes with her as she runs from her oppressive home life. But as the scenes and times of day change, we see different mixes of the same items: the sweater is worn over the jumper and belted at the waist, making it look like a sweater and skirt combination. On Garbo, the look is timeless, as suitable today as it was then. Even more influential was the scene where she shyly put on Clark Gable's pajamas while her wet clothes were drying. Happily, the pajamas had a belt, creating a slouchy soft, figure-defining look on Garbo. So appealing does she look in them that it is not too far a leap to suggest that the rise in popularity of pajamas for women in the 1930s had, if not its start, then certainly an enormous push forward, courtesy this movie. And of course, the pajamas had pants.

Straight trousers – men's style trousers – for women in the early 1930s were daring, especially if worn on the street. Knickers and beach pajamas, and even on rare occasions, shorts, for resort, campus and leisure wear had made their appearance in the previous decade, but never would they have been accepted anywhere else. However, in 1930 when Marlene Dietrich, in her first American movie, appeared in a tuxedo and top hat in Josef von Sternberg's *Morocco*, the world sat up and took notice.

Dietrich certainly was not the first woman to wear men's clothing to great effect. But the time had come to experiment, to display, and to accept the look worldwide. Dietrich wore trouser suits throughout the 1930s – she had a great body for them, broad-shouldered, long-legged and lean-hipped, and an icy, uninvolved androgyny that fit well with the masculine attire. The other trouser-wearing star of the 1930s was, of course, Katherine Hepburn. Although it is scarcely fashionable these days to look any further than Dietrich in the 1930s, I believe Hepburn had a far greater influence. After all, she was American, an athletic upper-class Connecticut Yankee. Her audiences would have related to her better than they did to the exotic, remote Dietrich. Hepburn came to Hollywood with a style all her own, and soon after she arrived, revealed a carefree disregard for the conventions and niceties that ruled Hollywood at that time. Although she told an amusing story about the Elizabeth Hawes-designed outfit she carefully selected to make the right impression on her arrival by train in

California, it soon became clear that her preference was for comfortable sportswear, a new kind of clothing in the 1930s.[2] Indeed, in the popular press of the time, much was made of her participation in sports – swimming and tennis especially – perhaps to explain her eccentric choices in clothes.

Her thin body, a quintessentially 1930s body, made the most of the tailored, pleat-front trousers or the rolled-cuff dungarees and boat shoes that were a natural part of her personal wardrobe (and of course, would have shown up in the movie magazines, even the fashion magazine articles, about her). Her impulse to wear pants was completely different from Dietrich's, who wore them to shock, to express her sexual ambiguity, to be noticed. Hepburn's trousers were unconventional, but were a completely natural expression. She was unconcerned with the reactions to them, even when George Cukor, the director of her first movie, *Bill of Divorcement* (1932), complained about them (Edwards 1985). The next year, she made *Christopher Strong*, a story about an aviatrix and her affair with a married

Figure 5.2 Katherine Hepburn as 'Sylvester' Scarlett in *Sylvia Scarlett*, 1935. Image donated by Corbis-Bettmann.

man. Dorothy Arzner directed. With her customary abruptness, Hepburn reported, 'Dorothy Arzner – popular woman director. She had done many pictures. Was very good . . . She wore pants. So did I. We had a good time working together' (1991: 156).

If wearing pants was the criterion, she must have had a great time making *Sylvia Scarlett* in 1935. For more than half the movie, she is dressed as a sort of scruffy English boy in a suit and dashing fedora over her boyish haircut, or just a man's shirt and pants (Figure 5.2). Although she carries the look with considerable élan, this movie was not a success. Hepburn's own singular personal style began appearing in her movies. In *Stage Door* (1937), she played one of a number of young aspiring stage actresses living in a rooming house in New York. Hepburn's character was different from all the rest (played by Ginger Rogers, Lucille Ball and Ann Miller, among others): her character, like Hepburn herself, had come from a wealthy, well-bred East Coast family. Her clothes were different from anyone else's throughout the movie. But one pants outfit, designed by Muriel King, who designed for both the New York custom trade and for Hollywood, was startlingly different. It was a dark blue tailored waist-length belted shirt-jacket and matching straight trousers, monogrammed and piped in white. It was pure Hepburn – casual, elegant, sporty and unique for the time. She wore it as if it were a pair of pajamas and a bathrobe – unselfconsciously, indifferently.

The ultimate Hepburn look came with *The Philadelphia Story* (1940), which Philip Barry wrote for her, tailoring the part to her personality. The costumes by Adrian were equally tailored to her own personal style. They were lady-like, elegant and sporty as needed. But in the indoor, private shots showing Tracy Lord with her mother and little sister, Hepburn was costumed in comfortably casual trouser outfits rather than skirted casual wear. One seriously doubts that, had the leading actress been someone else, the choice would have been to put her in pants. Instead, the lead was Katherine Hepburn, a unique star in her own time and over her long career. She gave the look of freedom and comfort upper-class elegance no matter what role she played, even as the 'boy' in *Sylvia Scarlett* or the sweet, gauche working-class misfit in *Alice Adams*. And the audience of millions of women watched.

To lay the adoption of trousers for women at the feet of Marlene Dietrich and Katherine Hepburn would, of course, be simplistic. It had been coming slowly for a long time – from ardent nineteenth-century reformers to bohemians, soldiers and pioneers donning men's garb, from physical education and gym bloomers to swimming suits, from jodhpurs, knickers and shorts to pajamas and dungarees. Pants had been there. What had been lacking was acceptance. Even into the 1930s, trousers were acceptable only on beaches, in resorts, occasionally on campuses, or in back yards of private homes – and then, primarily only on young women. Never would a fashionable woman wear trousers to work, to shop, or to do any serious activity that women participated in during that period. In fact, the claim is often made that it was the Second World War that broke that convention. In reality, the convention was not really broken until well into the 1970s, after it became permissible for women to wear trousers to work; even then trousers were acceptable only for support staff, for secretaries. Professional women had to wait another decade or more to feel comfortable (read be taken seriously) wearing trousers to work. But the convention of trousers took a giant leap forward in the decade of the 1930s, brought about in no small measure by seeing favorite stars wearing them in the movies.

Another type of film stimulated a different kind of trouser wear in the 1930s. That was the movie musical, and the trousers were often shorts. Shorts generally were limited to summer vacations and the beach, for play rather than sports. However, with the onset of talkies, Hollywood took every opportunity to exploit the new sound technology in the movies, offering musical interludes to the more pedestrian dialogue.

In 1933 Darryl Zanuck invited the choreographer and director Busby Berkeley to breathe new life into the musical form with Warner Brothers' proposed *42nd Street*. This new production revealed the rigor of long rehearsals as the dancers and cast prepared for a theatrical show within the movie. And here, from the first rehearsal, we are privy to rehearsal clothes (Figure 5.3). They were a mix of playsuits and sportswear: Una Merkl wore linen slacks with a short-sleeved polo shirt; others wore jumpsuits and shorts or tight short bloomers and shirts. Ruby Keeler, the ingénue star, wore the best-looking shorts and a huge puffed-sleeve blouse that remained tidily tucked in throughout. All of them wore high heels. Second lead Bebe Daniels rehearsed in dressy, satin trousers, a 'pajama' outfit; she was accompanied by chorus boys wearing regular, slightly wide-legged trousers and slim pullovers. However, despite the routine use of all lengths of trousers as practice clothing in the theater rehearsals, not one actress wore trousers, short or long, in her scenes off-stage. This pattern held throughout other Busby Berkeley movies of the early 1930s. At the risk of hammering home the point, for audiences seeing these movies, typically young and looking for the new, the rehearsal clothes would be an eye-opener. The look of the chorus girls wearing shorts would have been tried by many, especially when Bernard Waldman and his ilk were there to provide the means to do so.

Figure 5.3 Ruby Keeler in her neat little playsuit is chastised by Warner Baxter
(in tweed pants and a dress shirt) as Ginger Rogers looks on. Ginger
wears a playsuit with slim-fitting shorts and a sailor-style top. Note
the variety of rehearsal costume of the chorus girls. *42nd Street*,
1933. Image donated by Corbis-Bettmann.

Other hit movies that influenced fashion were *Top Hat* (1935) and *The
Gay Divorcee* (1936). As with many of the Astaire – Rogers movies of the
1930s, the plots were silly and almost interchangeable, but the sets were
lavish, and the music, dances and clothes memorable. *Top Hat* is the movie
where Ginger wears the feathered dance dress that seems to float, encircling both her and Fred Astaire as they dance 'Cheek to Cheek.' But it is
also the movie where Rogers wears a classic hacking jacket, jodhpurs, a
soft felt hat and gloves, and short boots, ready to go riding, and looking
perhaps more elegant in this perfectly tailored sporting outfit than she does
in most of her other costumes (Figure 5.4). The singing and dancing chorus
of blondes and their opposite numbers of boys in *The Gay Divorcee* all
wear sports clothes. Since the plot of the movie has them at a 'marvelous'
English resort hotel, the cast is free to wear sports clothing, if only in this
one scene. They wear slacks, beach pajamas, flannels, halters, t-shirts,
bathing suits – the entire scene is like a fashion show of casual resort wear.

Figure 5.4 Ginger Rogers, dressed in immaculate riding clothes, dances with Fred Astaire while they wait for a sudden shower to pass in *Top Hat*, 1935. Image donated by Corbis-Bettmann.

It's notable, though, that none of the stars (except the comic, Horton) appears in anything other than 'regular' clothes. But the outfits on the chorus in their fairly extended number are appealing and new.

An often overlooked factor that helped make trousers acceptable is the ideal climate of southern California, where warm weather, sunshine and casual living went hand in hand with the film industry. The movie magazines, read by millions, promoted the stars, their make-up, their hairstyles, their clothes, and often depicted them at ease in their homes, in their back yards or by a swimming pool – all the places where young beautiful people wore their new, casual clothing. The clothes of southern California, comfortable in response to the demands of climate and place, were seen in the movies and soon audiences demanded to wear them too. According to *Vogue*, clothes were fodder for gossip: the striped blue and white sailor's pullover purchased by the Prince of Wales in St. Tropez made him look 'young and boyish' (Hall 1985). Shorts became the trousers of choice, overwhelming (according to a perhaps overenthusiastic *Vogue*) the pajamas that had been the favorites of the 1920s. The *Elegants* spent their days entertaining at the pool in bathing suits, now one-piece knits, belted, with tops styled like today's tank tops, and bottoms cut off at the top of the legs. By the end of the decade, they were sporting two-piece, midriff-baring suits. Blouses were sleeveless, backs were bare, tans were golden, and all kinds of trousers, whether masculine and straight-legged or feminine, full and graceful, short or long, were photographed for the fashion magazine readers to marvel at (Hall 1985: 136–7).

But even with this evident popularity, a couple of things must be remembered: this casual, relaxed way of dressing still only appeared in warm weather, and only in a resort or beach setting. For chillier climates, even when dressing for sporting activities, women wore skirted suits or skirts and sweaters, even when men appeared in knickers. Further, the circulation of these glossy fashion magazines was not huge and was directed towards a select readership. Movies, on the other hand, hit the world. So the movie chorus girls in their shorts and tops, so similar in style to the dashing casual wear of the rich, but seen by millions, without doubt had greater impact. Once again, as it was with the *Letty Lynton* dress, it is impossible to say where the ideas came from. It is the nature of fashion to have the ideas 'out there,' almost invariably coming from several overlapping sources at once. But, for sheer numbers alone, no wonder it was the movies that people copied (Jarvie 1970: 95).

Sports, sportswear and fashion overlap on other fronts in the 1930s. Perhaps one of the more interesting examples, and certainly the most American, concerns the dress we know today as the shirtmaker or shirt-waist dress. It first appeared as a 'sports dress,' for golf, tennis and for spectator sports. According to Milbank (1989), Best & Co. promoted its American 'shirtmaker frocks' in 1926. No real mention of the dress occurs for some time after that in the popular press. However, with an eye towards a new sensibility, in 1935, the McMullen Company of Glens Falls, New York introduced a new line, 'shirt frocks' for women. McMullen had existed since 1902 as a manufacturer of fine men's shirts, but the Depression sent it in search of new markets. Women seemed the answer. The following year, McMullen hired designer Dorothy Cox, who translated the well-made masculine shirts into one and two-piece sports dresses for women, tailored with the same fine detail as the men's shirts were. She used cotton broadcloth, chambray and wool flannel for her designs, with wholesale price points from $4.75 to $12.75 (equivalent to $58.99 to $158 today). Advertising to the industry in 1936 declared, 'Shirtmaker to

Women,' thereby naming the dress. The company from then on was known as a manufacturer of shirtmaker or shirtwaist dresses, 'not just for the famous few, but for Miss and Mrs. Average American' (Milbank 1989: 150–1). There is no doubt that these dresses were intended as sportswear rather than for more formal activities.

Many influential magazines acknowledged the wider acceptance of the sports dress and used the term 'shirtwaist' happily. *Life* ran a cover article on 'Summer Sports Style' (thereby linking the ideas of sports and attractive fashion) in May 1938. Shirtwaists were there as 'classic shirtwaists' or 'shirtwaist dinner dresses' which, *Life* informed its readers, could range in price from $16.95 (the one they chose to highlight) to $135, $200 to $2375 in today's dollars (May 9, 1938: 19). This major *Life* feature left no doubt whatsoever that sportswear had arrived. It had transformed from leisure/vacation clothing to high fashion. It covered everything from the dinner dresses to slacks, playsuits and tennis dresses, made out of cottons, synthetics and silks, and bathing suits, by now made out of satin lastex and other fibers. And all the sportswear was American, giving the look of the American woman – casual, confident, open, sporty, but sleek and well dressed.

Although many of the sportswear pieces listed above were a part of movie costuming by this time, the shirtwaist seemed to have been ignored, or relegated to a very specific use in the movies. Primarily, it clothed servants or inmates, at least until the end of the 1930s. A very restrained, basic cotton version did appear as a crisp little prison uniform in the 1934 movie *Hold Your Man*. An incarcerated Jean Harlow gave it a certain air. But the aim of Hollywood in the 1930s was to present an invented world, populated by beautiful women immaculately dressed, and the simple shirtmaker was far removed from the elegantly designed gowns, dresses and suits of that decade. The movie world of the 1930s was rife with rich people living in extraordinary surroundings, served by men and women dressed in trim uniforms. For the women servants, these uniforms were the basic shirt dress, covered usually with little aprons worn with caps. It is interesting to realize that the style of shirt dress worn for sports found its way into maids' closets – or perhaps the maids' uniform found its way into sports because of its great simplicity and practicality. Whatever the answer, by the time *The Women* was released in 1939, it appeared in that movie in both its guises, as domestic uniform and as elegant at-home wear. Adrian, who designed the gowns, dressed the star, Norma Shearer, in two versions, both full-length. One was an at-home robe, probably in a light-weight wool, with long shirt sleeves and a collar with a matching stiff belt covered in the same material, the other, worn for entertaining women friends at home, was made of a soft jersey and was short-sleeved with a wide, shaped, sparkling beaded belt. Though very different in feel, both were shirt dresses, complete with breast pockets. So, by the end of the 1930s, the shirt dress had found its place in American wardrobes. Perhaps this one simple dress represents as clearly as any other American garment the transformation that came about in women's clothing at this time. It started out as a sports dress, but with the increasing popularity and acceptance of trousers for women, especially for sports, it withdrew from that field. As a straightforward dress, simple in line and design, it became a basic of American women's wardrobes.

On other fashion fronts, American designers were emerging from their Seventh Avenue anonymity by the 1930s, to a significant extent because French couture markets had dried up with the onset and deepening of the Depression. Women like Elizabeth Hawes, Dorothy Cox, Jo Copeland and Claire McCardell knew how to design for the athletic-bodied American woman. In a stroke of genius, Dorothy Shaver, vice-president of Lord & Taylor in 1932, started featuring American designers in Lord & Taylor ads, and gave them coverage in in-store displays and windows. Although dresses and suits routinely appeared, the emphasis was on sportswear. Not only did sportswear answer the needs of the American woman who wanted versatile clothing that was comfortable and easy, it was made out of less expensive fabrics than imported European clothing, was simpler in design, could easily be mass-manufactured, and was cheaper – all qualities Americans loved (Milbank 1989).

The decade of the 1930s, then, was a decade of transformation in fashion, brought about in large measure, ironically, by upper-class sports, the Great Depression and the movies of the masses. Many of the impulses that created the American Look had begun earlier, in the 1920s, and many came to full fruition after the Second World War in the 1940s. But post-war America, as in Europe, fell back into admiration and emulation of the French *haut style* with Dior's New Look. It would take another decade after that to regain the true American Style that had emerged during the 1930s. Sportswear, however, remained throughout, little changing through the decades. It answered the needs of a casual American way of life, of lean athletic bodies and their loose-jointed mannerisms. Sportswear was about practicality and comfort; mass-manufacture and mix-and-match; and menswear was transformed into a feminine form. Once it began to emerge, fortified by strong, clean design and codified by the movies, it found its place in classic styles that suggested leisure, good taste and standing, and all in the American setting that Hollywood projected so well. It remains with us today, still carrying the same messages. Indeed, it is sometimes startling to watch movies from the 1920s and 1930s and recognize clothing that is virtually unchanged today. It came out of sports but because of its simple effectiveness, spread into all but the most formal occasions. It is quintessentially American. And the movies sold it to the world.

Notes

1. That look has been attributed to the overall lack of nourishment in the Depression by some authors, but the ideal images of any period come from the top, not the bottom of the social scale. Hence, as the camera became more and more a driving force in the culture, the desire to look one's youthful, slender best, whether it be Pickford or someone else, overtook any other impulse. Interestingly, cosmetic surgery, beautification tool extraordinaire, began to be practiced at this time as well by the rich and famous. It was the Duchess of Windsor, however, a product of this era, who linked body size and wealth irretrievably together with her *bon mot*, 'You never can be too thin or too rich.'

2. In 1932 she went to Elizabeth Hawes, 'New York's highest-priced designer,' as Hepburn said in her memoir, to have an appropriate outfit made 'to wear getting off the train in California.' Hawes was the first truly American designer in New York to have her own shop, which she opened in 1928. Hepburn described her outfit:

> It was a sort of Quaker gray-blue silk grosgrain suit. The skirt was flared and very long. The coat was rather like a nineteenth-century riding coat with tails. The blouse was a turtleneck with a ruffle around the top of the turtle. And the hat. Oh!
>
> Well, the hat was a sort of a gray-blue straw dish upside down on my head. I had long hair, screwed up tight. Someone once said, '*a la concièrge.*' The dishpan sat on top of this–a bit formal and more than eccentric.
>
> But it had been very expensive, the whole costume, and I had great faith in it.
>
> Gloves, bag, shoes–dark navy.
>
> It was, I realize now, hardly an appropriate costume to arrive in, in Pasadena on July 4th with a temperature of ninety-odd. A sweatshirt and an old pair of white pants would have been more appropriate. (Hepburn 1991: 127–8)

References

Ballio, T. (1993), *Grand Design: Hollywood as a Modern Business Enterprise 1930–1939*, 28, vol. 5, C. Harpole (ed.), *History of the American Cinema*, New York: Charles Scribner's Sons.

Basinger, J. (1993), *A Woman's View: How Hollywood Spoke to Women, 1930–1960*, Hanover, NH: Wesleyan University Press.

Desser, D. and G.S. Jowett (eds) (2000), *Hollywood Goes Shopping*, Minneapolis: University of Minnesota Press.

Eckert, C. (1978), 'The Carole Lombard in Macy's Window,' *Quarterly Review of Film Studies* 3(1), winter.

Edwards, A. (1985), *A Remarkable Woman*, New York: William Morrow & Co.

Ewing, E. (1992), *History of 20th Century Fashion*, revised by A. Mackrell, New York: Costume & Fashion Press.

Eyman, S. (1990), *Mary Pickford, America's Sweetheart*, New York: Donald I. Fine.

Fuller, K.H. (1996), *At the Picture Show*, Washington DC: Smithsonian Institution Press.

Gaines, J. and C. Herzog (eds) (1990) *Fabrications: Costume and the Female Body*, London: Routledge.

Hall, C. (1985), *The Thirties in Vogue*, New York: Harmony Books.

Hepburn, K. (1991), *Me: Stories of My Life*, New York: Ballantine Books.

Jarvie, I.C. (1970), *Movies and Society*, New York: Basic Books, Inc.

Ladies Home Journal, February 1938.

La Valley, S. (1987), 'Hollywood and Seventh Avenue: The Impact of Period Films on Fashion,' in *Hollywood and History*, Los Angeles: Los Angeles County Museum of Art and Thames and Hudson.

Life, May 9, 1938.

Massey, A. (2000), *Hollywood Beyond the Screen*, Oxford: Berg.

Milbank, C.R. (1989), *New York Fashion*, New York: Harry N. Abrams.

Mulvagh, J. (1988), *Vogue History of 20th Century Fashion*, New York: Viking Press.

Palladino, G. (1996), *Teenagers: an American History*, New York: Basic Books, Inc.

Schreier, S. (1998), *Hollywood Dressed and Undressed*, New York: Rizzoli International Publications.

Seeling, C. (2000), *Fashion: The Century of the Designer, 1900–1999*, Cologne: Könemann Verlagsgesellschaft mbH.

Stanlaws, P. (1921), 'The Art of Dress,' *Photoplay*, April: 49–50.

Thorpe, M.F. (1939), *America at the Movies*, New Haven: Yale University Press.

Warner, P.C. (1997), 'The Thin Ideal: A Matter of Proportion and History,' in *International Textile and Apparel Association Proceedings*.

—— (1992) 'Clothing as Barrier: American Women in the Olympics, 1900–1920,' *Dress*, 24: 55–68.

Filmography with known costume designers

It, 1927
Our Dancing Daughters, 1928
Susan Lenox, Her Fall and Rise, 1931 (Adrian, gowns)
Bill of Divorcement, 1932 (Josette Di Lima, uncredited)
42nd Street, 1933 (Orry-Kelly)
Hold Your Man, 1934

It Happened One Night, 1934
Sylvia Scarlett, 1935 (Muriel King for Hepburn)
Top Hat, 1935 (Bernard Newman, gowns)
The Gay Divorcee, 1936 (Walter Plunkett)
Stage Door, 1937 (Muriel King)
The Women, 1939 (Adrian, gowns and fashion show)
The Philadelphia Story, 1940 (Adrian)

6

Promoting American Designers, 1940–44: Building Our Own House

Sandra Stansbery Buckland

Editors' Introduction: Although the movies bolstered the communication of new fashion ideas including casual sportswear, the major influence on fashion during the 1940s was the Second World War. The war broke the long-established business relationship between Paris designers and American manufacturers and retail stores. With the occupation of Paris by the German army, American designers were suddenly without one of their major sources of style inspiration. In New York, merchants, manufacturers and the Mayor himself, saw an opportunity to further develop their own fashion industry. American women's wear designers were suddenly thrust into the limelight. They focused on style features that had developed in the late 1930s – broad shoulders, knee-length skirts, and high heels to show off (nylon) stockinged legs. Against this backdrop, New York promoted its own fashion designers, mostly creators of ready-to-wear garments. Newspapers and department stores aided the cause by promoting American designers. Sandra Buckland relates how the United States 'built its own house' during the war years.

In March 1940, *Harper's Bazaar* editor Carmel Snow, along with American fashion buyers from New York's most prestigious stores, packed for Paris's spring openings. This would be no ordinary buying trip. War blazed across Europe, so couturiers arranged a circuitous, but still dangerous, route for their American friends who first sailed to Italy, then traveled to Paris aboard unheated, unlighted trains filled with soldiers. Couturiers wielded the power to secure precious seating, and the Americans were willing to risk their lives in homage to Paris's design leadership.

America had its own talented designers – Claire McCardell, Elizabeth Hawes, Clare Potter and Norman Norell – but before 1940, they worked without the publicity or authority of French designers. The American and French industries were very different, and those differences kept the American designers in the shadows.

French couturiers were celebrities who created artistic, custom models for their wealthy clients. Most American designers worked anonymously, interpreting Paris designs for ready-to-wear manufacturers who targeted middle-income consumers. French couturiers luxuriated in an atmosphere of artistic freedom provided by the economic backing of French textile mills. American designers' creativity was hobbled by the need to generate sales. And Paris couture evoked a mystique not yet awarded to American designers. Susan Hay said: 'Ordering and wearing a dress from Paris meant that a woman could have as her own a small bit of the unique life of the world's most distinguished elite in the world's most exciting city' (2000: 21).

Vecchio and Riley described the American fashion industry's dedication to Paris design:

> Twice a year, as though impelled by some migratory urge, the buyers, merchants, designers, manufacturers, publicists, and journalists of the United States flock like birds to the couture salons of Europe. There they hope they will learn what the women of America will be wearing next season – or, rather, what they will be able to adapt, produce, promote, and sell to these women. (1968: 1)

Vogue editor Emmy Ives reported that the 'French were thrilled to see Americans come' and they 'made such a great effort to show us beautiful things, that the air fairly crackled with sparks of love' (*Fashion Group Bulletin*, March 1940: 1). The love affair between America and Paris was long-standing and mutual. The American fashion industry depended on Paris for design leadership, and Paris catered to America's manufacturers and store buyers, because they provided a major source of revenue for the couture industry.

In June 1940, Paris fell under Nazi occupation. Historians have speculated about the extent of couture's collaboration, or business for the sake of survival (de Marly 1980; Taylor 1995; Veillon 2002), but ultimately, Paris no longer held openings that Allied nations could attend. Therefore, while the couture industry continued to design, it temporarily lost its influence in the fashion world.

Wilson and Taylor wrote that 'the absence of style leadership from Paris created an unprecedented situation. The whole international organization of mass produced clothing for women was built around the designers' and buyers' seasonal visits to the French capital' (1989: 122). They continued that without Paris, 'British ready-to-wear looked to New York, as well as to its own London designers for inspiration' (1989: 122). McDowell viewed France, Britain and America as protagonists in a battle over who would 'command the world fashion trade . . . The issue was the fashion hegemony of Paris (1997: 124). With Paris under occupation and England struggling with severe shortages and the government's Utility Scheme, New York luxuriated in an unforeseen opportunity. Yet, New York was caught off guard and unprepared, because few believed that Paris would fall. With Paris silent, the American industry faced critical questions. Should it wait for Paris to be liberated? Would Paris ever be the same? Would American women buy dresses designed without French inspiration?

The New York fashion industry fretted and debated, but in the end, it dared to break with its past and forge a new direction. The unprecedented opportunity presented by the Second World War prompted the American fashion industry to revolutionize its business practices and launch its own campaign for design leadership. The war years marked an incredible moment, a watershed, for the New York industry. It gambled its economic future and created the international fashion industry that we know in the twenty-first century. Until recently, historians have neglected this remarkable story. This chapter explores how it happened through the examination of trade papers, press coverage and personal accounts. To fully understand this revolution, one must first look at the power of Paris and then follow New York's creative initiatives that resulted in a new leadership role for American designers.

Laying the Foundation

Throughout the nineteenth century, the United States fashion industry developed expertise in the manufacturing, promoting and retailing of fashion apparel. Paris, however, dictated the design of fashionable women's garments. By the beginning of the twentieth century there was a growing dissatisfaction with couturiers who 'kept trying to replace the simple American shirtwaist and walking skirt with more ornate garments.' This action brewed 'the idea that there was a native American fashion suitable for independent American women had been brewing' (Milbank 1989: 56).

The First World War created great hardships, but it also created opportunities for women to gain a new independence in both behavior and dress. In the United States, the war caused such a drain on manpower that women stepped into jobs and service positions vacated when husbands, fathers and brothers left for the war front. These independent women expressed their new roles through their dress and presented a market in search of a new style direction – an American style. To address this market, the First World War fashion industry in the United States turned its attention to American designers. In 1914, under the auspices of its 'American Clothes for the American Woman' slogan, *Harper's Bazaar* sponsored an all-American fashion show at the New York Roof Garden on Times Square that proved to be a great success (Herndon 1956: 58). *Vogue* reported on the event but also demonstrated its continuing allegiance to France:

> For the first time in the annals of dress New York has essayed the role of designer in an effort to show what it can do if called upon to make fashions of its own or go fashionless next spring ... If these fashions showed strongly the influence of Paris, this is neither to be wondered at nor regretted for is not Paris the master and New York the pupil who, now that the master is otherwise occupied, seeks to prove that by constant study and appreciation it, too, has learned something of the art of making clothes? (Levin 1965: 211–12)

With the end of the First World War, French couture houses struggled under shortages of both materials and craftsmen. Yet, despite its hardships and the efforts of American designers, Paris once again eclipsed the American industry and dominated world fashion throughout the 1920s.

American buyers aided Paris's economic recovery by returning to their practice of attending fashion openings where they purchased 'several dozen copies of each model' for resale to their wealthy clients (Laver 1969: 246). Retail store buyers also purchased models to be reproduced in their custom salons. When the copies were ready, the stores advertised that line-for-line French copies were available for purchase. Manufacturers, however, took a less direct approach to copying. They purchased couture originals for use by in-house designers who interpreted French fashions for the American public. The Paris couture industry encouraged and profited from these copying practices.

Paris's reign over the fashion world again slipped with the Great Depression. From 1926 to 1930 French exports declined by over 40 per cent (Milbank 1989: 98). Part of this decline occurred when the American government imposed a 'duty of up to 90 percent on the cost of the original model,' while *toiles* (muslin patterns) remained duty free (Laver 1969:

246). The *toiles* came complete with instructions that manufacturers could use in reproducing inexpensive copies of the originals. Sonia Delaunay closed her couture house in 1931 because she saw that 'the future of fashion lay with industrial couture, what we call today "ready-to-wear"'(Steele 1991: 74).

The Depression also caused declining sales for American retailers, so they looked for innovative advertising promotions. Elizabeth Hawes recalled that, 'The public was holding onto its nickels. It needed something startling to pry them loose' (1940: 195). In 1932, Lord & Taylor launched what Hawes termed a 'press stunt' designed to boost lagging sales (1940: 194). Dorothy Shaver, vice-president and director of Lord & Taylor's style bureau, developed the 'American Fashions for American Women' campaign that initially promoted American designers Elizabeth Hawes, Annette Simpson and Edith Reuss, then Clare Potter and Muriel King. The campaign quickly made an impression on industry insiders:

> The last person to receive recognition in America was the first person to become famous in Paris – the designer. Recently the tables were turned – and by a woman . . . And names were mentioned! America's ability to create styles was recognized.
>
> America herself was ready for this step. The Americanization of America was in the wind . . . The chain that held Americans to the Old Fashion World was broken!
>
> Now American names such as Elizabeth Hawes, Clare Potter, Adrian, stand shoulder to shoulder with those of Schiaparelli, Molyneux and Chanel. The American designer has come into her own. The customs of centuries have been discarded. America is the recognized fashion capital of the world. (Oglesby 1935: 23–4)

Shaver, however, did not intend to send the message that America's reliance on French design was at an end. Instead, in introducing the campaign, she paid homage to a continuing allegiance to Paris:

> We still doff our hats to Paris. Paris gave us our inspiration, and still does. But we believe that there must be clothes which are intrinsically American, and that only the American designer can create them. That is why we turn today to commend the spirit and the enterprise of these young New York women who are working so successfully to create an American style. (Hawes 1940: 194–5)

The designers enjoyed a temporary fame as their names were widely publicized and advertised, and a 'flood of articles on American Designers came out in newspapers and magazines all over the U.S.A' (Hawes 1940: 196). Shaver's promotion of American designers by name, just as French designers' names were used, was revolutionary at the time. Until then, retailers had opposed using designers' names, except for French copies, because they thought that anonymity was good for business. *Vogue*'s Jessica Daves explained that: 'Anonymity made the store name more important, gave an impression of exclusivity, and permitted pricing to be an individual store decision' (1967: 53).

Dorothy Shaver's 'American Fashions' promotion generated positive consumer support, and some retailers joined Shaver in her campaign to feature American designers (Webber-Hanchett 2003). Other retailers did not follow her lead. Sally Kirkland worked for Lord & Taylor during this time and later wrote, 'The main reason other American stores and the press had not followed Dorothy Shaver's courageous example in promoting American designers in the '30s was the almost total belief in the French Couture as the source from which all new fashion in daytime or evening clothes flowed' (1985: 36). Even Lord & Taylor continued to rely heavily on Paris designs offering special orders for couture garments in its custom salon while at the same time promoting American designers. Milbank said that 'the entire American fashion industry remained dependent on French designs' (1989: 112). Hawes later wrote that the American design movement was destined to fail because there weren't enough trained designers in 1932, and that by 1934 one heard 'comparatively little of the American Designers' (1940: 260–1).

The American fashion industry had years of experience and tremendous technical skills gained through the government's Works Progress Administration. Production innovations gave American manufacturers the ability to produce an economically competitive product that allowed American ready-to-wear to steadily increase its share of French and English apparel markets (Crawford 1948: 220). Many Americans, however, firmly held to what Elizabeth Hawes called the French legend: 'All beautiful clothes are made in the houses of the French Couturieres and all women want them' (1940: 1). Perhaps, though, the legend continued because the consuming public so rarely read American designers' names. The *New York Times* maintained a policy of using French designers' names, but not those of American designers (Buckland and O'Neal 1998). Phyllis Feldkamp remembered that even fashion magazines avoided featuring American designers. She reminisced, 'It took us ages to break the French connection . . . There really aren't any mentions of any designers in any of the ads, much less the picture credits, the editorial ones, and it was just Paris, Paris, Paris . . . It made it hard for American design didn't it?' (Lambert 1977: 18).

Occasionally, retailers or publications highlighted American creations, but this attention was exceptional, breaking the routine coverage of Paris. For example, *Vogue* periodically published an Americana issue. Its

February 1, 1938 issue wore a patriotic cover, and the editorial said that the issue strove to portray the nation's beauty, power and excitement. One feature article discussed the importance of America's garment industry and its contributions to making American women 'better dressed, more fashion-conscious than any others on the face of the earth.' The article talked about the size, sales and scope of the industry, then compared the French and American industries. Ironically, the article failed to include the name of a single American designer. Instead, it gave design credit to manufacturers stating that American women knew only a few manufacturers' names because their products carried the store labels. Throughout the entire issue, *Vogue* lauded American design, but gave the credit to the retailers, the fabric companies or the manufacturers. The only place where American designers received any recognition was in the advertisements. Bergdorf Goodman's ad highlighted five designers – Peggy Morris, Leslie Morris, Mark Mooring, John Dean and Mrs. Gleason – while Lord & Taylor's ad featured Nan Westley. *Vogue* played a leading role in promoting fashion to American women, yet, less than two years before Paris fell, its Americana issue carried no editorial mention of American designers. America possessed a strong foundation of design talent, but its praises seemed grudgingly sung.

Even those who advocated an American style, such as Dorothy Shaver, eschewed an entirely American campaign in favor of smart business practices. Paris held the prestige, and stores wanted as much of that fashion authority as they could create in the public's mind. The public simply didn't recognize American designers, and they voted for Paris-inspired creations with their purchasing dollars. These consumers may not have recognized, however, that America already had its own style. The American woman needed functional clothes for her busy life, and she did not have time for the multiple fittings required by haute couture. Vera Maxwell, for example, along with other designers like Claire McCardell, created innovative mix-and-match separates as early as the 1930s (Martin 1985: 18). Figures 6.1 and 6.2 illustrate typical McCardell designs for outdoor and weekend wear from the 1944 season.

American designers knew how to cater to the American woman, but their anonymity made them the stepchildren of the fashion world. Finally, the war gave them an opportunity to take center stage. When news of Paris's occupation reached New York, the fashion industry mourned the loss of its design leader and expressed grave concerns for friends and colleagues. American fashion industry leaders, though, wasted little time in tackling a crucial question, 'Now that Paris is closed . . . What shall we do now?'[1]

Figure 6.1 'Lumberjack Plaid for Outdoor Wear.' Publicity photograph, June 30, 1944. Lumberjack plaid slack suit with matching flat shoes designed by Claire McCardell. Author's collection.

Building an American House

The American fashion industry had many resources, but it lacked an organizing body. Fashion leaders operated in an autonomous manner, so, in New York, many voices asked the question of what to do without Paris. There was no one forum, no one voice of leadership around which this industry could rally. Instead, throughout the summer of 1940, a variety of leaders

Figure 6.2 'Brief but Big.' Publicity photograph, June 16, 1944. Playsuit in black cotton with white topstitching designed by Claire McCardell. The play-suit was part of a weekend ensemble that included a skirt and middy shirt with a matching white jacket. Author's collection.

from all parts of the New York fashion world joined in the discussions of where to begin. Many discussions occurred at monthly luncheons hosted by the Fashion Group, an organization of women fashion professionals. One point stood out clearly in everyone's mind – the summer of 1940 would mark a distinct revolution in how the American fashion industry developed and promoted its designs. The industry planned its 'unveiling' for Fall 1940. Tobé Fashion Reports (July 16, 1940: 15) predicted:

The fall of 1940 will go down in history as the year in which the whole structure of the fashion business had to be rebuilt.

... The destiny of American fashions lies in the hands of American designers. The two questions upper-most in the minds of everyone concerned with fashion is [sic] – 'Are the American designers *able* to do it?' – and second, 'How should it be done?'

As the American fashion industry built its own house, it looked in several directions for leadership. Some eyes looked westward. California was home to a thriving apparel industry that specialized in casual sports-wear styles. California was also home to the movie industry. Sally Kirkland described the industry saying, 'The West Coast had been known right along for its active sportswear from swim to skiwear . . . But the evolving concept of casual simplicity in total dress was given a bit of dash by the man-tailored, trench-coated glamour of the movie stars Marlene Dietrich, Greta Garbo and Katherine Hepburn' (1985: 35). The Hollywood film industry included designers such as Gilbert Adrian and Irene who were stars in their own right. Hollywood provided perhaps the only venue where designers enjoyed the same prestige as Paris designers. This Hollywood glamour even drew a number of couture designers, including Chanel, Lanvin, Patou and Schiaparelli, to the United States for the opportunity to design for films.

Throughout the 1930s, glamorous film stars provided a diversion from the hardships of the Depression, and American women eagerly followed the fashions created for the silver screen. Off-screen, actresses such as Marlene Dietrich and Katherine Hepburn validated trousers as acceptable public dress for the average woman (Shaw 2000: 121; Warner, this volume). This influence also reached European women. France's occupation government launched a propaganda campaign against 'the pernicious influence of American cinema, accusing it of having led astray a whole section of female youth' (Veillon 2002: 128).

Apparel manufacturers and retailers regularly copied Hollywood designers' on-screen creations. Moviegoers eagerly bought these garments because movie designers carried a fashion authority and status seldom afforded to New York designers. The American public recognized names promoted in movie credits or publicity stories. In the late 1930s, MGM executive Louis B. Mayer sent Gilbert Adrian to New York to investigate a career on Seventh Avenue. Mayer hoped to make a deal with garment industry wholesalers that might offset part of Adrian's movie salary, but the designer was not interested (Riley 1975: 24). A number of Hollywood designers, including Adrian, eventually capitalized on their movie fame and entered the ready-to-wear market, but, generally, Hollywood displayed little interest in leading the apparel industry.

In New York, the atmosphere was entirely different. Industry leaders feared that without Paris's inspiration, American women would lose interest in fashion and stop buying dresses. Apparel manufacturers faced a variety of operational challenges such as new piece-work rates under development with the labor unions and the loss of business to other manufacturing centers such as Kansas City and Chicago. The loss of Paris's leadership worried these businessmen. While in retrospect it might seem unlikely, they feared that between the war and Paris's silence, the industry would soon be out of business.

Everyone seemed to agree that something had to be done to promote American designers as talented and capable of producing designs suited to the American woman. The problem remained that few consumers knew American designers by name. Most designers worked for manufacturers, so they had no name recognition and certainly carried little fashion authority. On August 8, 1940 Tobé told her subscribers that something needed to be done fast, so that any remaining fashion momentum would not die. She suggested that the public was questioning whether or not designs would be as good as they had been when Paris led the way. She wrote:

> It's up to you to answer them – and answer them soon! Your answers must be strong enough to be convincing and dramatic enough to catch and hold the public attention . . .
>
> The American woman must be thoroughly sold that American designers can design the smartest thing in *any line* that she needs – and that *she can buy* it *from you.*

Without a governing body to coordinate the drive to build American design authority, promotional campaigns took numerous forms and came from some unexpected sources including politicians, manufacturers, union leaders, retailers and publishers.

New York City Mayor Fiorello H. LaGuardia recognized that the fashion industry made enormous financial contributions to his city's economy. He knew that if the industry suffered, the city would suffer. The Mayor may also have recognized the possibility that Hollywood could take the lead in the changing fashion world, but there was no question in this politician's mind as to which coast should take control. It also appears that the Mayor was monitoring the war in Europe. Three months before Paris fell, the Mayor spoke to a Fashion Group monthly meeting. He shared his opinions stating, 'New York City is the center of fashion of the entire world . . . I don't see why we have to take our fashion from any other country . . . And I hope to see the time come when people will be copying New York models' (LaGuardia 1940: 4–8). The Mayor may not have understood fashion, but he recognized a threat to his city's well-being. He soon became actively involved in the campaign to promote American designers.

Throughout the summer of 1940, many fashion industry leaders expressed opinions about the course to follow. Mayor LaGuardia quickly sensed the discord within this vital industry. In August 1940 the Mayor called a press conference and invited twelve New York fashion editors to his office. Among these editors were Virginia Pope of the *New York Times*, Alice Perkins of *Women's Wear Daily* and Katherine Vincent of the *Herald Tribune*. As Pope reported, LaGuardia told the editors, 'I never had a press conference cause so much excitement as this one . . . I'm interviewing you today . . . I want to learn something about the fashion business. What's all the conflict about in the dress designing field?'('Mayor Has Plan' 1940: 22). The editors explained the challenge facing the fashion industry as it transitioned to a new way of operating, and the Mayor revealed that he was aware of several groups competing for control. The Mayor also hinted at a plan of his own that would aid the industry in its 'moment of confusion.' He further offered the opinion that American designers would be in the clear if they could go for two years without missing Paris. 'Then if France regains her soul and Paris comes back,' he said, 'we will have established a wholesome and stimulating rivalry.' The Mayor kept his plan quiet for months, but he actively participated in fashion promotions and was photographed at many fashion shows.

New York: The Fashion Capital of the World

In September 1940 a group of retailers launched their contributions in promoting American designers. Six top Fifth Avenue retailers including Bergdorf Goodman and Saks Fifth Avenue presented a series of fashion openings. In a remarkable show of cooperation, these retailing competitors coordinated their events so that the public and the press could attend each opening. The stores presented 800 original American designs in the glamorous French tradition ('Designers' 1940: 14). Furthermore, the stores promoted their designers, by name, during the show and allowed those names to be published. This was a true break with the industry's traditions – normally publicity of any kind was avoided ahead of a fashion season. To allow advance publicity was to risk unauthorized, less expensive copies. The stores also gambled that promoting individual designers would not lessen the retailers' fashion prestige or authority. On September 5, 1940 Tobé reviewed the openings with the comment, 'The week of September 3rd–7th 1940 may well go down in fashion history as the time in which American designed fashions at last came into their own.' Virginia Pope summarized the importance of the openings when she editorialized, 'For the first time New York stepped out of the position of understudy and took over the stellar role' ('New York,' 1941: 8).

Several significant changes in the way the press covered American fashions followed closely on the heels of the American openings. First, the *New York Times* changed its editorial policy to include designers' names in its editorials. Then in September 1940, *Vogue* magazine placed a large ad in the *New York Times* promoting its forthcoming issues. *Vogue* usually paid little attention to American fashions, but with Paris occupied, the magazine had little choice. The British fashion industry continued throughout the war, but its skills favored couture dresses rather than the ready-to-wear dresses mastered by the American industry (McDowell 1997: 133). The American press periodically reported on the British Utility Scheme for conserving fabric, but these stories seemed more inclined to show Americans how Europe was suffering rather than to report on fashion. Still, *Vogue* sent a very dramatic message to the public through its ad in the *New York Times* on September 5, 1940. The ad spoke to the heart of the industry's challenge when it said:

FOR THE FIRST TIME IN FASHION HISTORY, America is on its own – without the direct inspiration of Paris . . .

The first completely American Collections are now ready. They settle, once and for all, the question agitated in the headlines of every newspaper, 'Can America Design?' . . . American women will *keep* their reputations as the best dressed women in the world!

Vogue is proud to review the American Openings (the most important ever held in this country) in its two September issues. They are reported with the same authority, the same critical judgment, the same brilliant picturing of the mode by top-flight artists and photographers, that Vogue has brought to the reporting of the Paris openings, during the past fifty years.

The magazine's policy change was particularly significant because *Vogue* did not attend American showroom openings. *Vogue* also seemed to think that it was important to stress to the public that it would put all of its resources into these special issues and present American designers, for the first time, on an equal footing with Parisian designers. The magazine's staff realized that if American women were to respect the skills of American designers, then opinion leaders such as the editorial staffs of the major fashion publications would need to set the example. *Vogue* editor Edna Woolman Chase told a Fashion Group meeting in January 1942 that the group faced the challenge of 'expressing publicly our views, or shaping, or helping to shape the views of many other women in America' (1942: 1). She continued that the group had a duty to provide leadership to 'millions of other women all over America' who would look to them. Along with these editorial changes in the fashion publications, the public also saw a change in retailers' advertisements.

Before Paris's occupation, many fashion advertisements in both magazines and newspapers carried references to Paris. Often the stores announced that they either had original Paris models or that their copies of Paris designs were ready. During the summer of 1940, very few retail ads mentioned any design source at all. Instead, the New York stores spent the summer months developing new advertising messages to support their Fall openings. In September 1940, retailers unveiled new ads with increased references to American inspiration and to American designers.

In a full-page ad in the *New York Times* on September 25, 1940, Lord & Taylor announced the ten designers (Charles Cooper, Frances Troy Stix, Vera Jacobs, Karen Stark, Zelma Golden, Fritzie Hannah, Vera Host, Bertha Altholz, Will Saunders, Pat Warren) that would be featured in their Designers' Shop. Perhaps the most revolutionary part of the new shop was that the store acknowledged the designers' skills by sewing in labels bearing each designer's name. Furthermore, the store promoted this policy in its ads. One ad said, 'Yours – for your very own, in your size, your color, your most flattering lines – the signed originals of these talented ten.' According to Dorothy Shaver, the store selected the designers because they were known in the professional world and their clothes were worn by thousands of women, but the public did not know them ('Smart New York Store' 1940: 20).

Other retailers also adopted the American theme: Franklin Simon introduced a new campaign entitled 'American Genius,' Bergdorf Goodman offered its first 'All-American collection,' Russeks advertised an 'All-American Costume Suit' and Arnold Constable promoted its 'American Creators' which carried both designers' names and photographs. Even stores that did not regularly feature designer goods promoted American designs. Macy's placed a full-page ad in the *New York Times* on September 22, 1940 that read, 'The Importance of New York! Macy's bows low to New York . . . undisputed fashion capital of the world . . . May she long remember all the wonderful things Paris taught her!' Clearly, Paris was silent, but not forgotten. Perhaps McCreery's paid the highest compliment to the American designers in a very simple ad in the

New York Times on September 9, 1940 that read, 'the new American designers say . . .'

One part of the New York fashion industry watched the September openings and thought that more needed to be done. In November 1940, the International Ladies Garment Workers Union, as a preliminary to its December contract negotiations, announced that it would ask manufacturers to join with the unions in an effort to introduce more efficient production methods and '[advertise] New York as a style center' ('Seek Industry Aid' 1940: 18). Union representatives first funded a study of institutional advertising used for other industries along with recommendations as to how those types of advertisements might be used to promote New York City as a fashion center. Based on this study, the unions devised their own promotional plan that they presented to the dress manufacturers. The union offered to donate $100,000 to a fund that would be used to finance advertisements and two fashion shows. The union asked that manufacturers purchase union labels to sew into every dress constructed in the New York area, thereby donating to the fund. In return for the manufacturers' cooperation, the union offered to forego any pay increase requests in the forthcoming contract negotiations.

This unlikely alliance of unions and manufacturers grew out of fear for their jobs. New York had been home to many dress manufacturers for years, but both parties watched as other United States' cities lured prized jobs from New York. These allies seized this moment of transition in the fashion industry and capitalized on the opportunity to slow the migration of precious jobs. The unions and manufacturers used their fund to establish the New York Dress Institute. In July 1941, both Mayor LaGuardia and First Lady Eleanor Roosevelt joined in launching this initiative by sewing the first labels into dresses. Everyone soon realized that, despite the war, women did not lose interest in purchasing dresses. With so many resources called into service for the war effort, women had little else to purchase, so the Dress Institute's funds grew.

Mayor LaGuardia kept his promise to promote the fashion industry. In the spring of 1941 he hosted a two-day fashion event called 'New York's Fashion Futures.' This joint effort between the city's Commerce Commissioner and The Fashion Group promised to 'dramatize New York City's leadership in the fashion world' ('City to Promote "Fashion Future"' 1940: 34). Dorothy Shaver, of Lord & Taylor, told the organizing committee that the show would 'clarify the now confused production of heterogeneous modes and create the focus that Paris formerly supplied for American clothes' ('Ten Billion Involved' 1940: 34). The importance of the show even reached the White House. First Lady Eleanor Roosevelt was a

Figure 6.3 'Color for Morale.' Publicity Photograph for an 'original Ellbi creation.'
The neck piece was described as 'a cascade of ruffled net that boasts
a flourish of American garlands whimsically embroidered in subtlest
pastels . . . the perfect accessory to swish up your best black
number.' Author's collection.

member of The Fashion Group and agreed to serve on the show's advisory
committee. Over tea in the Red Room, she discussed details of the show
with members of The Fashion Group ('Aids Fashion Show' 1940: 40). The
press participated by providing coverage for the Mayor's publicity visits to
dress manufacturers.

The show opened to rave reviews in the press and to a packed house.
This innovative presentation of American design set the pattern for other
shows that followed. Organizers wisely sought to involve participants from
all aspects of the industry including textile producers, manufacturers and
retailers. The Chairman of the Mayor's Business Advisory Committee esti-
mated that the show would affect industries with a total value of
$10,500,000,000 ('Ten Billion Involved' 1940: 34). His estimate illustrates

the enormity of the city's and the industry's concern that the American fashion industry continue to prosper. The loss of this major industry would have been catastrophic for the economy of the city and the nation. In addition to their participation in the show, retailers further articulated the prestige of the event when they included references to specific dresses in their newspaper ads. The show proved to be a success for all including the British War Relief fund that received the proceeds from the ticket sales.

Throughout the spring and summer of 1941 fashion coverage followed the pattern set during the fall openings. American women did not lose interest in purchasing dresses, so the fashion industry enjoyed its successful promotion of American design (Figure 6.3). The war in Europe, however, overshadowed business accomplishments and garnered front-page coverage. Retailers acknowledged this threat by featuring soldiers in their ads and by encouraging women to dress for their men. Then, on December 7, 1941 the Japanese bombed Pearl Harbor and America declared war. The fashion industry shifted its focus from establishing New York designers as world leaders to concentrating on how the industry could best help to win the war.

For the Duration

Bonwit Teller summarized the fashion industry's attitude toward wartime promotions in an ad in the December 21, 1941 *New York Times* that featured women dancing in evening gowns. Under the heading, 'Dress up . . . Heads up,' the copy said, 'Today America doesn't want its women dreary. It wants you looking nice. Not only because it's good for what ails you. Or because the boys, God bless 'em, like to see you that way. But because there are other important reasons too.' The ad explained that the fashion industry provided economic support for the soldiers and that America's fashion business was staffed by women. This type of campaign followed the pattern of British *Vogue*'s 'Beauty is Your Duty' campaign. The fashion industry had now charged America's women with the moral duty of buying beautiful dresses for the sake of the morale of the nation.

The case for American designers, at least for the moment, was well established as evidenced by enthusiastic sales of women's dresses. Periodically, reports of Paris couture's activities trickled out of France, but for the most part, Paris provided little competition for New York. London, too, looked to New York for fashion leadership (Wilson and Taylor 1989: 122).

American women took on new roles for the duration, and these roles shifted the demographics of the buying public. Scores of women worked in the war industries, and their paychecks elevated many of them to middle-class status. For many, defense paychecks gave them their first opportunity to purchase the fashions that they had previously only read about. This, coupled with the media's pressure to look beautiful for the morale of the nation, spurred sales. Consumers realized that the government was diverting resources to the war effort, and they feared that clothing would be rationed. Then in April 1942 the government announced Limitation Order 85, which imposed styling regulations designed to conserve fabric. The fashion industry soon found itself trying to promote its products to an eager market without generating too much consumer demand. The industry determined that its best course was along a patriotic theme that stressed quality, investment purchases and women's responsibility to look attractive for morale.

America's wartime struggles placed American designers in a unique position. On the one hand the designers now created for working women who spearheaded the civilian efforts to win the war, while at the same time they led an industry that made crucial contributions to the nation's economy. Designers, therefore, earned a new, almost heroic, status. Despite wartime constraints, the fashion industry launched several new promotional campaigns that pushed American designers even farther into the spotlight. In January 1942 Coty announced the creation of the American Fashion Critics Award. The Coty Award would go to the designer who set a trend that the industry followed. Coty used this award to encourage designers to work toward a unified style instead of following their own interests. In January 1943 Mayor LaGuardia participated in presenting the first award to designer Norman Norell with additional citations given to Adrian, Hattie Carnegie, Clare Potter, Charles Cooper, Mainbocher, Claire McCardell and Valentina ('Designer Honored' 1943: 10). In addition to public promotional events, the Mayor also worked behind the scenes.

In August 1943 Mayor LaGuardia announced his own plan for promoting American design. He established a committee to develop a mammoth post-war building project that he called 'The World Fashion Center' ('Style Center' 1943: 18). The announcement caused a surge of controversy over the feasibility of, the need for and the location of the center. The mayor's project was never built.

In this era of innovative promotions, the *New York Times* developed two successful initiatives. The first was a new section devoted to expanded coverage of the fashion industry's seasonal openings. This coverage is particularly noteworthy in light of the severe paper shortages that plagued newspapers. At a time when newspapers turned down advertising because of paper shortages, the *New York Times* created fashion features that gobbled up precious newsprint. On September 13, 1942 fashion editor

Virginia Pope inaugurated the new 'Fashion Forecasts' section by writing: 'A new fashion season is dawning, one of the most vital in the history of American design. Operating under wartime restrictions and completely freed from any foreign influence, designers have met the challenge and are creating authentic all-American styles, suited to the needs of the emergency.' This new feature contained photographs of the new fall styles complete with designer credits. More notably, the section also included photographs of ten American designers, their comments on American design and their predictions for the future. The paper had not given such star treatment even to couture designers.

Beyond this expanded fashion coverage, the *New York Times* also presented the first of what became a series of yearly fashion shows. On September 15, 1942 the paper announced that it would sponsor a fashion show that would highlight 'the progress in American fashion leadership after two years of independence of the former style capital.' The paper repeatedly stressed that this show, eventually called 'Fashions of The Times,' would not be like ordinary fashion shows. Instead, the emphasis would be on innovations in both designs and fabrics necessitated by the war. The patriotic theme did not hamper the collective efforts of designers, textile manufacturers, set designers or retailers as they created a glamorous forum that presented American designers as celebrities and stars. With each presentation, the shows gained in popularity, and tickets soon became scarce.

By the end of 1943, however, the industry began looking towards victory in the war and the possibility of Paris's liberation. At that point, American designers had worked free of competition for over two years, but no one knew what would happen if and when Paris regained its freedom. Perhaps as a pre-emptive strike, the *New York Times* began a new series of articles on New Year's Day, 1944. The series ran during the following three months and each article contained the biography of at least one American designer. The articles highlighted the quality and distinctiveness of American designers' work. They also provided an opportunity for these designers to express their design philosophy and to contrast New York and Paris creations. At a time when quality and value represented patriotism, this positioning aligned the designers with American nationalism and, presumably, sought to reinforce consumers' allegiance to both the United States and its designers.

Retailers consistently used designers' and manufacturers' names in their wartime promotions, but with the prospect of renewed competition with Paris, the stores increased this coverage and developed several new features. For example, in an effort to place previously unheralded designers in the spotlight, Saks Fifth Avenue premiered a half-page ad called 'Saks Fifth AveNEWS' with the first installment featuring Sophie Gimbel, the store's custom designer and supervisor of its Salon Moderne. Saks started placing her name at the forefront, but the store also used her name to align her designs, and the store's name, with the larger national concern for quality and conservation. In the following months, the ads addressed a variety of style issues and regularly featured Gimbel's work.

One of the most telling events in the effort to promote American designers came as a result of an article in *Life* magazine entitled 'American Designers' in May 1944. The magazine carried an American design on its cover, then devoted seven pages to the designers and their work. The introduction said: 'The U.S. fashion world is becoming very proud of U.S. clothes designers. As long as Paris ruled in the realm of style, Americans were apologetic about their designers. But when Paris fell Americans began to appraise and appreciate their own.' On the following Sunday, May 7, 1944, Bonwit Teller placed a full-page ad in the *New York Times* with a picture of the magazine cover. The copy told readers that Bonwit carried the creations of seven of the designers and that those designs were in the store's windows. Lord & Taylor, the first store to promote American designers, fired a return volley the next Sunday. In a similar full-page ad, the store said, 'Let's get this question of American Designers straightened out right now!' First the ad chastised *Life* for only featuring ten designers, then it reminded readers that Lord & Taylor had been first to promote American designers. Finally, it listed the names of twenty-nine designers whose work was available in their store. Not to be outdone, Saks Fifth Avenue also ran an ad on May 14, 1944 with a picture of the store front, a list of fourteen designers featured in their store and a message that Saks was proud of the work they had done in promoting American design. Clearly, the campaign to establish and promote American designers had been a success. This war of words could not have happened just four years earlier.

In August 1944 the Allies liberated Paris and the couture industry sought to re-establish its place in the fashion world. The American fashion industry cheered, and the *New York Times* scrambled for news coverage of Paris fashions. One unidentified source told reporters that, 'Every store wants to be the first one to show Paris models, but that doesn't mean at all that they have forgotten the fine work done by American designers in the past few years' ('Paris Not to Dim' 1944). The fashion industry soon demonstrated that its loyalty to American designers would last longer than just 'for the duration.' The *New York Times* continued its fashion shows and retailers expanded their advertising coverage of designers' work. The debates of what to do raged in a variety of forums, but one point remained clear – the fashion world had changed forever. French designers might lead the couture industry, but America now had equal respect for its own design capabilities. Paris could no longer dictate and expect America to follow. Instead, the American fashion industry had built its own house and shown the world that it could stand on its own.

Note

1. This was used as the topic for The Fashion Group's monthly luncheon held in New York on July 11, 1940. The Fashion Group International, Inc., Archives, New York, p. 1.

References

'Aids Fashion Show' (1940), *New York Times*, December 18.
'American Designers: U.S. Public is Getting to Know their Names and Styles' (1944) *Life*, May 8: 63–69.
Buckland, S.S. and G.S. O'Neal, (1998), '"We Publish Fashions Because They Are News": *The New York Times 1940–1945'*, *Dress*, 25: 33–41.
Chase, E.W. (1942) to The Fashion Group, Inc., in *The Fashion Group Bulletin*, 8(1), February: 1.
'City to Promote "Fashion Future"' (1940), *New York Times*, October 30.
Crawford, M.D.C. (1948), *The Ways of Fashion*, New York: Fairchild.
Daves, J. (1967), *Ready-Made Miracle: The American Story of Fashion for the Millions*, New York: G.P. Putnam's Sons.
'Designer Honored' (1943), *New York Times*, January 23.
'Designers' (1940), *New York Times*, August 28.
The Fashion Group Bulletin (New York), January 1, 1940–December 31, 1945.
The Fashion Group, Inc., Meeting, Biltmore Hotel, July 11, 1940, transcript, The Fashion Group International, Inc., Archives, New York.
Hawes, E. (1940), *Fashion is Spinach*, New York: Grosset & Dunlap.
Hay, S. (2000), 'A & L Tirocchi: A Time Capsule Discovered,' in *From Paris to Providence: Fashion, Art, and The Tirocchi Dressmakers' Shop, 1915–1947*, Providence, RI: Museum of Art, Rhode Island School of Design.
Herndon, B. (1956), *Bergdorf's on the Plaza: The Story of Bergdorf Goodman and a Half-Century of American Fashion*, New York: Alfred A. Knopf.
Kirkland, S. (1985), 'Sportswear for Everywear,' in R. Martin *All American: A Sportswear Tradition*, New York: Fashion Institute of Technology, 34–43.
LaGuardia, F.H. (1940) to The Fashion Group, Inc., Biltmore Hotel, New

York City, March 20, The Fashion Group International, Inc., Archives, New York.

Lambert, E. (1977), Interview by Phyllis Feldkamp, December 8, Oral Histories Project of the Fashion Industries, Gladys Marcus Library, Fashion Institute of Technology, New York, 28.

Laver, J. (1969), *A Concise History of Costume*, London: Thames and Hudson.

Levin, P.L. (1965), *The Wheels of Fashion*, New York: Doubleday.

Lewis, M. (1940), 'What shall we do now?' To The Fashion Group, Inc., Biltmore Hotel, New York, July 11. The Fashion Group International, Inc., Archives, New York.

de Marly, D. (1980), *The History of Haute Couture 1850–1950*, New York: Holmes & Meier Publishers, Inc.

Martin, R. (1985), 'All American: A Sportswear Tradition,' in *All American: A Sportswear Tradition*, New York: Fashion Institute of Technology, pp. 8–21.

'Mayor Has Plan to Aid Fashion Bid' (1940), *New York Times*, August 22.

McDowell, C. (1997), *Forties Fashions and the New Look*, London: Bloomsbury.

Milbank, C.R. (1989), *New York Fashion: The Evolution of American Style*, New York: Harry N. Abrams.

'New York: Two Fold Fashion Center' (1941), *New York Times*, January 5.

Oglesby, C. (1935), *Fashion Careers American Style*, New York: Funk & Wagnalls.

'Paris Not to Dim' (1944), *New York Times*, September 2.

Riley, R. (1975), 'Adrian,' in S.T. Lee (ed.), *American Fashion: The Life and Lines of Adrian, Mainbocher, McCardell, Norell, Trigere*, New York: Quadrangle/The New York Times Book Co., pp. 1–107.

'Seek Industry Aid' (1940), *New York Times*, November 25.

Shaw, M. (2000), 'American Fashion: The Tirocchi Sisters in Context', in S. Hay (ed), *From Paris to Providence: Fashion, Art,And the Tirocchi Dressmakers' Shop, 1915–1947*, Providence, RI: Museum of Art, Rhode Island School of Design.

'Smart New York Store' (1940) *New York Times*, September 25.

Steele, V. (1991), *Women of Fashion: Twentieth-Century Designers*, New York: Rizzoli International Publications.

'Style Center' (1943), *New York Times*, August 23.

Taylor, L. (1995), 'The Work and Function of the Paris Couture Industry during the German Occupation of 1940–1944', *Dress* 22: 34–44.

'Ten Billion Involved' (1940), *New York Times*, December 10.

Tobé Fashion Reports (New York), January 1–December 31 1940.

Vecchio, W. and R. Riley (1968), *The Fashion Makers: A Photographic Record*, New York: Crown Publishers.

Veillon, D. (2002), *Fashion Under the Occupation*, Oxford: Berg.

Webber-Hanchett, T. (2003), 'Dorothy Shaver: Promoter of "The American Look",' *Dress* 30: 80–90.

Wilson, E. and L. Taylor (1989), *Through the Looking Glass: A History of Dress from 1860 to the Present*, London: BBC Books.

Archives

The Fashion Group International, Inc. Archives, New York.
Tobe Fashion Reports Archives, New York.

7

The Onondaga Silk Company's 'American Artist Print Series' of 1947

Amy Lund and Linda Welters

Editors' Introduction: After the Second World War ended in 1945, most Americans resumed family life. The GI Bill sent many veterans back to school to further their educations. Women gave up their wartime jobs and retreated to their homes to raise children.

During the war, the US government had regulated the manufacture of most clothing. The conservation of resources that resulted from these regulations continued for several years after the war. When Christian Dior introduced his feminine, narrow-waisted, full-skirted 'New Look' in early 1947, it created quite a stir. While some women protested such a radical change in fashion, the 'New Look' once again established Paris as the center for women's fashion.

In the meantime, the promotion of American art and fashion continued in the second half of the 1940s. Amy Lund and Linda Welters discuss the collaboration of the Onondaga Silk Mills with the Midtown Galleries of New York City to create a line of printed fashion fabrics called the 'American Artist Print Series' based on the work of American artists. The Onondaga Silk Company worked with American artists to create the textile prints and American fashion designers to create the dresses. The fabrics and fashions were introduced to consumers in cities across the US in January 1947, just a month before Dior unveiled the 'New Look' in Paris.

In the years immediately following the Second World War, the Onondaga Silk Company collaborated with the Midtown Galleries of New York City to create the 'American Artist Print Series.' This collaboration, drawing upon the established practice of using internationally renowned artists – Raoul Dufy, Salvador Dali, and Fernand Léger for example – as textile designers, resulted in a collection of dress fabrics inspired by works of lesser-known American artists. The company called on American ready-to-wear designers to create fashionable garments from the fabrics. The collaborators presented the complete series, from original paintings to finished garments, to the American public in the spring of 1947 through exhibition in museums and department stores.

The 'American Artist Print Series' serves as an example of the continuing promotion of American art and design during the 1940s. It succeeded in advancing both American art and American textile design through ready-to-wear fashion. Fashion became the vehicle to present American art to the public. The idea for turning art into fashion was unique for this period. This chapter explores the development of the concept, and considers the ingredients for its success. These include the choice of artists, the selection of their paintings, and the transformation of the latter into textile motifs by industrial designers. The chapter likewise examines the production of the garments by leading ready-to-wear designers, the impact of the exhibition on Americans and the importance of its legacy today.[1]

Artists and Textile Design

Collaboration between artists and textile companies was well established by the 1940s. The practice had developed between the world wars, most notably in France and England. While some artists designed the textiles themselves, others agreed to have their artwork adapted for textiles by industrial designers. In the years before the Second World War, Ascher, Ltd; Bianchini-Ferrier; Edinburgh Weavers, Ltd and Allan Walton depicted contemporary artists' works on their textiles (Duncan 1988: 179; Robinson 1969: 158–9). Artists such as Salvador Dali, Vertès, Raoul Dufy and Fernand Léger designed some of these textiles ('Art into Living' 1947). Several of these artists worked for more than one company. Henri Matisse, Pablo Picasso, Alexander Calder, Angelo Testa and Henry Moore also explored the medium of textiles around this time.

In the United States, companies such as Stehli Silk and HR Mallinson & Co. employed textile designers, including American textile artists, to create their prints. Ilonka Karasz had designs produced by HR Mallinson, as did Marion Dorn and Ruth Reeves (Schoeser and Blausen 2000).

At the close of the Second World War, the use of actual paintings as inspiration for textile designs had become quite common. For instance, in 1945, Ascher, Ltd produced a series of head scarves called 'Modern Art for Daily Wear' based on work by English artists (Mendes and Hinchcliffe 1987: 24). Zika Ascher believed in bringing art out of museums so it could be enjoyed by everyone.

One of the factors besides employment that attracted artists to textiles was the development of screen-printing as a surface design technique (Schoeser 1986: 28). Until the 1930s, most textiles had been printed with rollers. Printing with flat screens allowed for much larger patterns because the designs were no longer confined to the eighteen-inch repeat dictated by the circumference of a roller (Humphries 2004: 215). Additionally, screen-printing, which is based on the principle of stenciling, can reproduce a variety of effects including those once only possible with woodblocks or copperplates (Harris 1993: 39). This method led to more calligraphic designs.

The textile designs that emerged from the collaboration between artists and screen-printers featured a common visual style. These early screen-printed textiles featured calligraphic motifs combined either with washes of color in the background or as contrasting amorphous shapes. This style was often called biomorphic or semi-abstract (Goodrich and Baur 1961: 197). Printed textiles from this period are similar to painted works by Arshile Gorky, Joan Miró, mobile artist Alexander Calder, and furniture designer Eero Saarinen. This biomorphic style became well established in the 1940s, although it was not the only style used.

Some American textile firms had developed specifically American themes in their designs by the late 1920s. HR Mallinson produced series inspired by national parks, caves, and American Indians (Shaw 2003). In the 1930s a distinct American style of printed textile design had emerged based on American realism (Schoeser and Blausen 2000).

Another influencing factor was the post-war shift of art and industrial design from Europe to the United States (Payant 1946). Many artists sought refuge from the chaos of Europe or strove to explore the developing art of modern industrial America (Rose 1986). Additionally, as we have seen in Chapter 6, American fashion designers had gained stature during the war years. Thus, the stage was set for the collaboration between American fine artists and the American textile and fashion industry.

The Idea

The Onondaga Silk Company of New York got the idea for a collection of screen-printed textiles for use in fashionable apparel entitled the 'American Artist Print Series' in late 1945. The company had worked with artists to design textile prints, specifically Raoul Dufy (Duncan 1988: 173), but this was the first time it had singled out American artists and taken the designs directly from previously painted works as opposed to having the artists create designs especially for textiles.

The Onondaga Silk Company, founded in 1918, had merged with the Old Colony Silk Mills of New Bedford, Massachusetts by 1930. It had mills in Syracuse and Ogdensburg, New York, and Easton, Pennsylvania, as well as offices in Chicago and Los Angeles. The company produced a wide range of fabrics including plain weaves, jacquards, velvets, and printed rayons and silks for use in ties, linings and fashionable apparel.[2]

The idea for the 'American Artist Print Series' was the inspiration of Mary Gruskin, the wife of Alan D. Gruskin, the director of the Midtown Galleries of New York City, who presented it to Onondaga ('From a Kingman Watercolor' 1947). In an article in the *New York Times* (December 17, 1947: 41), Philip Vogelman, Onondaga's president, described the goal of the collaboration as: 'not to turn the painter into a textile designer, but rather to make intelligent and expert use for fashion of the motifs, coloring and style expressed by his special talents.' Vogelman and others thought that this project was highly original and 'one of the most unusual and exciting ventures ever undertaken in American Art or in American Fashions' (Letter to Elizabeth McCausland, December 6, 1946, Midtown Galleries Records).

From the commercial viewpoint, both the textiles and the fashions had to appeal to consumers' tastes and to their fascination with art to assure sales. As *Art News* stated, 'Painting into this season's dress – quite an order!' (Frost 1947: 31).

Choosing the Artists and the Paintings

The group of six American artists eventually chosen by Onondaga – William Palmer, Waldo Peirce, Dong Kingman, Gladys Rockmore Davis, Doris Rosenthal and Julien Binford – regularly exhibited their work at the Midtown Galleries in New York City. Some had exhibited there since the 1930s. The artists worked in oils, watercolors and pastels. Each artist had his or her own style and favorite subject, and the textile designs produced from their paintings reflected their individuality. None of these artists could be termed avant-garde. Their work did not reflect the surrealism of Salvador Dali or the abstract expressionism of Jackson Pollack or Wassily Kandinsky. Instead they were reminiscent of traditional, literal painters and American scene painters such as Edward Hopper, Grant Wood and Andrew Wyeth (Rose 1986). These artists found their showcase in the Midtown Galleries: Gruskin, Midtown's owner, promoted academic and realist painters and purposely avoided abstract art (Midtown Galleries Records).

William Palmer's paintings and murals portrayed landscapes and scenery of New York State (*American Artists* 1985: 253). Waldo Peirce produced impressionistic landscapes and still lifes in oils and watercolors (*National Cyclopedia of American Biography* 1974: 376). Dong Kingman – a painter, illustrator and muralist – worked with watercolors to depict city scenes ('The Watercolor Series' 1947). Gladys Rockmore Davis preferred the medium of pastels to portray theatrical imagery (Collins and Opitz 1980; *Who Was Who in America* 1968: 233). Doris Rosenthal incorporated Meso-American images into her paintings and lithographs (Collins and Opitz 1980; *Who Was Who in America* 1973: 621). Julien Binford painted watercolors and oils inspired by his native Virginia (Hastings 1985: 55).

The process of selecting the paintings, producing the textiles and creating the dresses took over a year. Selection started on December 5, 1945, when Midtown Galleries began sending paintings to Onondaga to consider. The first group included twenty-six paintings by four of the artists – Waldo Peirce, Dong Kingman, Gladys Rockmore Davis and Julien Binford. In March of 1946, Midtown Galleries sent Onondaga paintings by two additional artists, Doris Rosenthal and William Palmer. The sending and returning of paintings continued into mid June. Midtown Galleries sent Onondaga at least fifty-five paintings by the six artists to consider for the series. Eventually, Onondaga selected just twenty-two paintings ranging in date from the late 1930s to 1946. A list of paintings with the names of the textiles derived from them in parentheses appears below.[3]

Palmer   *Horses* ('Horses'; 'Horses and Corrals')
            Sun, Water and Air ('Sun, Water and Air')

Peirce   *Lilac Garden* ('Jardin Aux Lilas')
            Autumn Leaves with Kittens ('Kittens at Play')
            The Catch, or *Fish in Net* ('Fish in Net')
            Trout Fishing ('Trout Fishing')

Europa and the Bull ('Sea Fantasy')
The Dogwood's Last Stand ('Clouds and Trees')
On the Penebscot, or *Cider Press* ('Cider Press')

Kingman   *White House* ('New Orleans')
Trees ('Trees')
Red Poppy ('Red Poppies')
Back Yards ('Chickens in Squares')

Davis   *Ballet Slippers* ('Ballet Slippers')
Carousel #1 ('Carousel')
Giselle ('Giselle')

Rosenthal   *Children and Corn* ('Corn Foliage')
Flowers and Fruit, or *Tropical Foliage* ('Tropical Foliage'; 'Papayas')
Fruit on Table ('Papayas')

Binford   *Rooster(s) in the Coal Bin* ('White Chickens')
Scythe Sharpener of Fine Creek Mills ('Fine Creek Mills')
Woman With (a) Hat ('Woman with a Hat')

Onondaga paid the artists $150 in advance royalties for each design considered. The company made payments on some designs that did not make it into production. The final selection included two works by William Palmer, *Sun, Water and Air* and *Horses*, which exhibit the subjective expressionism often evident in American scene painting (Rose 1986). Waldo Peirce's seven works evoke the ethereal quality of American scene painting, although his style is impressionistic (Hulick 1984). The selected paintings range from sweeping landscapes and allegorical subjects to realist scenes from Peirce's native state of Maine. His choice of subject in *Europa and the Bull* shows the neoclassical influence on design during the 1930s and 1940s from Italian Art Deco (Woodham 1990: 166).

In contrast to the works of Palmer and Peirce, Dong Kingman's four selected paintings interpret everyday scenes characteristic of American realism. Kingman's style can be compared to that of other regionalists through his choices of subject matter; but unlike the regionalists, he did not limit himself to American scenes. He chose his subjects from his environment by walking around until he found an image that fascinated him. This environment could be San Francisco, New York, New Orleans or Bangkok (Gruskin 1958; Kingman 1958).

Gladys Rockmore Davis' themes were often mythical, idealistic and romantic. Her images featured with recognizable figures derived from the theater and children's stories, which she frequently illustrated (*Who Was Who in America* 1968; Collins and Optiz 1980). The painting titled *Ballet Slippers* depicts a scene backstage at a ballet while *Carousel* shows children in a park with a merry-go-round.

Doris Rosenthal painted primarily tropical subjects. Her work showed a fascination with Mexico and Guatemala. She had visited Mexico twice in the 1930s on Guggenheim fellowships (Collins and Optiz 1980: 621). Even Rosenthal's less obvious subject in *Children and Corn* seems to have originated from a sketch made in Guatemala.

Julien Binford is less well known than the other painters. He followed the path of the regionalists. His scenes of rural Virginia often focussed on farming activities.

The final selection of paintings featured traditional artistic styles from the 1930s – regionalism and American scene painting – rather than the avant-garde styles of European surrealism or the emerging abstract expressionism. Both painting style and visual content featured elements unique to American painting of the period.

Designing the Fabric Prints

After the final selection, Onondaga's art department translated the paintings into suitable designs for dress fabrics. The actual process of selecting motifs from the paintings and rendering them into repeat designs for textiles is unclear. Frost (1947) credited Onondaga's art director with selecting the motifs and overseeing their development into textile designs by the company's anonymous industrial designers; however, some of the artists themselves had a hand in rendering the motifs. Another artist represented by Midtown Galleries, Emlen Etting, apparently worked out thirteen textile designs submitted to Onondaga on April 1, 1946 (Midtown Galleries Records). To further complicate our understanding of the process, the company's advertisement on the back cover of the January 1947 issue of *Art News* names Philip A. Vogelman, Onondaga's president, as the stylist. Whether or not all the artists participated in the process, in the end it was the industrial designers who finalized the textile designs, making them appropriate for use by dressmakers and, thus, encouraging their commercial acceptance.

The industrial designers did not confine themselves to literal interpretations of the paintings but often chose sections or specific motifs for their adaptations. They tried to stay as true to the original character and style of the paintings as possible, but occasionally modified the motifs ('From a Kingman Watercolor' 1947).

In this series, William Palmer's painting *Sun, Water and Air* was simplified into a white silk crepe printed with a design of hills and trees outlined in black and accented with splashes of yellow and pink (Figure 7.1). The alternating oblique repeats measure fifteen inches high by twenty-and-a-half inches wide. This arrangement of the repeats leaves little open space, making the pattern more visually interesting than if each scene were aligned horizontally.

Palmer's other painting, *Horses*, was ultimately translated into two different textile designs. Both evoked the feeling of the American West. The first interpretation, 'Horses and Corrals,' was a very linear, horizontal representation with pairs of horses galloping across the fabric (Figure 7.2). The other textile design, 'Horses', more closely mirrored the image from the painting; it focussed on individual horses and de-emphasized the scenery.

Waldo Peirce's *Europa and the Bull* was retitled 'Sea Fantasy.' The final design depicts a green-and-yellow-clothed Grecian nymph in the place of the nude Europa seated on the back of a bull. Scenes from Peirce's other scene paintings translated into overall patterns. In 'Trout Fishing,' for example, the fisherman fades into a pattern of trees and rocks (Figure 7.3). The textile designers managed to retain the impressionistic qualities of the original paintings.

The designers were intrigued by Kingman's work because of its graphic qualities. They interpreted his paintings less directly by choosing selected motifs for repeated prints. The painting *White House* was adapted into a textile titled 'New Orleans' (Figure 7.4): 'These motifs were "lifted" from Dong Kingman's colorful watercolor of an old New Orleans street corner, re-arranged by the industrial designer into an all-over, closely packed pattern and then printed by the manufacturer with nice attention to color' (Midtown Galleries Records). The resulting silk crepe fabric featured images of the car, street lamp, posts and fence interspersed with trees and a doorway in alternating horizontal rows, which created a vibrant urban scene.

Kingman tried his hand at textile design; he worked out a red-and-yellow checkered pattern from a detail in his painting *Back Yards* (Frost 1947: 32). The painting included chickens as part of the back yard scenery. In the textile design, the chickens became the focus. A label accompanying the exhibition of the series remarked: 'In Dong Kingman the fabric industry has uncovered a highly skilful [sic] designer – if he could be tempted away from

Figure 7.1 'Sun, Water and Air.' Textile print adapted from *Sun, Water and Air* by William Palmer. Onondaga Silk Company, RISD 47.121.

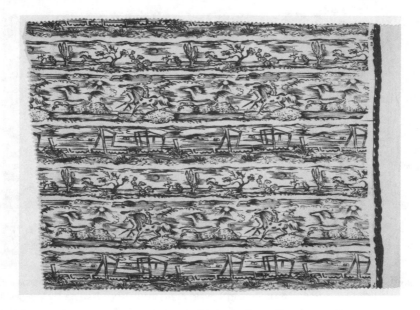

Figure 7.2 'Horses and Corrals.' Textile Print adapted from *Horses* by William Palmer. Onondaga Silk Company, RISD 47.114.

his own highly creative way of painting' (Midtown Galleries Records). The finished design 'Chickens in Squares' featured a more complex pattern and colorway than Kingman's sketch to be printed on Enka® rayon crepe.

The industrial designers used large-scale motifs for their translations of Davis's works. 'Carousel' is almost an exact reproduction of the painting minus the children in the foreground (Figure 7.5). It displays radial

Figure 7.3 A window display at Gilmore Brothers department store, Kalamazoo, Michigan. 'Trout Fishing' textile print, from *Trout Fishing* by Waldo Peirce. Midtown Gallery Records, 1904–97, Archives of American Art, Smithsonian Institution.

symmetry in that the carousel motif repeats around a point. 'Ballet Slippers' displays images of ballerinas, crowns of roses, pairs of slippers and pointed hats taken directly from Davis' painting.

Doris Rosenthal sketched corn stalks, adapted from *Children and Corn*, that became the repeating motifs in 'Corn Foliage.' Her other works inspired two textile designs entitled 'Papayas.' The first, originating from either *Fruit on Table*, or *Flowers and Fruit*, is quite large with motifs of pineapples, papayas and leaves. Another large-scale 'Papayas' depicted branches of banana trees; it was derived from *Flowers and Fruit* (Figure 7.6).

The designs adapted from Julien Binford's paintings featured two rural farm scenes, one of chickens being fed near a coal bin and the other of farming activities. The first design, entitled 'White Chickens,' almost directly reproduced the painting, but added the figure of a farmer to connect the multidirectional images of the hens and roosters. It was printed on both silk and rayon crepe (Figure 7.7). The textile entitled 'Fine Creek Mills' featured a farmer plowing with a team of horses. It is illustrated without attribution in *American Ingenuity: Sportswear, 1930s–1970s*, the catalog of an exhibition of the same name at the Metropolitan Museum of Art (Martin 1998: 63).

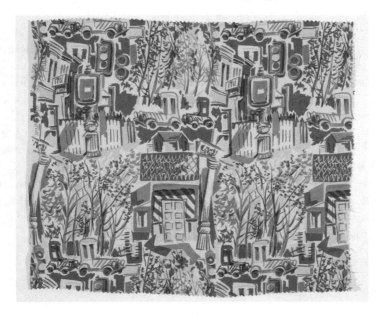

Figure 7.4 'New Orleans. Textile print adapted from *White House* by Dong Kingman. Onondaga Silk Company, RISD 47.129.

Figure 7.5 'Carousel.' Textile print adapted from *Carousel #1* by Gladys
Rockmore Davis. Cleveland Museum of Art, 47.105.

Binford's 'Woman with a Hat' was deemed 'one of the most successful
carry-over patterns from paintings to fabric designs in the exhibition'
(Midtown Galleries Records). The design featured repeats of a tiny, thin
woman under an oversized hat (Figure 7.8). It was printed in black on
either green or bright pink silk crepe.

Many of the textile designs produced through this collaboration of
painters and industrial designers exhibit calligraphic lines combined with
washes of color typical of textile prints produced in the late 1940s, particularly those by Ascher, Ltd and Bianchini-Ferrier. The finished prints also
echo the abstract expressionist art gaining in popularity after 1945, even
though the original art did not. The designs combined the traditional styles
of the original paintings with contemporary design trends.

Creating the Garments

The next step was to create garments from the printed fabrics. For this
stage of production, Onondaga sent fabrics to thirteen leading New York
fashion designers who had used their fabrics before. These designers had

Figure 7.6 A model at the Midtown Gallery in a dress made from 'Papayas,' a
textile derived from Doris Rosenthal's *Flowers and Fruit*. Photograph
by Larry Gordon. Midtown Gallery Records, 1904–97, Archives of
American Art, Smithsonian Institution. Doris Rosenthal.

exclusive use of the fabrics for a period of time, until the summer of 1947,
when fabrics became available as yard goods.

As discussed in Chapter 6, the United States had grown strong in the
fashion world during the war years. New York and California ready-to-
wear fashions had gained status as an affordable, fashionable alternative to
custom-made clothing. As a result, leading department stores across the
country, such as Lord & Taylor, Bergdorf Goodman, Marshall Fields and
Neiman-Marcus, sold clothes by American designers at this time.

Figure 7.7 A window display at Gilmore Brothers department store, Kalamazoo, MI. 'White Chickens' textile print, from *Rooster(s) in the Coal Bin* by Julien Binford, Midtown Gallery Records, 1904–97, Archives of American Art, Smithsonian Institution.

The designers/manufacturers for the 'American Artist Print Series' included:

Brownie of Foxbrownie
Eta of Ren-Eta
Jo Copeland of Pattullo
Joset Walker of David M. Goodstein, Inc.
Sally Milgrim

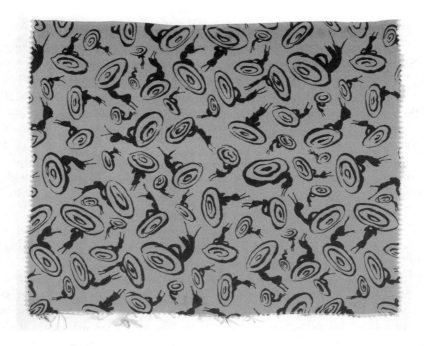

Figure 7.8 'Woman with a Hat.' Textile print adapted from *Woman with (a) Hat* by Julien Binford. Onondaga Silk Company, RISD 47.128.

Morris Kraus of Zuckerman and Kraus
Ben Reig (Omar Kiam, designer)
Bruno of Spectator Sports
Anna Miller
Nettie Rosenstein
Sophie of Saks
Emmet Joyce of Samuel Kass, Inc.
Jamison Classics

Two of the designers, Sophie of Saks and Sally Milgrim, were considered 'couturiers' (Milbank 1989). Sophie of Saks was one of the best-known. Since 1931 she had been the in-house designer for Saks Fifth Avenue's Salon Moderne. She made the cover of *Time* magazine on September 15, 1947, the first American designer to do so. Sally Milgrim designed for private clients at Milgrim, a Fifth Avenue specialty store. She created the inaugural gowns for Mrs. Warren Harding, Mrs. Calvin Coolidge and Eleanor Roosevelt (Milbank 1989: 117). She also designed a ready-to-wear label known as 'salymil' that sold at her shop and at other stores around the country.

The others were ready-to-wear designers or manufacturers. Jamison Classics was a manufacturer who did not identify its designer. Most specialized in day dresses, evening dresses, suits and blouses. A few, like Joset Walker, developed a reputation for sporty looks. Nettie Rosenstein and Brownie of Foxbrownie were known for ensembles made from printed silk, often with matching gloves. Jo Copeland and Omar Kiam (designer for Ben Reig) designed unique lines that did not follow the dominant silhouette of the time.

Styles during the war years featured square padded shoulders, natural waistlines, and knee-length hems, creating a trim, hard-edged silhouette. Draped or shirred fabric treatments, which had appeared in the late 1930s, became more prominent in the 1940s. The rationing of fabric resulting from war restrictions encouraged creation of economical, spare designs that did not use excess fabric. These styles persisted after the war ended, although a desire for new softer looks was in the air.

The fabrics in this collection were lightweight silk and rayon crepes measuring approximately 40 inches wide. 1940s fashion featured a wide range of crepe fabrics in both prints and solids. The designers offered variations on the successful designs of the war years but also tried new ideas with different focal points for a less severe silhouette. Crepe was easy to drape, thus many of these designers employed simple draping for their designs.

As *Art News* stated: 'the scheme required dresses which would respect the original inspiration and at the same time fulfill the requisites of spring 1947' (Frost 1947: 31). In July of 1946, the Onondaga Silk Company sent fabrics to these designers/manufacturers so that garments could be constructed, photographed, and ready for showing by October and November for the previews of the spring fashions. Their designs would arrive at the retailers by January of 1947. The fabrics were made into day dresses, dinner and evening dresses, blouses, scarves and gloves.

The fashion designers faced several challenges. To preserve the imagery on the textiles, they avoided elaborate drapery, bias cutting or excessive seaming. Several of the designers stayed with simple day dresses. Binford's 'White Chickens,' in the hands of an unidentified designer, became a short-sleeved, belted shirtdress (Figure 7.7). Foxbrownie used Binford's 'Fine Creek Mills' for an uncomplicated dress with a matching yellow-gold wool jacket lined in the same printed silk (Martin 1998: 62). It also had matching gloves. Peirce's 'Trout Fishing' (Figure 7.3) became a dress with tiers of pleated ruffles for collar and skirt.

Draped evening dresses with minimal construction offered another solution for the designers. Sophie of Saks and Emmet Joyce designed elegant sleeveless floor-length evening dresses from, respectively, 'Jardin Aux Lilas' and 'Sun, Water and Air.' Matching gloves and/or shawls provided another opportunity to display the print designs derived from landscapes.

A limitation with some of the prints was the large scale of the designs. The motifs in Davis's *Carousel*, for example, measured twenty-and-a-quarter inches high by thirty inches wide. Designer Nettie Rosenstein created a successful suit and blouse combination by using the carousel as a border design in the blouse and jacket lining (Frost 1947). Other designers utilized some of the large-scale designs in simple draped evening dresses, particularly those adapted from Doris Rosenthal's work. Foxbrownie created a long-sleeved gown draped at the side using 'Corn Foliage' (Frost 1947). The dress designer drew on a similar approach with the print 'Papayas' from *Flowers and Fruit* (Figure 7.6). The dramatic evening dress used the print to advantage as surface design at the shoulder and on the skirt. The smaller-scale designs worked well as blouses. Kingman's 'Red Poppies' was deemed a success for a blouse design by Morris Kraus (Frost 1947).

Designers also diluted the vibrant prints by adding fabrics of solid colors. Eta of Ren-Eta draped a gold swag on a halter-necked evening dress of Peirce's 'Clouds and Trees' (Frost 1947). Joset Walker used a neutral-colored solid fabric under a draped bodice for a day dress of Binford's 'White Chickens' (Frost 1947).

Palmer's 'Horses and Corrals' created problems because of the horizontal arrangement of one of the prints. Foxbrownie used it for a simple sport dress. Sophie of Saks created a fashion-forward evening dress with the other print, 'Horses,' which had a circular arrangement of motifs. The evening dress had a scalloped neckline and fitted bodice, along with a wide, full skirt trimmed with net along the hem (Frost 1947). The fitted bodice and full skirt resembled Dior's 'New Look,' which was about to be unveiled at the Paris shows in February 1947.

Nettie Rosenstein created two different dresses with the print from Peirce's 'Cider Press.' One was an evening dress with a soft, bertha collar and draped sleeves; the other was a day dress with matching gloves. The latter is in the Costume Institute's collection.

Jo Copeland designed a simple summer dress with a draped neckline using the 'New Orleans' print from Kingman's *White House* ('From a Kingman Watercolor' 1947). Copeland's design balanced simple construction with complex print design. She designed a similar dress from Kingman's 'Chickens in Squares' (Frost 1947). The draped neckline offset the geometric nature of the textile design. Copeland successfully balanced the print motifs with the lines of the dresses.

Ultimately, the consumer would determine the success or failure of the textile designs, their interpretations, and the garments themselves. The fabrics and garments made with these Onondaga prints were carried by leading department stores in the United States and advertised alongside those of current European designers.

Presentation and Promotion

Onondaga presented their printed designs as a complete package – paintings into garments – on the afternoon of December 16, 1946 in the Ritz Carlton Ballroom in New York City. The event included the paintings, yard-long samples of the fabric prints, and the finished garments. A color film also was made to record the creative process behind the production and to be shown along with the exhibition.[4] Invitations were sent to newspapers, radio stations and magazines (Midtown Galleries Records).

Midtown Galleries exhibited the paintings and drawings together with swatches of fabric in January 1947. As had been their practice, they sent the exhibition on tour. The exhibition traveled to the following art museums and design schools from January 1947 through May 1948:

Atlanta Art Association and High Museum of Art, Atlanta, Georgia
Cleveland Museum of Art, Cleveland, Ohio
City Art Museum of St. Louis, St. Louis, Missouri
Toledo Museum of Art, Toledo, Ohio
Kalamazoo Institute of Arts, Kalamazoo, Michigan
Wilmington Society of Fine Arts, Wilmington, Delaware
Dayton Art Institute, Dayton, Ohio
Rochester Memorial Gallery, Rochester, New York
Munson-Williams-Proctor Institute, Utica, New York
Springfield Museum of Art, Springfield, Missouri
Fort Wayne Art School and Museum, Fort Wayne, Indiana
John Herron Art Institute, Indianapolis, Indiana
Brooks Memorial Art Gallery, Memphis, Tennessee
Addison Gallery, Andover, Massachusetts

The Museum of Art at the Rhode Island School of Design included the textiles in an exhibition entitled 'Textile Panorama' in April 1947 ('Textile Panorama' 1947). Requests for the exhibition continued into November of the same year (Midtown Galleries Records). In some cases, only part of the original exhibit was sent depending on the installation space. Some pieces traveled to different sites.

During this same period the show traveled to major department stores where the designer garments were being sold, such as the RH Sterns Company in Boston, Massachusetts; Rich's in Atlanta, Georgia; Bloomingdale's in New York City; and Gilmore Brothers in Kalamazoo, Michigan (Midtown Galleries Records). The stores displayed the clothes next to the artwork (Figures 7.3 and 7.7). Bloomingdale's produced an advertising catalog for promotion of the dresses. (The catalog is in the Costume Institute at the Metropolitan Museum of Art.) The fabrics became available to home sewers as piece goods in July.

The financial success of the fabrics can be determined by the royalty figures paid to the artists (Lund 1993). The sales figures indicate the amount paid for the yardage sold for each textile design. Oddly, the figures for 'Horses,' adapted from William Palmer's work, are missing. No sales figures are available for the completed garment designs. Nevertheless, some conclusions can be drawn from the available information on yardage (Midtown Galleries Records).

The 'American Artist Print Series' sold over 51,000 yards of fabric through March 31, 1948. 'White Chickens' (Figure 7.7), the adaptation of Julien Binford's painting, was the best-seller at 7,931 yards. The next highest amounts were for sales of approximately 4,000 yards each for 'Sea Fantasy,' 'Cider Press,' and 'Trout Fishing' (Figure 7.3), all adapted from Waldo Peirce's art. The textile print 'Horses and Corrals,' adapted from William Palmer's *Horses,* came in a close fifth at 3,835 yards. Sales from textiles adapted from Kingman's work – 'Trees,' and 'New Orleans' – as well as Binford's 'Fine Creek Mills' ranged from about 2,500 to 3,000 yards. Most of the prints sold from 1,000 to 2,000 yards. The least successful prints, Peirce's 'Kittens at Play' and 'Jardin Aux Lilas,' Davis's 'Giselle,' and Rosenthal's 'Papayas' (Figure 7.6) sold under 900 yards.

Most of the sales took place within the first half of 1947 with a few exceptions. Five of the designs enjoyed substantial sales through the remainder of 1947: 'Cider Press,' 'Fish in Net,' 'Sea Fantasy,' 'New Orleans' and 'Trees.' 'Sea Fantasy' continued to sell well in 1948.

Generally, each of the outfits required a minimum of three to four yards; the evening dresses used more fabric than the blouses, while gloves and scarves obviously used smaller amounts of fabric. Estimating four yards per garment, enough fabric for about 12,500 dresses was sold, with about 300 yards reserved for gloves or scarves. This would have been a fairly large number of garments sold in this series.

These dresses probably sold in department stores for somewhere between $125 and $500 judging by comparable garments advertised in *Harper's Bazaar* in 1946–7, including a dress by Jo Copeland of a different

Onondaga silk. These prices are above the cost of mass fashion, but well below couture prices, which could be several thousand dollars. Such price points targeted upper-class or upper-middle-class women who would have appreciated the source of the print designs.

From the amount of fabric sold, it appears that the 'American Artist Print Series' succeeded financially. The exhibition tour to museums and galleries in major cities proved popular and likely contributed to sales throughout 1947 and into 1948. It would have assured a continued interest in the line of fabrics beyond its opening season. The effect Dior's 'New Look,' shown in February 1947, had on the sales of this series was slight as the series was already launched by the time the 'New Look' arrived in American stores. *Harper's Bazaar* did not show Dior's new silhouette until their April issue ('First Notes from the Paris Collections'). Copies of the Dior originals were only available on a made-to-order basis at leading department stores. The ready-to-wear clothes made of Onondaga's fabrics had been in the stores since January. Additionally, some of the fashions in the series showed features similar to those that appeared in Dior's line.

Additional evidence points to the success of this particular series. The Onondaga Silk Company collaborated with another gallery, the Kennedy Art Galleries of New York City, on a line of fabrics that focussed on bird imagery in art for the fall of 1947. Nine designers interpreted the work according to an August 5, 1947 story in the *New York Times* (p. 28). The Midtown Galleries set plans in motion to produce with Onondaga another series of this type titled 'Contemporary American Silk Print Series' in 1948. Davis, Palmer, Rosenthal, Peirce and Kingman contributed paintings to this series. Over the next few years the Midtown Galleries also sent paintings to Onondaga by other artists including Lenard Kester, William Thon, Henry Billings, Cecile Belle and Fred Meyer (Midtown Galleries Records).

Besides these two collaborations with the Midtown Galleries, little else is known about the Onondaga Silk Company. These art series seem to have been the only major ventures by Onondaga. After these exhibitions, the Onondaga Silk Company drifted back into the relative obscurity from which it had arisen to capture the brief interest of the fashion world.

Notes

1. Sources include artwork, textile samples and garments as well as newspapers, periodicals and business records. The Midtown Galleries Collection at the Archives of American Art, Smithsonian Institution, contains records, textile samples and

photographs; additional textiles, garments and records of the exhibitions are in a number of collections listed in the References under Archives.

2. Company history was compiled from several sources. See 'Mill Notes,' *American Wool and Cotton Reporter* June 9, 1925, p. 75; 'Textile Cos Helped by Outside Experts,' *New York Times* July 20, 1930, sec. N, p. 19; a *New York Times* article dated April 2, 1930 in the Midtown Galleries Records; and *Davison's Textile Blue Book*, Ridgewood, NJ: Davison Publishing Company, Inc, 1945–55.

3. The painting titles are not consistent in the records; comparison with published sources did not clear up the problem.

4. Unfortunately, the film has yet to be discovered. It was mentioned in press releases and published reports about the series (Midtown Galleries Records).

References

American Artists: An Illustrated Survey of Leading Contemporary Americans (1985), New York: Facts on File Publications.

'Art into Living: Silk Prints 1947' (1947), *Art News*, 45(11): pp. 34–8+.

Collins, J. and G.B. Opitz (eds) (1980), *Women Artists in America 18th Century to the Present (1790–1980)*, Poughkeepsie, New York: Apollo.

Duncan, A. (1988), *The Encyclopedia of Art Deco*, New York: E.P. Dutton.

'Fashion Designer Sophie Gimbel: Who Wants the New Look?' (1947), *Time*, September 15: 87–92.

'First Notes from the Paris Collections' (1947), *Harper's Bazaar* 81, April: 186–7.

'From a Kingman Watercolor into a Silk Print for Onondaga' (1947), *American Artist*, March: 44–6.

Frost, R. (1947), 'Silk in Search of Six Painters,' *Art News* 45(11): 30–3+.

Goodrich, L. and J.I.H. Baur (1961), *American Art of Our Century*, New York: Frederick A. Praeger Publishers.

Gruskin, A.D. (1958), 'The Story of the Artist,' in A.D. Gruskin (ed.), *The Watercolors of Dong Kingman, and How the Artist Works*, New York: The Studio Publications, pp. 21–61.

Harper's Bazaar, (1946–7).

Harris, J. (ed.) (1993), *Textiles, 5,000 Years*, New York: Harry N. Abrams.

Hastings, P. (ed.) (1985), *Who Was Who in American Art*, Connecticut: Sandview Press.

Hulick, D.E. (1984), *Waldo Peirce: A New Assessment 1884–1970*, with essay by R.F. Brown, Orono: University of Maine.

Humphries, M. (2004), *Fabric Reference*, 3rd ed., Upper Saddle River, NJ: Pearson Prentice Hall.

Kingman, D. (1958), 'The Making of a Watercolor,' in A.D. Gruskin (ed.), *The Watercolors of Dong Kingman, and How the Artist Works*, New York: The Studio Publications, pp. 113–33.

Lund, A. (1993), 'Art and Textile Design: The Onondaga Silk Company's

'American Artist Print Series' of 1947,' master's thesis, University of Rhode Island.

Martin, R. (1998), *American Ingenuity. Sportswear 1930s–1970s*, New York: Metropolitan Museum of Art.

Mendes, V.D. and F.M. Hinchcliffe, (1987), *Ascher: Fabric, Art, and Fashion*, Cambridgeshire: Balding and Mansell.

Milbank, C.R. (1989), *New York Fashion: The Evolution of American Style*, New York: Harry N. Abrams.

National Cyclopedia of American Biography (1974), vol. 55, New York: James T. White.

Payant, F. (1946), 'Design in America,' *Design* 48(3): 3.

Robinson, S. (1969), *A History of Printed Textiles*, Cambridge, MA: The MIT Press.

Rose, B. (1986), *American Painting: The Twentieth Century*, New York: Rizzoli International Publications.

Schoeser, M. (1986), *Twentieth Century Design Fabrics and Wallpapers*, London: Bell and Hyman.

Schoeser, M. and W. Blausen, (2000), '"Wellpaying Self Support": Women Textile Designers,' in Pat Kirkham (ed.), *Women Designers in the USA 1900/2000*, New Haven: Yale University Press.

Shaw, M. (2003), 'American Silk from a Marketing Magician: HR Mallinson & Co,' *Silk Road, Other Roads: Proceedings of the Eighth Biennial Symposium of the Textile Society of America*, September 26–28, Northampton, MA. [CD-Rom].

'Textile Panorama' (1947), *Museum Notes* 5(3), Providence: Museum of Art Rhode Island School of Design.

'The Watercolor Series: Dong Kingman' (1947), *American Artist*, September: 42–5.

Who Was Who in America (1968) vol. 4, Chicago: Marquis Who's Who.

Who Was Who in America (1973) vol. 5, Chicago: Marquis Who's Who.

A Woman of Fashion, Spring–Summer (1947), New York: Bloomingdale Bros, pp. 32–4.

Woodham, J.M. (1990), *Twentieth-Century Ornament*, New York: Rizzoli International Publications.

Archives

Addison Gallery of Art, Phillips Academy, Andover, Massachusetts

Midtown Galleries Records, 1904–1997. Archives of American Art, Smithsonian Institution, Washington, DC

Cleveland Museum of Art, Cleveland, Ohio

Costume Institute, Metropolitan Museum of Art, New York

New Britain Museum of Art, New Britain, Connecticut

Rhode Island School of Design Museum of Art

St Louis Art Museum

8

The Beat Generation: Subcultural Style

Linda Welters

Editors' Introduction: During the 1950s, Americans were conservative in their attitudes (Miller and Nowak 1977). They lived with the threat of the Cold War, the 'Red Scare,' and the atom bomb. The average family lived in the newly formed suburbs where mothers stayed at home and fathers headed off to work. On Sundays, families went to churches of predominantly Protestant denominations. Many middle-class men worked for 'the organization' and adopted corporate values as their own (Whyte 1956). Immigrant groups and racial minorities often struggled to attain the American Dream.

A neat, well-groomed appearance was valued. Attitudes about dress were conservative. Men customarily wore suits, often gray flannel, to work and casual clothes on the weekends. Men with blue-collar jobs donned work shirts and trousers. Their hair was short, and their faces clean-shaven. Women wore suits, dresses or skirts with nylons and heels. Bermudas and slacks were worn for casual activities during the day, but not at night. Women's hairstyles were predominantly short.

However, not everyone accepted the strictures of this post-war lifestyle. As discussed by Linda Welters, a small cadre of writers began expressing their dissatisfaction with the American life through poetry and novels, labeling themselves the 'Beat Generation.' Their message was met with enthusiasm across America, and their numbers grew. They loved bebop jazz, abstract expressionist art, Theater of the Absurd, and existentialist philosophers. Although no particular style was associated with early Beats, eventually those who wanted to be affiliated with the movement developed a subcultural look that is still recognized today. The message of the Beat Generation was just the tip of the iceberg. It formed a springboard for the values of the hippies in the 1960s.

For many Americans, the Beat Generation evokes mental images of shabbily-dressed men sporting beards, sandals and sunglasses, and women dressed in black. The contribution of the Beats to twentieth-century fashion is poorly documented and depicted in just a few sentences in a handful of books, none of which agree on what were the components of Beat style. Even the most substantial treatment is only a short section in Ted Polhemus' *Street Style* (1994) that raises more questions than it answers. This chapter aims to fill this void by examining the style of the American Beat Generation, but first the stage must be set by introducing the Beat phenomenon as a literary movement that grew into a subculture.

The Beats as Writers and Poets

The so-called Beat Generation arose in the post-war years, giving voice to the discontent of the 1950s. The movement started in New York City in 1944 with three aspiring writers: Jack Kerouac, Allen Ginsberg, and William S. Burroughs. Kerouac, the son of French-Canadian immigrants to Lowell, Massachusetts, had arrived in New York on a Columbia University football scholarship, but dropped out after a year. Allen Ginsberg, son of a high school teacher from Patterson, New Jersey, also studied at Columbia. Burroughs, grandson of the inventor of the Burroughs adding machine, had drifted from one city to the next after graduating from Harvard in 1936. When their paths crossed in the area around Columbia University, a literary movement was born. Together they developed a credo called the 'New Vision.' This included: 1. Uncensored self-expression as the seed of creativity; 2. Expanding the artist's consciousness through non-rational means (derangement of the senses via drugs, dreams, hallucinatory states and visions); and 3. Allowing art to supercede the dictates of conventional morality (Watson 1995). Using this 'New Vision,' Kerouac began writing *The Town and the City* (1950), an autobiographical novel about growing up in Lowell.

Gradually their circle spread to include other individuals ranging from petty criminals to college graduates. One of the petty criminals was Herbert Huncke, a Times Square hustler and drug addict who introduced Burroughs to heroin. Huncke first used the word 'Beat,' a slang word from the drug world, to mean 'defeated,' unwilling or unable to 'make it' (Charters 2001: 238). Kerouac, however, got credit for labeling the Beat Generation in a 1948 conversation with John Clellon Holmes when he said: 'You know, this really is a *Beat* Generation' (Holmes 1952a: 22). Holmes defined 'Beat' as a 'sort of nakedness of mind, and ultimately of soul.' It meant being 'pushed up against the wall' or going 'for broke' (Holmes 1952b: 22).

Holmes wrote the first novel about the Beat Generation, entitled *Go*, which was published in 1952. The characters and story mirrored real-life events in the new underground scene that had surfaced in New York City after the war. That same year he wrote an article for the *New York Times Magazine* entitled 'This is the Beat Generation,' drawing the public's attention to this new group.

Another member of the group was Neal Cassady, a one-time juvenile car thief from Denver who met Kerouac and Ginsberg in 1946 through a mutual friend, Hal Chase. Cassady charmed the group, and developed close friendships with Ginsberg, Burroughs and Kerouac. Together, Kerouac and Cassady traversed America in the late 1940s, setting in motion the plot for *On the Road* (1957), Kerouac's most successful novel. Kerouac started writing *On the Road* in 1948, revising it in 1951. Cassady was the inspiration for the character Dean Moriarity in *On the Road*, and the title character in *Visions of Cody* (1959).

William S. Burroughs and his wife Joan Vollmer left New York in 1947, living first in Texas, then in Louisiana, finally settling in Mexico City where he wrote *Junky* (1953). He accidentally shot and killed Joan in 1951. After he was cleared of criminal charges, he moved to Tangiers where he remained until 1958. It was there that he wrote *Naked Lunch* (1959).

During these formative years for the Beat writers, Allen Ginsberg struggled with the reality of his mother's schizophrenia and his own homosexuality. He experienced a vision involving the poet William Blake. He was arrested for harboring Huncke's stolen property and subsequently admitted to a psychiatric hospital as a condition of his sentencing. Upon his release in 1950, he dedicated himself to becoming a poet. It was through Allen that the writers Carl Solomon and William Carlos Williams and the poet Gregory Corso became associated with the Beats (Watson 1995).

The Beat message began to spread, even though people were not yet conscious of it as a movement. Poets and writers started congregating in San Francisco in 1950, giving birth to the 'San Francisco Renaissance.' Allen Ginsberg moved there in 1954, and met the established poet Kenneth Rexroth, who advised him on matters of form. Soon the city became known for poetry readings, jazz and art galleries. It was there that Ginsberg first read his famous poem 'Howl' at the Six Gallery in 1955. The poem began 'I saw the best minds of my generation destroyed by madness, starving hysterical naked, dragging themselves through the negro streets at dawn looking for an angry fix' (Ginsberg 1956: 62). It touched on all the fears and beliefs of the Beat Generation, becoming one of its best-known works. Lawrence Ferlinghetti, founder of San Francisco's City Lights Bookstore, published 'Howl' late the next year. It sold briskly and went into a second printing. Early in 1957 he was arrested on obscenity charges. Although he was eventually cleared, the trial made the Beat writers famous. When *On the Road* was finally published in late 1957, it was an instant success, and the Beats were firmly ensconced in American culture. By then Ginsberg had moved to Paris with his lover Peter Orlovsky where they were eventually joined by Corso and Burroughs (Miles 2000). Together they took up residence at the so-called Beat Hotel in the Latin Quarter where they lived and worked off and on until 1963. Kerouac remained in the United States.

Gilbert Millstein's review of *On the Road* in the *New York Times* on September 5, 1957 prophesied that it would become the testament to the Beat Generation, which it has. Other critics were not so generous. The intellectual Norman Podhoretz dismissed Kerouac, Ginsberg and Burroughs as 'know-nothing Bohemians' in the *Partisan Review* (Podhoretz 1958). He damned the characters depicted in *On the Road* and Kerouac's subsequent book, *The Subterraneans*, as 'the poisonous glorification of the adolescent in American popular culture' (Podhoretz 1958: 493).

The popular press and television began focussing a penetrating lens on the Beats. Articles appeared in newspapers and in magazines such as *Mademoiselle*, *Time*, *Life*, *Esquire* and *Playboy*, reaching a zenith in 1959. With the exception of the *Mademoiselle* article (February 1957) which drew attention to 'the lively arts in San Francisco,' the media coverage was almost uniformly derisive. Herbert Caen, columnist for the *San Francisco Chronicle*, coined the word 'beatnik' on April 2, 1958 after the launch of the Russian sputnik. He described a party *Look* magazine hosted in preparation for an article to which fifty 'beatniks' had been invited. The name caught on immediately. Movies and television soon featured 'beatnik' characters.

The Beats continued writing, holding poetry readings, publishing literary magazines and making public appearances on radio and television. Kerouac wrote the script for *Pull My Daisy* (1959), the most authentic Beat film. His novel *The Subterraneans* was made into a movie starring George Peppard in 1960.

Most of the major Beat writers were men. Although a few of them were openly homosexual, women were involved as friends, lovers or long-suffering wives, who cooked and worked to support their men (Charters

2002). Some of these women – like Diane di Prima, Hettie Jones and Joyce Johnson – were also aspiring writers living in Greenwich Village. They had studied English at women's colleges like Swarthmore and Barnard. In their writing, they characterize themselves as intellectuals who felt like misfits during the repressive 1950s. These women instantly identified with the Beat Generation after reading about it (Johnson 1983; di Prima 1969). However, with few exceptions, women fit in as 'minor characters' as Joyce Johnson titled her memoirs.

Beat Subculture

The credo articulated by the early Beats as the 'New Vision' evolved into a way of life that later defined the Beat scene. In almost every aspect it conflicted with mainstream American values. Other contemporary artists and intellectuals reflected the same dissatisfaction with post-war life, specifically abstract expressionist painters, playwrights of the Theater of the Absurd, Lee Strasberg's method actors, and the existentialist philosophers. The works of these intellectuals, artists, writers and poets are linked by freedom of expression and spontaneity, a core element in Beat philosophy.

The early Beats loved jazz, particularly the expressionist form known as bebop. They were regulars at jazz clubs in New York City, San Francisco and other cities in between. Jazz musicians were their early heroes, specifically Dizzy Gillespie and Charlie Parker of bebop fame. Beat writers made constant references to playing jazz records and going to jazz clubs to hear jazz musicians 'blow' their horns and play bongo drums. Beginning in San Francisco in 1957, the Beats read poetry to jazz music. Jazz continued to be the music the Beats identified with into the early 1960s as folk singing and rock and roll gained prominence.

The Beats' admiration for the 'negro' hipster led to harmonious relationships with African Americans. Two prominent Greenwich Village Beats – LeRoi Jones and Ted Joans – were African Americans. Interracial relationships were accepted without prejudice, resulting in marriages such as the one between LeRoi Jones and Hettie Cohen Jones. Whites mingled freely with blacks in Harlem neighborhoods and clubs. As Ted Joans stated: 'there were no hassles in those days' (Nicosia 1982a: 131).

Beat culture included an extensive vocabulary derived from the hipster jive talk of the 1940s. This vocabulary functioned to separate the Beat subculture from mainstream society through words. Men were 'cats,' women were 'chicks' or 'birds,' apartments were 'pads,' something that was really good was 'gone,' and people who were not 'hip' were 'squares.'

Spirituality played a part in Beat thinking. Kerouac, who grew up as a Catholic, incorporated some of its aspects into his writing, in particular a concept he termed 'beatitude.' Ginsberg, who was raised Jewish, became a Zen Buddhist after Gary Snyder introduced him to Zen Buddhism in San Francisco.

Beat life embraced wide experience; there were practically no taboos or inhibitions regarding behavior. Beats searched out and regularly used mind-altering substances, mainly Benzedrine, marijuana (called 'tea'), heroin and alcohol. Freedom of expression extended to sex. Although the Beats married and divorced, they also embraced the bohemian notion of free love. Both men and women experimented with same-sex relationships even if they were heterosexual. The absence of taboos extended to flirtation with death, as evidenced by the accidental shooting of Joan Vollmer in a William Tell incident (*Naked Lunch*).

The Beats did not like to work at regular jobs, which was seen as getting in the way of experiencing life and creating literature. They often mooched off their friends. To make money, they took menial short-term jobs. The character Dean Moriarity in *On the Road* worked as a parking lot attendant and as a railway brakeman. Diane di Prima (1969) worked as an artist's model and in a bookstore. Some in the Beat circle were not above petty thievery or selling drugs.

Consequently, the Beats sought cheap living arrangements. In every place in which they congregated – New York City, San Francisco's North Beach and Venice, California – Beat enclaves developed in low rent neighborhoods (Miles 1993; Maynard 1991). Some of the housing was substandard; Diane di Prima (1969) describes living in an unheated cold-water flat, sleeping in the back room of a bookstore where she worked, and sleeping on park benches. Furnishings were minimal: depictions of Beat 'pads' show little more than mattresses on floors where friends could 'crash.' The Beats did not believe in owning lots of possessions to restrict their mobility. Because they did not attach importance to their living arrangements, the Beats spent considerable time in hangouts such as cafes, coffee houses, tea rooms, bars, bookstores and galleries.

Mexico became a favorite country to visit because it offered cheap living as well as mind-altering drugs. Burroughs lived in Mexico City for a period of time, then traveled further into South America in search of a hallucinogenic drug called *yage*. In 1953 he moved to Tangiers where he could live inexpensively and obtain the drugs he needed to maintain his habit. Kerouac and Ginsberg visited him there.

As the Beat message spread, disenfranchised youth across the US began to adopt the outward symbols of Beat behavior, including the lingo, a love of jazz music and poetry, and sexual freedom. The Beat subculture appealed to artists and intellectuals; thus it found fertile ground on college campuses. As with other subcultures, personal appearance took on importance as a badge of identification and a Beat style developed.

Beat Style

The original Beats did not project a uniform image as far as style was concerned. Old photographs, descriptions of clothing and appearance in their writings, and interviews with people who lived during the era reveal a preference for casual clothes – chinos, jeans, T-shirts, sweatshirts, sweaters and a variety of shirts – foreshadowing the wide acceptance of such attire for most occasions by the late 1960s and 1970s. The exception was William S. Burroughs, who was frequently pictured wearing a suit, tie and hat. Yet by the late 1950s, a 'beatnik' stereotype emerged in the media that is instantly recognizable to anyone who lived during that era: 'chicks' in black leotards and 'cats' in black turtlenecks, jeans, berets, goatees and dark glasses (Maynard 1991).

Where did this stereotype originate? By studying a wide variety of sources – Beat literature, contemporary literature about the Beats, photographs, films and oral histories – I was able to divide Beat style into three time periods: 1944–9, 1950–6 and 1957–63. My analysis was informed by the work of sociologist Stanley Cohen (2002), whose research focused on working-class youth culture in Britain in the 1960s. Cohen's theory, first published in 1972 as *Folk Devils and Moral Panics*, argues that public reaction to society's deviant groups, which he labels 'folk devils,' is largely a product of media attention. He describes the sociological process as follows: the initial deviance leads to an inventory of words and images (including appearance) that eventually become symbols of deviance. Both the deviant group and the control culture feed off each other in a process he calls sensitization. The deviant group is presented to the public in a stylized and stereotypical fashion by the mass media. Morality is upheld by the authorities, coping mechanisms result, and the deviant group dissipates as a societal threat. Cohen recognizes that clothing and hairstyles play an important role in this process because they help identify the group seen as threatening. He lists the developmental stages of a stereotypical look as follows: style worn by a few, rapid growth and diffusion, commercialization and exploitation, slackening off, stagnation, then preservation as a nostalgic memory (Cohen 2002: 169).

1944–9

This was the period in which the group formed, articulated their vision, gave themselves a label, and developed the words, symbols and behaviors that characterized them as a generation. During this period, the young writers wore the conventional clothing of the 1940s. A 1944 photograph of Hal Chase, Jack Kerouac, Allen Ginsberg and William S. Burroughs near Columbia University (www.corbis.com) shows them in suits, ties and topcoats. Burroughs, several years older than the others, wears a hat. Only Kerouac, with a cigarette hanging out of his mouth, looks mildly disheveled. In their writings about the period, the Beats reveal two sartorial images: one modeled after the black 'hipsters' they admired; the other based on a newer, more casual 'Beat' image.

The 'hipster' look had been in place since the late 1930s (Polhemus 1994). The jazz musicians who were the chief proponents of the look wore zoot suits, drape suits, distinctive headgear and dark glasses indoors. Anatole Broyard provides a portrait of the hipster as an underground man: 'He brandished his padded shoulders . . . flourished his thirty-one-inch pegs like banners . . . his two-and-seven-eighths-inch brim was snapped with absolute symmetry . . . And he always wore dark glasses, because normal light offended his eyes' (1948: 45). Kerouac later described hipsters who looked like criminals 'creeping around Times Square'; yet he socialized with them because he liked the same things they liked, 'personal experience and vision' (1959b: 361–2). In *On the Road*, he described the scene around Times Square: 'a great mob of young men dressed in all varieties of hoodlum cloth, from red shirts to zoot suits' (Kerouac 1957: 131). He wrote admiringly of a musician wearing a 'sharkskin plaid suit with the long drape and the collar falling back and the tie undone for exact sharpness and coolness' (240). Holmes also described 'natty sharp-suited hipsters' in *Go* (1952a: 52). The word 'sharp' appears to have defined the hipster image.

The Beats themselves borrowed elements of 'sharpness.' Bull Lee, the Burroughs character in *On the Road*, wears 'long striped sharpster pants' (Kerouac 1957: 144). When the young men in *On the Road* dress up, they 'sharp up for the big night,' and look 'sharp in a suit' (52–3). Both the characters based on Neal Cassady – Dean Moriarity and Cody Pomeray – purchased natty pencil-stripe suits in New York (Kerouac 1957; Kerouac 1959a). Two photographs survive of Cassady himself wearing such a suit which he purchased from a Chinese tailor in New York City (www.corbis.com).

The ultimate hipster was Dizzy Gillespie, the public face of bebop (Ward and Burns 2000). His music so inspired his fans, both black and white, that

Figure 8.1 Dizzy Gillespie, *c.* May 1947. Photographed by William Gottlieb for
Down Beat magazine. Courtesy of William Gottlieb.

they imitated his look. Three of his sartorial trademarks eventually entered
the style vocabulary of the Beats: beret, eyewear and goatee (Figure 8.1). In
his autobiography, he described himself as 'pretty dandified' (Gillespie 1979:
279). He began wearing a beret, probably emulating crew members he had
observed when sailing to France on the *Isle de France* in 1937. He recalled:

Perhaps I remembered France and started wearing the beret. But I used it as headgear
[that] I could stuff into my pocket and keep moving. I used to lose my hat a lot. I liked
to wear a hat like most of the guys then, and the hats I kept losing cost five dollars
apiece. At a few recording sessions when I couldn't lay my hands on a mute, I covered

the bell of the trumpet with the beret. Since I'd been designated their 'leader,' cats just picked up the style. (Gillespie 1979: 279–80)

Wearing dark glasses on stage shielded Gillespie's sensitive eyes from the stage lights; as a youth he had suffered from eye infections. (Although Gillespie did not use heroin, many jazz musicians were seriously addicted and light hurt their eyes.) Gillespie preferred horn-rimmed glasses to rimless glasses because they did not break. Horn rims became the preferred eyewear of the Beats, particularly Allen Ginsberg, as seen in numerous photographs. Dizzy grew a goatee during his days with Cab Calloway because the 'tuft of hair' cushioned his mouthpiece and 'was quite useful to him as a player.' Previously, when he had shaved, the spot under his lip 'prickled and itched' and felt uncomfortable (Gillespie 1979: 280). By 1948, Dizzy's male fans adopted his blue beret, his horn-rimmed spectacles and dark glasses and grew hair on their lower lips. One club where he played sold paste-on goatees (Ward and Burns 2000).

The second image of the male Beat emerged in the literature set in the late 1940s. Kerouac (1957; 1959b), Holmes (1952a) and Johnson (1983) describe young men in faded jeans, chino pants, T-shirts, frayed sweaters, worn shirts, old Army jackets and Levi's jackets. Kerouac ascribes to the clothes a 'Beat' quality, as in 'a Beat sweater and baggy pants' (1957: 16). By 'Beat' he meant worn out; for example, 'Beat shoes that flap' (Kerouac 1957: 6). But Beat also meant sad, like the wool plaid shirt Sal Paradise, Kerouac's alter ego, retrieved from someone he'd loaned it to: 'It was there, all tied up, the whole enormous sadness of a shirt' (Kerouac 1957: 59). Kerouac repeatedly described Moriarity in old clothes, but in an approving sort of way: 'his dirty workclothes clung to him so gracefully' (1957: 7); 'muscular and ragged in T-shirt, unshaven' (1957: 109).

The early Beats were not particularly concerned with cleanliness or whether clothes or shoes were worn looking unless they were trying to pick up girls. When Sal Paradise in *On the Road* hitchhiked or rode the bus, his canvas bag contained just two shirts, two sweaters, huaraches and an extra pair of pants. In Oakland, he picked up a second-hand army coat for $3.

The women who associated with Beat men during this early period followed mainstream fashion. Holmes (1952a) described a woman in a green draped dress; Kerouac wrote of doll-like, well-dressed women who accompanied men dressed in suits. He wrote admiringly of women in slacks, which would still have been viewed as novel then, especially for dressy occasions. Joyce Johnson (1983) described Trotskyite women she encountered in the Village in 1949 who wore dark clothes and long earrings, or men's shirts over faded jeans.

Johnson identified certain emblems of bohemianism in her memoirs such as huaraches and free-form jewelry. Huaraches, she said, were 'the mark of the New York Bohemian intellectual back then' (Johnson 1983: 22). Sal Paradise wears Mexican huaraches on his first hitchhiking trip, but finds them 'not fit for the rainy night of America' (Kerouac 1957: 11). Johnson described long earrings and belts from a store called 'The Sorcerer's Apprentice' as 'badge[s] of membership in the ranks of the unconventional' (1983: 31).

By 1950, then, several elements had entered the wardrobes of the Beats although their adoption was by no means universal. These include berets, horn-rimmed glasses, dark glasses worn indoors, jeans, T-shirts and other casual clothes. At this time, such clothes were available everywhere at reasonable prices. Jeans manufacturers included Levi's, Wrangler and Lee. T-shirts, which had been issued as undergarments during the First World War, were available from Hanes, Fruit of the Loom, and Sears-Roebuck by 1938 (Fresener 1995). T-shirts were tight-fitting, white or striped, and not yet printed with words. However, none of these elements was considered threatening to mainstream America because the dominant culture as yet knew nothing of the Beats.

1950–6

During this period, the Beat scene spread to San Francisco. John Clellon Holmes' novel *Go* and his article about the Beats appeared in 1952, alerting those who read his works to a new underground of youth. About this time deviant youth icons appeared in the movies. Marlon Brando's gang in *The Wild One* (1953) clad themselves in black leather jackets, black jeans and T-shirts. The movie was based on an incident with a motorcycle gang that took place in Hollister, California over the July 4, 1947 weekend. The teenage James Dean in *Rebel Without a Cause* (1955) wore a T-shirt and jeans after school. He touched a chord with rebellious middle-class American youth who felt restless and misunderstood. These cinematic characters provided ideas for deviant dress at the same time that the Beat movement was surfacing, but only for men. In both of these movies, the young women associated with the heroes wore conventional clothing.

The number of alienated youth grew. Beat style began to emerge as a symbol of group affiliation. Michael McClure wrote that: 'as our hair grew longer, we were inventing a style' (1999: 34). The hipster suits disappeared while the casual, shabby style ascended. Men continued to prefer checked shirts (particularly red ones), sweaters, chinos, jeans, T-shirts, army jackets and crepe-soled shoes. A few wore sandals and berets; others donned

Hawaiian shirts in warm weather. Some men, like Diane di Prima's lover 'Dirty John,' did not bathe often (di Prima 1969).

Yet there still was no consensus on what to wear if you identified with the Beat Generation. Holmes did not mention appearance in his article in the *New York Times* other than to identify the 'clean young face[s] . . . making the newspapers' for drug possession and other deviant behavior (1952b: 223). Some Beat men looked just like any other casually dressed men of the period, particularly Kerouac and Ginsberg. Photographs of Kerouac show a handsome man with groomed hair wearing checked shirts and casual jackets. Ginsberg sports horn-rimmed glasses, sweaters and jackets in photographs. The few who had beards, like poet Gary Snyder, clearly signified a departure from clean-cut 1950s fashion.

The dichotomy between the sloppy, shabby Beat and the regularly dressed Beat is no more evident than in the attire Snyder and Ginsburg chose for the poetry reading at the Six Gallery in 1955. Snyder wore jeans and sported a beard while Ginsberg wore a conservative charcoal gray suit, white shirt and tie.

Beat women, on the other hand, developed a distinctly recognizable style by the end of this period. They gave up trying to follow fashion, opting instead for loose men's shirts over slacks or faded jeans, or skirts with black stockings. Turtlenecks or leotards were common choices for tops. Joyce Johnson, who began the decade dressing in plaid kilts and wool sweaters while attending Barnard in 1951, ended it in black stockings. In December 1956, she charged 'a sleeveless black velvet dress with a long satin sash' to her Lord & Taylor account to wear to a New Year's Eve party (1983: 125). She claimed that it was her last attempt at 'bourgeois elegance' for fifteen years.

Diane di Prima was one of the first to develop a Beat style. While a freshman at Swarthmore in 1951, she observed that: 'blonde girls in cashmere sweaters, with single strands of pearls, seem to own this place' (di Prima 2001: 88). She, however, 'dressed like nothing they ever saw on this campus' (di Prima 2001: 89). Her hair was long to her waist and she wore ballet slippers. She often wore a black nylon leotard with jeans and a colorful sash. Still, she referred to Levi's and sweatshirts as her 'eternal costume' (di Prima 1969: 130). However, during the times when she was seeking employment in the corporate world, she donned a skirt and high heels. At one point *c.* 1955, she chopped off her hair in a crew cut and wore men's shirts to hide her body; she preferred plain white cotton or dark green corduroy shirts.

Carolyn Cassady, wife of Neal Cassady, also appears to have dressed for both worlds. Pictures of her in the late 1940s and early 1950s show a fashionable blonde in suede-jacketed suits and jersey dresses. But in 1952, when she set out to seduce Jack Kerouac, she wore jeans and a white shirt with a dab of cologne (Cassady 1990: 453). At the time, Kerouac was living with the Cassadys and Carolyn resented her exclusion from the fraternity of Jack and Neal.

Kerouac described the appearance of Mardou Fox, the black heroine in *The Subterraneans*, in very attractive terms. In the early 1950s, Mardou wears jeans, black slacks, and thonged sandals. She looks 'so hip, so cool, so beautiful' in her black velvet slacks and 'so cute' in her jeans. He describes her as a sort of fashion icon who wears a 'red raincoat over the black velvet slacks and cuts along, with black short hair . . . like someone in Paris' (Kerouac 1958: 107).

By the mid 1950s, black was a favorite color for the Beats. Allen Ginsberg wore frayed black turtlenecks (Johnson 1983); Diane wore her black leotard, and Mardou her black slacks. Polhemus (1994) credits existentialism as an influence, but offers no solid evidence. Robert Duncan recalled that years before the Beats arrived in San Francisco, 'when the Sartre–existentialist thing came after the war, the North Beach filled with young and black-stockings with doleful looks who huddled around the bars being existentialists' (1982b: 26). However, Duncan separated them and their behavior from the Beats, who came later.

Black also appeared in fashion circles at this time. During the late 1940s American fashion designer Claire McCardell created casual styles in black jersey. She had been prominently featured as part of the American designer campaign during the war (see Chapter 6). Her jersey tops and leggings as well as Capezio ballet shoes influenced young women. Two outfits with black jersey tops and black stockings, photographed by Irving Penn, appeared in *Vogue* in 1950 (Yohannan and Nolf 1998: 53). Patricia Campbell Warner, a graduate of the University of Toronto, recalls a black wool jersey top she wore with a black skirt to coffee houses and jazz clubs from 1956 to 1958 (Warner 2003). Her friend, an art major, took the black concept further: she wore black turtlenecks, skirts, stockings and shoes – and she had long straight hair.

Wini Breines (1994) offers another interpretation of the preference for black. Based on interviews with 'bad girls' from the 1950s, she posits that black signified that the wearer was dark, dissident, different, a threat. Pastels, light colors and well-groomed hair represented goodness and innocence in suburban teens. Girls who wore black fantasized about 'bad' boys. One woman stated: 'I dumped out my inheritance of pastel colours and princes and collected a new bag of black sweaters, jeans, psychopaths and Beat fantasy.' Another said, 'I just wanted to be a beatnik. I quit wearing pink and orange and always wore darker colors. I was one of the first people in Charleston [South Carolina] to get dark stockings' (Breines 1994: 399). Whichever reason or combination of reasons behind the adoption of black by the Beats, by the mid 1950s the Beats, women particularly, gravitated toward the color to signify their deviance from mainstream society.

By the end of 1956, Beat enclaves had formed on the East and West coasts. Yet those who were living the Beat life did not know how large their numbers had become. Diane di Prima (1969) guessed that there were forty or fifty in New York City, another fifty in San Francisco, and about a hundred scattered throughout the country. At that point she was given a copy of Ginsberg's poem 'Howl,' identified with it, and realized that 'a new era had begun' (di Prima 1969: 164).

1957–63

The year 1957 was transitional. In February, *Mademoiselle* covered the San Francisco scene as a literary and artistic phenomenon, but never identified the artists, writers and poets in the article as 'Beats' ('The Lively Arts' 1957). *Funny Face* (1957), starring a long-haired Audrey Hepburn as a reluctant bohemian model, opened mid-year. Hepburn, as a Greenwich Village bookseller, wore a tweed tunic and skirt over a black sweater and long black stockings. In Paris, where she was to model, she wore black slacks, tops and flat Capezio-like shoes. Again, no one said the word 'Beat' in the movie, yet all the components were there to affiliate Hepburn's character with the Beat Generation. She worked in a bookstore, read existentialist philosophy, went to coffee houses and listened to jazz. In Paris's Latin Quarter, she went to cafes where she mixed with intellectual men in black turtlenecks or striped T-shirts and long-haired girls in jeans. Fred Astaire played the photographer, who was modeled after real-life fashion photographer Richard Avedon. Hubert de Givenchy, a new young couturier, designed the clothes Audrey modeled. In the guise of Audrey Hepburn's character, Jo, the American girl Beat did not appear threatening.

But soon the 'moral panic,' as Cohen would call it, set in. The 'Howl' obscenity trial had made the Beat Generation famous. In October of that year, Kerouac's *On the Road* was published with a great review in the *New York Times* and became a bestseller. Suddenly, everyone was interested in this new literary movement. The public now associated the term 'Beat' with the writers. Negative publicity started and lasted for several years. Magazines published photos of sparsely furnished Beat 'pads' and messy-looking intellectual types in sandals, chinos and turtlenecks, shocking the 'squares' ('Squaresville' 1959; O'Neil 1959). The negative commentary stressed the lack of a work ethic and nonconformist attitudes among Beats. Paul O'Neil (1959), a staff writer for *Life*, wrote the first serious piece about the Beats published in a popular magazine. The article, titled 'The Only Rebellion Around,' investigated the Beat phenomenon beyond the superficialities. At this time, police started raiding poetry readings and closing coffee houses.

The Beat stereotype congealed: bearded men wearing berets and dark glasses, sandals, striped jerseys, or black sweaters with chinos or jeans; women with long, straight hair and black slacks and leotards or black stockings and chunky sweaters with tweed skirts (Maynard 1991; Watson 1995). As the media highlighted certain aspects of appearance, Beat followers adopted the image. The Beats' shabby, unkempt appearance became a badge of defiance in the neat, well-groomed 1950s. This is the process Cohen called sensitization. Hebdige (1979) expands on the subversive implications of style, explaining that appearance signifies difference and becomes a form of revolt.

The Beat writers only partially fit the stereotype. Jack Kerouac (Figure 8.2)

Figure 8.2 Jack Kerouac, 1957. Photographed for *Mademoiselle* magazine. Image donated by Corbis-Bettmann.

was photographed for the *Mademoiselle* article wearing a checked shirt. Many photographs show him wearing checked or plaid shirts. In this particular photograph, his collar does not lay flat, his hair is windblown and he needs a shave, giving him a 'Beat' appearance. He had just returned from two months alone in the mountains. Kerouac explained that although he usually combed his hair, Gregory Corso had encouraged him not to (Kerouac 1959b). Allen Ginsberg wore checked shirts and turtleneck sweaters, sometimes with jeans. During this period he and other Beat writers grew beards. The poet Gregory Corso was derided as 'a dark little man who boasts that he has never combed his hair' ('Manners and Morals' 1959). Like the 'obscene' comedian Lenny Bruce, the Beats began to employ shock value: Ginsberg once took his clothing off to silence a heckler during a poetry reading; his lover Peter Orlovsky read a poem in his underwear (Lipton 1959; McDarrah and McDarrah 1996).

The appearance of the Beats at this time was more diverse than the stereotype, and there may have been regional variations. In New York, the public identified women in black stockings as Beats. Joyce Johnson, whom Kerouac called 'my little secretary in black stockings' (Johnson 1983: 205), was verbally abused by her neighbors who accused her of being a commu-

Figure 8.3 Beatniks inside The Gaslight, a Greenwich Village coffee shop, February 3, 1959. Image donated by Corbis-Bettmann.

nist and sleeping with bums. Photographs of girls in Greenwich Village show lots of variety, including full-skirted dresses and heels as well as slacks and sandals. Folk or ethnic garments were sometimes worn. Figure 8.3 depicts a young woman in a Greenwich Village coffee shop wearing white (not black) pants with an embroidered Mexican blouse and strappy sandals. Women's hair could be short, although long hair was an appearance cue that signified membership with the Beats. Long hair was viewed as wilder and looser than the short, hair-sprayed dos of the 'squares.' Figure 8.4 shows three casually dressed young people, only one of whom has a beard and a beret.

In Venice, California beards signified membership in the Beat community. Larry Lipton's *The Holy Barbarians* (1959), the first book-length treatment of a Beat community, discussed beards at length. A character named Angel could not get a job because he had a beard. When he shaved, he was hired. Chuck, bearded and barefoot, was a former ad man who burned his gray flannel suit. He considered his beard to be a 'letter of resignation from the rat race' (50). Other stereotypical aspects of appearance prevailed: men wore sunglasses because 'light hurts the eyes if you're a pot head' (71). Lipton criticized the weekend Beats, who came in from the

Figure 8.4 Beatniks gather at a Greenwich Village coffee house, November 14, 1959. Image donated by Corbis-Bettmann.

suburbs to experience bohemian life for a night or two, labeling them 'squares' (26).

Lipton's picture of Venice, California is countered with a 1958 scientific study of the San Francisco Beat Community by psychotherapist Francis Rigney (Maynard 1991). He found that his subjects came mostly from middle-class backgrounds. The majority of the men were clean-shaven and nearly half wore business suits every day. About a third of the men in his sample wore sandals. The women presented a more uniform picture by wearing black stockings, black dresses and leotards, although this clothing was not universal. His point was that the stereotype did not exist.

Some people dressed to fit the stereotype in an attempt to join the 'scene.' Eileen Kaufman was a weekend beatnik from Sacramento when she met poet Bob Kaufman in San Francisco in 1958 (Kaufman 1982). Her Beat outfit consisted of a poncho over a black leotard and a T-shirt. She had long hair and wore black eyeliner. He was wearing a red corduroy jacket, striped T-shirt, non-descript pants, sandals and a wine-colored beret and sported a black goatee. It was love at first sight for Eileen.

Harry Washburn, who embarked on a road trip to San Francisco upon graduation from Dartmouth College in 1959, eventually settling in New York, said that Beat style 'was very plain – khaki pants and a button-down shirt with the sleeves rolled up' (Washburn 2003). In Providence, Janice Fontes left her conservative home before putting on her Beat outfit to go to the local tea room; she wore jeans, eyeliner and white lipstick, and had long straight hair (Fontes 2003).

The dominant culture entertained notions that Beats were dirty and smelled bad. Diana Trilling, the solidly middle-class wife of literary critic James Trilling, wrote after attending a poetry reading in 1959 at Columbia: 'I took one look at the crowd and was certain that it would smell bad. But I was mistaken.' She was self-conscious about being seen in such a shoddy-looking crowd. She noted 'so many young girls, so few of them pretty, and so many dreadful black stockings,' and 'so many young men, so few of them – despite the many black beards – with any promise of masculinity' (Trilling 1959: 571).

Almost simultaneously, the moral panic, as Cohen would say, started diffusing. One method of disempowering a threat is to ridicule it, which is what happened when Herbert Caen coined the word 'beatnik' in 1958. In 1959, enterprising Greenwich Villager Fred McDarrah started a 'rent-a-beatnik' scheme where a beatnik, 'badly groomed but brilliant,' would attend a party for a fee of $40 plus $5 for each additional beatnik (McDarrah and McDarrah 1996). Photos of Beats who did this show men in beards, berets and dark glasses, and women in black. The volume of articles peaked in 1959, the same year the Maynard G. Krebs beatnik character appeared in *The Many Loves of Dobie Gillis*. The Beats filmed a movie called *Pull My Daisy* in 1959 and Kerouac's *The Subterraneans* was made into a film in 1960. That same year *Mad Magazine* published a Beat parody.

Kerouac, in an article he authored for *Playboy* in 1959, was upset with the way that society absorbed the Beat message. He said that the Beat Generation had simply become a slogan or label for a revolution of manners in America. He observed that the pseudo-beat girls 'said nothing and wore black' (Kerouac 1959b: 362). He speculated that respectable people would soon be 'nattily attired in Brooks Brothers jean-type tailoring and sweater type pull-ons, in other words, it's a simple change in fashion' (1959b: 366). Joyce Johnson observed that the Beat Generation 'sold books, sold black turtleneck sweaters and bongos, berets and dark glasses, sold a way of life that seemed like dangerous fun – thus to be either condemned or imitated. Suburban couples could have beatnik parties on Saturday nights and drink too much and fondle each other's wives' (1983: 187–8).

Kerouac and Johnson were right. Fashion designers soon drew inspiration from Beat style. In 1959 *Life* showcased Beat fashions in a feature on college back-to-school looks. Several American designers had created 'Beat-knits, loose sweaters that are respectable versions of those Beats live in' that were available in college shops across the country. The photos showed dark-colored sweaters over tight black trousers, skirts and leotards for a 'real gone' look ('Real Gone Garb For Fall' 1959: 48–9).

The look reached the couture level the next year. Yves St. Laurent, then head designer at Dior, created a collection based on Beat style for fall–winter 1960. It featured cashmere turtlenecks and crocodile jackets trimmed with mink, all in black. But it did not sell well, as the customers objected to wearing styles that too closely resembled those of the hooligans they saw around the Latin Quarter in Paris. It ultimately proved to be his undoing at Dior. After serving his obligatory military time, Yves St. Laurent's contract at Dior was not renewed (Rawsthorn 1996).

By the early 1960s, the Beats were no longer seen as a menace to society. They continued publishing, but time moved on. The musical preferences of the upcoming baby boomers shifted to folk music and rock and roll. Bob Dylan and the Beatles recorded their first albums at this time. The easy relations between blacks and whites in the Beat subculture disintegrated with the onset of the civil rights movements and the race riots of the 1960s. While some of the original Beats successfully transitioned into the 1960s, others did not. Allen Ginsberg appeared at happenings and be-ins, becoming the nation's poet-at-large during that tumultuous decade. He lived a long and rich life. Burroughs lived in Paris, then moved to London, finally settling in Lawrence, Kansas. He had recovered from his heroin addiction and lived to his eighty-third year. Ginsberg and Burroughs died within months of each other in 1997. Neal Cassady drove the Magic Bus for the Merry Pranksters, whose saga formed the story of Tom Wolfe's *Electric Kool-Aid Acid Test*. Sadly, Cassady died on a railroad track in Mexico in 1968 after mixing barbiturates and alcohol, and Kerouac died of alcoholism in Florida in 1969. Kerouac and Cassady had burned 'like fabulous yellow roman candles' (Kerouac 1957: 5), but were not destined to grow old. As early as the 1970s, renewed interest in the Beat Generation and its culture manifested itself in the form of books, conferences and exhibitions.

The Beats in Cultural Memory

The Beat Generation began as a literary movement in the post-war years, gathered strength in the 1950s, finally bursting into national consciousness in 1957 with the 'Howl' trials and the publication of *On the Road*. The media, particularly *Life* and *Time*, cast the Beats in the role of folk devils who threatened the moral fiber of America. As we have seen, appearance played an important part.

Although many Beats were not distinguishable from other people throughout the time periods discussed, certain sartorial traits became associated with them. In the first period, 1944–9, bebop fans adopted the beret, eyewear and goatee of Dizzy Gillespie. Additionally, sandals were recognized as a visual marker of bohemianism. However, the jeans, T-shirts and second-hand clothes worn by the Beats were also worn by others in the post-war era. During the second period, 1950–6, images of Marlon Brando and James Dean in jeans and T-shirts aided rebellious youth across America in finding a look to go along with their changing values. Women began wearing clothes that distinguished them from fashion-conscious Americans: jeans, men's shirts, sweatshirts, black leotards and stockings. By 1957, when the Beat phenomenon became widely known, the public had picked up on certain components of Beat appearance – the shabbiness, the beards and unkempt look, the black – as presented in the media and the stereotype congealed. The Beats and their followers responded by picking up elements of the stereotype in their appearance. Looking a certain way helped people with similar values to find each other, like Bob and Eileen Kaufman, and to tell the world who they were. Humor and ridicule can diffuse a threat, as they did in relation to the Beats with the many spoofs and parodies that appeared on television and in print. By 1963, it was all over and the image of the Beats became a memory.

The memory of the Beats as 'cool' sells merchandise. The Gap used a 1950s image of Jack Kerouac to promote its khaki pants in a late 1990s ad campaign (*The Source* 1999). The text said simply: 'Jack wore khakis.' The photograph shows a look so contemporary that it sold clothes forty-some years after it was taken.

The Beat stereotype is also one of nostalgia and humor. We look back fondly on the earnest bongo-drumming, poetry-spouting beatniks, as evidenced in the film *Down with Love* (2003) starring Renee Zellweger. Set in 1962, it includes a scene of a Greenwich Village beatnik party complete with long-haired girls in black turtlenecks and tights, and men in chunky turtlenecks sporting beards, goatees and berets.

In truth, the Beats' fondness for jeans, T-shirts, sandals and second-hand clothes persisted into the hippie era, ultimately affecting the way all but the most conservative Americans dressed. The attitudes about dress that the Beats set in motion are still prevalent today.

References

Breines, W. (1994), 'The "Other" Fifties: Beats and Bad Girls,' in J. Meyerowitz (ed.), *Not June Cleaver: Women and Gender in Postwar America, 1945–1960*, Philadelphia: Temple University Press, pp. 382–408.

Broyard, A. (1948), 'A Portrait of the Hipster,' in A. Charters (ed.) (2001), *Beat Down to Your Soul: What Was the Beat Generation?* London: Penguin, pp. 43–9.

Cassady, C. (1990), *Off the Road: My Years with Cassady, Kerouac, and Ginsberg*, excerpt in A. Charters (ed.), *The Portable Beat Reader*, London, Penguin, pp. 449–64.

Charters, A. (ed.) (1992), *The Portable Beat Reader*, London: Penguin.

—— (ed.) (2001), *Beat Down to Your Soul: What Was the Beat Generation?* London: Penguin.

—— (2002), 'Foreword,' to R.G. Johnson and N.M. Grace (eds), *Girls Who Wore Black: Women Writing the Beat Generation*, New Brunswick, NJ: Rutgers University Press.

Cohen, S. (2002), *Folk Devils and Moral Panics: The Creation of the Mods and Rockers*, 3rd ed., London: Routledge.

di Prima, D. (1969), *Memoirs of a Beatnik*, London: Olympia Press.

'The Disorganization Man' (1958), *Time*, June 9: 98, 100, 102.

—— (2001), *Recollections of My Life as a Woman: The New York Years*, New York: Viking Press.

Fontes, J. (2003), Interview with author, East Greenwich, RI, June 20.

Fresener, S. (1995), *The T-Shirt Book*, Salt Lake City: Smith.

Gillespie, D. (1979), *To Be, or Not . . . to Bop: Memoirs*, New York: Doubleday.

Ginsberg, A. (1956), 'Howl,' in A. Charters (ed.), *The Portable Beat Reader*, London, Penguin, pp. 62–70.

Hebdige, D. (1979), *Subculture: The Meaning of Style*, London: Methuen.

Holmes, J.C. (1952a), *Go*, Mamaroneck, NY: Paul P. Appel.

—— (1952b), 'This is the Beat Generation,' *New York Times Magazine* 16 November, in F.W. McDarrah, Reprint (1985), *Kerouac and Friends: A Beat Generation Album*, Hanover, NY: William Morrow and Co.

Johnson, J. (1983), *Minor Characters*, Boston: Houghton Mifflin Company.

Kaufman, E. (1982) 'Who Wouldn't Walk With Tigers,' in A. Knight and K. Knight (eds), *Beat Angels*, California, PA: vol. 12, *the unspeakable visions of the individual*, pp. 29–38.

Kerouac, J. (1950), *The Town and the City*, New York: Harcourt, Brace.

—— (1957), *On the Road*, New York: Viking Press.

—— (1958), *The Subterraneans*, New York: Grove Press.

—— (1959a), *Visions of Cody*, Reprint (1972), New York: McGraw-Hill.

—— (1959b), 'The Origins of the Beat Generation,' *Playboy*, June: 31–2, 42, 79. Reprint (1979) in S. Donaldson (ed.), *On the Road: Text and Criticism*, New York: Viking Press.

Lipton, L. (1959), *The Holy Barbarians*, New York: Julian Messner.

'The Lively Arts in San Francisco' (1957), *Mademoiselle*, February: 142–3, 190–1.

'Manners and Morals: Fried Shoes' (1959), *Time*, February 9: 16.

Maynard, J.A. (1991), *Venice West: The Beat Generation in Southern California*, New Brunswick, NJ: Rutgers University Press.

McClure, M. (1999), 'Painting Beat by Numbers,' in H. George-Warren (ed.), *The Rolling Stone Book of the Beats*, New York: Hyperion.

McDarrah, F.W. (photographer) and E. Wilentz (ed.) (1960), *The Beat Scene*, London: Corinth Books.

McDarrah, F.W. and G.S. McDarrah, (1996), *Beat Generation: Glory Days in Greenwich Village*, New York: Schirmer.

Miles, B. (1993), 'The Beat Generation in the Village,' in R. Beard and L.C. Berlowitz (eds), *Greenwich Village: Culture and Conterculture*, New Brunswick, NJ: Rutgers University Press, pp. 165–79.

—— (2000), *The Beat Hotel: Ginsberg, Burroughs, and Corso in Paris, 1958–1963*, New York: Grove Press.

Miller, D.T. and M. Nowak (1977), *The Fifties: The Way We Really Were*, New York: Doubleday.

Nicosia, G. (1982a) '"Sharing the Poem of Life": An Interview with Ted Joans,' in A. Knight and K. Knight (eds), *Beat Angels*, California, PA: vol. 12, *the unspeakable visions of the individual*, pp. 128–40.

—— (1982b) '"The Closeness of Mind": An Interview with Robert Duncan,' in A. Knight and K. Knight (eds), *Beat Angels*, California, PA: vol. 12, *the unspeakable visions of the individual*, pp. 13–27.

O'Neil, P. (1959), 'The Only Rebellion Around,' *Life*, November 30: 114–31.

Podhoretz, N. (1958), 'The Know-Nothing Bohemians,' in A. Charters (ed.) (2001), *Beat Down to Your Soul: What Was the Beat Generation?*, London: Penguin, pp. 481–93.

Polhemus, T. (1994), *Street Style: From Sidewalk to Catwalk*, London: Thames and Hudson.

Rawsthorn, A. (1996), *Yves Saint Laurent*, New York: Doubleday.

'Real Gone Garb for Fall, Beat but Neat' (1959), *Life*, August 3: 48–9.

'Squaresville USA vs Beatsville' (1959) *Life*, September 21: 31–7.

The Source (1999).

Trilling, D. (1959), 'The Other Night at Columbia: A Report from the Academy' in A. Charters (ed.) (2001), *Beat Down to Your Soul: What Was the Beat Generation?*, London: Penguin, pp. 561–77.

Ward, G.C. and K. Burns, (2000), *Jazz: A History of America' Music*, New York: Alfred A. Knopf.

Warner, P.C. (2003), Telephone interview with author, June 22.

Washburn, H. (2003), Interview by author, Cambridge, MA, March 15.

Watson, S. (1995), *The Birth of the Beat Generation: Visionaries, Rebels, and Hipsters, 1944–1960*, New York: Phantom.

Whyte, W.H. (1956), *The Organization Man*, New York: Simon and Schuster.

Yohaman, K. and N. Nolf (1998), *Claire McCardell: Redefining Modernism*, New York: Harny N. Abrams.

9

Space Age Fashion

Suzanne Baldaia

Editors' Introduction: During the 1960s, America exploded with political and social protest. The civil rights movement, dissent over the American involvement in Vietnam, and women's rights were just some of the factors that resulted in the wholesale rejection of the status quo. The old rules fell by the wayside for clothing too. Designers began creating pants suits for women to wear for formal occasions. Men broke out of their gray flannel suits and became peacocks. British rock groups, inspired by American blues singers, popularized a new form of music called rock and roll that influenced fashion on both sides of the Atlantic. Against this backdrop, the United States engaged in a race with the Soviet Union to go into outer space. Being modern was in style in art, architecture and design. Suzanne Baldaia illustrates how the American fashion magazine Harper's Bazaar signaled modernity by presenting clothing as part of the 'space age.'

'Dresses to wear on the moon.' 'Lipstick for space travelers.' 'New designs for unearthly beings.' Phrases like these in fashion magazines, often accompanied by stunning photography, showed American women how to dress for the modern world in the 1960s. Space age styles by André Courrèges, Pierre Cardin and Paco Rabanne bring to mind clean, crisp lines, geometric shapes, smooth leather or vinyl, sleek white jumpsuits, shimmering silver and helmet-like hats. The look seems 'modern' regardless of current fashion styles. In fact, *space age* is synonymous with *modern* according to *Roget's Thesaurus* (Morehead 1985: 530).

Consumers choose fashions not only because they are aesthetically pleasing but also because they mean or *signify* something about contemporary culture (Guy, Green and Banim 2001: 6). Precisely what a fashion signifies in a social context depends on shared knowledge. Shared meanings are expressed through signs and symbols. Regardless of the form of the fashion sign – word or image – the ultimate meaning of fashion is that of *modernity*. According to Blumer (1969: 116), fashion is always modern. For the American woman, fashion magazines provide signs and symbols to comprehend the modern world.

In this chapter, I examine the concept of modernity as expressed in space age fashion during the 1960s, particularly how *Harper's Bazaar*, an American fashion magazine published by the Hearst Corporation, portrayed a 'modern' space age world to promote the consumption of fashionable products. The study reveals how space exploration became part of the American consciousness and how signs and symbols associated with the space age became synonymous with modernity through the media. Analysis of the text and photographs in *Harper's Bazaar* reveals extensive borrowing of space age terminology and imagery to express modernity in fashion.[1]

The Space Age

Profound scientific achievements marked the space age, defined here as the period from the launch of sputnik in 1957 to 1972 when the United States and the Soviet Union signed The Intergovernmental Agreement on Cooperation in the Exploration and Use of Outer Space for Peaceful Purposes. The US space program was initiated for defense reasons (McDougall 1985: 104). However, by 1961 the civil space program for peaceful purposes was underway. President John F. Kennedy publicly made a passionate commitment to land an American on the moon by the decade's end, a commitment that was later carried out by his successor Lyndon Johnson (McDougall 1985: 404). The highly anticipated and publicized climax came in 1969 when Americans first landed on the moon. The final US lunar landing came in 1972.

As the US and the Soviet Union engaged in what was called 'the space race' – a simultaneously real and symbolic battle for superiority – the media broadcast images and sounds of space age phenomena and events (Mathews 1991). In the United States, portrayals of rocket building and launches, astronauts, space walks, splashdowns and lunar roving provided evidence to the public of an unmistakable 'American spirit.' It was against this backdrop that women viewed the space imagery in fashion magazines.

Signs and Symbols

Social and cultural theorists help us understand how fashion imagery acquires meaning. According to Grant McCracken, author of *Culture and Consumption*, the fashion object acquires meaning during a two-step process. In the context of space age fashion, for example, McCracken's theory would state meaning was first drawn from the cultural world (e.g. newspaper accounts of space flight) and then transferred to consumer goods by specialists whom he calls *agents of meaning transfer*, including fashion journalists, editors, photographers and advertisers, such as those at *Harper's Bazaar*. They affect the adoption and diffusion of fashion objects by the promotion of some fashions and the exclusion of others (McCracken 1988: 76). The meaning is appropriated by the consumer through the purchase or use of consumer goods (McCracken 1988: 71–89).

In this case space age meanings were contained in and transmitted through *signs*. According to Saussure (1985: 36–7), a *sign* is the union between a *signifier* – a word, sound, or image – and a *signified*, which is a concept. Further, Peirce identified three types of signs: *icon*, *index* and *symbol* (1985: 5–23). An icon is the simplest sign and signifies by resemblance. An index is a more complex sign that signifies through cause or indication. For example, smoke is a sign of fire because fire caused the smoke. Symbols are the most abstract class of signs and signify through social convention, that is, through a shared *code*. All words are symbols. Space age signifiers functioned as icons, indices and symbols depending on the context in which they were used to transfer meanings.

In *The Fashion System*, Barthes (1983) uncovered the systematic nature of meaning in the fashion magazine positing that three categories of fashion exist: the actual (real) garment, the written (described) garment, and the image (photographed) garment. Both written garment and image garment comprise the fashion magazine; however, it is the written garment, communicated through language, which Barthes considers central to fashion's function as a sign. Conversely, image or photographed clothing signifies meaning more ambiguously. With no authoritative structure such as language to guide its communicative effect, the fashion photograph uses its own language. In the case of fashion, the object, whether written about or photographed, always denotes 'fashion.' Barthes' description of how meaning is transmitted easily applies to space age modernist fashion as seen in *Harper's Bazaar* during the 1960s.

The development of a code is a learning process similar to learning a language (Eco 1976: 138) and requires time and is therefore historical.

According to Barthes, the interpretation of a photograph is historical because it depends on the reader's knowledge, just as though it were a matter of a real language (1977: 28). Historical knowledge contributes to the development of a stock of signs and a code by which to interpret them, a *symbolic terrain*. The notion of a symbolic terrain and that of shared meaning form a framework from which cultural meaning may be drawn for transfer to the fashion object for consumption by the user.

Expressing Modernity through Fashion

Modernity is the state of being up-to-date or of the current time period (Bullock and Stallybrass 1977: 397). Modernity is also intimately linked with the concepts of change and progress, which, according to Lauer and Lauer, are deeply rooted in American culture (1981: 174). A modernist style can be defined as a style that is cubic, geometrically organized, regular in form, constructed of materials such as concrete, steel, and glass and, ideally, pure white (Berman 1988: 43). Additionally, Fuller (1988: 117) stated that anti-ornamentalism remained one of the key tenets of the modernist movement in art and design. According to Berman (1988: 11) modernist design expresses modernist ideology, which includes faith in science and rationalism, belief in the progressive nature of technology, and celebration of the machine.

Based on the code of modernism, space age fashion may be defined first and foremost as *modernist*. In *Harper's Bazaar*, both words and images signified modernity by alluding to the space age.

The Space Age Fashion Code

In *Harper's Bazaar*, both words and images signified modernity by alluding to the space age.[2] During the earliest years of the space age, 1957–60, the media laid a foundation of space age meaning by introducing space age objects and phenomena to the general public. Over time, Americans connected space age words and images to forms and ideas on a deeper symbolic level. People recognized memories of previous connections between these elements, accumulating them to develop a *space age code*. Further, in the case of fashion magazines, space age signifiers, reiterated over time, contributed to the development of a *space age fashion code*.

Harper's Bazaar editors such as Carmel Snow, Nancy White, Polly Mellen, China Machado and Diana Vreeland, art directors, photographers, and their advertisers created a code by which the language of the space age was understood and served as a promotional tool for the consumption of fashion. They, along with designers, harnessed a pattern of stylistic formal elements to symbolize 'space age' that came to represent modernity. These elements included silver-colored materials and metals (e.g., chrome, platinum, aluminum, silver), white materials, encapsulating forms and helmet-shaped hats.

The compilation of space age signs appears in Table 9.1. These signifiers include words or phrases as explicit as 'space age' and 'astronaut' to denote space age imagery as well as signifiers less explicit such as 'launch' and pictures of planets from which connotations of space age imagery may be construed based on their use in context. Signifiers that functioned in a stand-alone capacity are termed primary signifiers, while signifiers combined with other signifiers to transfer space age meaning are called secondary signifiers.

One of the earliest editorial uses of space age imagery was 'The World of Now,' a nine-page fashion layout from February 1960, using Cape Canaveral as a backdrop. Canaveral was the site of American rocket launches and also served as an aerospace testing site throughout the 1960s. The photographer, Richard Avedon, included a highway sign with the words 'Cape Canaveral' in the opening photo with an actual rocket on the launch pad. The copy on subsequent pages explained the imagery employing basic yet scientific terminology, grounding the entire layout in a base of factual, tangible reality. Avedon takes us to the 'rarely glimpsed behind the scenes' location while the copy identifies less recognizable equipment as 'a rocket tracking antenna,' and a 'pied-a-terre – complete with launching pad and encasement called the umbilical cord' (78, 81).

'The World of Now' layout represents what Barthes termed the 'literal' style of a fashion photograph in which the association of ideas is objective, intentional and direct (1983: 302). However, written signifiers are essential in spelling out the precise motive in using Cape Canaveral to promote these specific fashions: 'Cape Canaveral . . . is the symbol of the pace at which the present is overtaking the future. It is the context in which we should think of today as well as the coming decade' (77). The fashions – straight, geometric and stripped of superfluous decoration – and the technological space age objects are linked conceptually through functional design. '[S]pare and bare' and comprised of 'ordered perfection,' 'the dresses, the antenna, in fact most of the artifacts of our times, are united in a similar austere concept of functional design. Recognition of this relatedness led *Harper's Bazaar* to approach the doors of Cape Canaveral' (77, 85). The motivation for using this specific layout for these particular fashions is

Table 9.1 Space Age Signs

Verbal (Written) Signs

Primary Space Age Signifiers

space age	extraterrestrial	Names of satellites, e.g.:
space ships	plashdown	Sputnik
space travel	earthling	Explorer
spacewalk	Martian	Names of US space exploration
space exploration	Venusian	missions, e.g.:
outer space	Names of astronauts, e.g.:	Project Apollo
rocket	John Glenn	Project Gemini
rocketship	Alan Shepard	Project Mercury
rocketfire	Edward White	Cape Canaveral
interplanetary	Neil Armstrong	Cape Kennedy
Astronaut		

Secondary Space Age Signifiers

missile	earth	constellation
launch	capsule	Names of constellations, e.g.:
universe	star	Aquarius
galaxy	meteor	Orion
milky way	celestial	Names of planets, e.g.:
nova	astral	Mars
cosmos	cosmic	Jupiter

Primary or Secondary Space Age Signifiers

space	orbit
moon	gravity
lunar	earth
satellite	earthly
alien	unearthly

Visual Signs

Primary Visual Signifiers

rocket	spaceship	space capsule	astronauts
spacesuit	spaceboots	space helmets	

Secondary Visual Signifiers

planets	moon	earth	black space with stars

made explicit. The written and visual signifiers are used to symbolize the relationship between the 'form' and 'spirit' of the context (a space age location) and the form and spirit of the fashion (linear, functional, spare). Space age meaning, infused with an emerging concept of a new modernity, could shift smoothly from the cultural world to the fashion good. This was the space age: the place, the fashion, the ideology of the 1960s.

Using locations that functioned as signs of the space age, such as Cape Canaveral, was a common tactic to exemplify modernity in fashion throughout the 1960s. In the case of the October 1965 fashion layout titled 'St. Louis Night in Space,' the reader is taken to McDonnell Aircraft Space Center, which manufactured space exploration vehicles. Signifiers of the space age, such as an actual astronaut in a space suit emerging from a space capsule, are used. Backgrounds include 'a mockup of a Gemini space capsule's electrical system,' and a 'retrograde module' which housed the rocket's breaking system (222–5). One model is called 'lady astronaut' while the other is '*Bazaar*'s space woman.' The outfits include Adolfo's 'exciting space helmet[s],' white and silver designs, described as 'full of pared-down precision.' Visual signifiers drawn from the world of real space technology, such as rockets and astronauts, supported by written space age signifiers, functioned to create space age meaning. Additionally, the fashion forms themselves – silver, white, helmet hat of precise geometric design – were becoming symbols of the space age and of 1960s modernity. The space age fashion code was unfolding.

Prior to the Cape Canaveral layout, the magazine's editors and the advertisers contributed to the symbolic terrain by publishing stories about space exploration. In July 1959 the editors printed a small photograph of a rocket ship being launched to accompany a short news article titled 'From Sputnik to Astronauts':

> as the decade closes seven hand-picked astronauts are vigorously training under the aegis of the U.S. government for man's first return flight into outer space. Glowing with health and confidence, they signal that the incredible day of Flash Gordon is at hand. Science has gone so far so fast, it seems incredible that the birth of the space age occurred less than two years ago when Sputnik I first beeped its way around the earth.

A two-page layout in January 1962 titled 'New Year's Revolutions' further illustrates the development of the space age code. It describes a modern world as seen through the eyes of a visitor to the upcoming World's Fair: 'Satellites will transfer calls through outer space'; and a 'crawling robot' is being developed to explore the moon and Mars. The copy continues: 'Names and terms symbolizing new and difficult concepts of science will gain for [women] the familiarity of the everyday – POGO, OGO, Ego, Echo, Tirus, Midas (the man-made satellites), Dyna-Soar (the Space Glider) . . . Nucleomitophobia (the fear of atomic energy) . . . exobia (extra-terrestrial life)' (85–6). Another example is from the June 1961 issue. Titled 'Avedon on Heroes,' the editorial photo spread by Richard Avedon introduces the 'heroes' of the early space age. Shown are Alan Shepard, the first American in space; John Glenn, the first American to orbit Earth; and Virgil Grissom, one of the first astronauts (who perished in a cockpit fire in 1967). Also introduced are the silver space suits complete with NASA logo patches (78–9).

Thus, we see that *Harper's Bazaar* introduced new words, objects, activities and concepts into the modern woman's vocabulary when publishing non-fashion space age phenomena. Over time the reader learned these signs and became familiar with the modern, space age code as it developed in the cultural world of science and technology.

During this early period, *Harper's Bazaar* not only laid the foundation for a general *space age code*, but also developed a *space age fashion code*. The magazine defined its terms and identified its rules. Likewise, during the middle period of the space age, the code developed, becoming more familiar and allowing the full flower of symbolic meaning in the fashion forms.

Recall the 1960s layout 'Cape Canaveral' where the fashions had the 'Canaveral spirit' and were 'bare' and 'spare,' 'sensib[le],' and comprised of 'ordered perfection.' The copy tells that the dresses and 'artifacts of our times are united in a similar austere concept of functional design.' According to *Harper's Bazaar*, space age fashion of the day was first and foremost functional, austere, spare, sensible and ordered. Therefore, it was modern.

In 'Moonshot,' a fashion editorial from September 1964, *Harper's Bazaar* transferred space age meaning to the fashion forms by simply juxtaposing the fashion photographs with several written space age signifiers. Photographed by Avedon, three fashionable ensembles are shown on two facing pages. The designers are Guy Laroche, Simonetta et Fabiani and André Courrèges. The caption reads 'Moonshot: the Missile Suits . . . Starlight Gleams Pink.' Both 'moonshot' and 'missile' are connotative of 'space age' and are connected to the fashion by simple contiguity or adjacency on the page.

Two of the ensembles are called 'missile suits,' and exemplify an *encapsulation* theme in their formal design. The encapsulating forms are defined here as objects which enclose the body or parts of the body effectively disguising the separation of body parts (similar to Figure 9.1.b). A close-fitting hooded hat is worn with a narrow jumpsuit tucked into boots, which emphasizes the whole unified form. An ensemble features 'bants' described in the copy as 'the combination shoes and leggings melded together.' The shoes are not separating the foot from the leg, but instead joining leg and foot and presenting a sleek line from head to toe. The lines or shapes of the fashion are like a slim missile or rocket, and are also like the spacesuits worn by astronauts which encapsulate and protect the body.

The significance of the models' poses and kinetic signs (signs of motion)

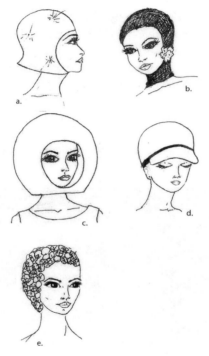

Figure 9.1 Helmet-like hats
　　　　(a) 'Sculpting the Sleek Modern Head,' *Harper's Bazaar*, December
　　　　1968: 131. Design by Mr. John.
　　　　(b) 'Space-Age Helmet,' *Harper's Bazaar*, December 1969: 147.
　　　　Design by Emmé.
　　　　(c) 'Nouveau Pink Helmet . . . Mr. John is First in Space,' *Harper's
　　　　Bazaar*, April 1965: cover.
　　　　(d) 'White Kid Helmet . . . Precise Enough for Spaceship Living,'
　　　　Harper's Bazaar, March 1966: 170. Design by St. Laurent.
　　　　(e) 'Reflection of a Modern Design I,' *Harper's Bazaar*, December
　　　　1969: 185. Design by Emmé.

must be noted. The fashions referred to in 'moonshot' and 'missile' are shown on the models jumping straight up, arms by their sides, toes pointed. The effect is that of a rocket or missile, the body as human projectile. The written signifiers make the poses clear. Without these signifiers the connotation may have been less clear. Barthes would call this written fashion. Connecting space age connotations in these specific fashion forms and these specific poses contributes to the development of an autonomous space age fashion code whereby particular fashion forms became symbols of the space age.

The one or two words used to transfer space age meaning to the fashions were replaced with an extended narrative in a May 1966 advertisement for Clairol 'Moon Babies' lipstick (Figure 9.2). The two-page ad uses numerous written signifiers to tell a story of beautiful otherworldly women called 'moon babies.' According to the story, these beauties use sorcery, extra-sensory perception (ESP) and witchcraft in addition to the lipstick to get their men. Combining a mythical fantasy of the moon babies with fashion rhetoric illustrates what Jakobson (1985: 147) identified as the poetic function of language. Poetic function concerns making a verbal utterance a work of art. The development of an extended narrative

Figure 9.2 Clairol 'Moon Babies' advertisement, *Harper's Bazaar*, May 1966: 26–7. Permission by Clairol/Division of Proctor & Gamble, courtesy of *Harper's Bazaar*.

drawing from a mythical story utilizes more complex connotation to create space age meaning.

The lipstick itself is frosted silver, described as 'New silver-sizzled pales with a sheen never seen on Earth before.' The word 'silver' appears throughout the ad, significant because early spacecrafts and spacesuits were silver colored. During the 1960s, make-up often shimmered with silver metallic particles, and was either denoted as 'space age' or placed in the context of space age imagery. Recall that in the previous discussion of modernist design 'love of machine' is one of the ideals of modernism. Machines are constructed of steel and in its basic form steel appears silver in color. Other metals, such as gold and copper, lack the inherent strength required to create machines used during industrialization and hence do not qualify as modernist materials. Silver is the choice for space age fashion forms.

A Pierre Cardin dress photographed by Bill King for a June 1968 editorial spread is described as space age based on its chrome halter neckline (Figure 9.3). The copy states: 'Cardin on silver . . . space age hanger for a straight drop of black crepe.' It reinforces why the dress is space age: 'Cool, hard gleam against soft . . . skin. Cardin's lucky stone – a diamond – like a rocket's headlight centered in the motif.' A hard-edged silver halter likened to the nose cone of a rocket, clearly denotes a space age fashion.

Fashion avails itself of new technology in many ways. During the 1960s advances in fiber and fabric technology for use in space exploration led to more comfortable and more affordable metallic yarns for fashionable clothing. As a result, fashions made of silver-colored fabric became more popular. In fact, Stanley Marcus wrote in 1982 that a silver nylon tricot nightgown advertised in a 1967 Neiman Marcus Christmas catalogue became 'the single biggest selling article of feminine apparel' sold in the catalogue (115). Not only does a 'silver' metallic finish signify 'modernism,' but the use of silver in fashion objects presents the body as machine-like, symbolically placing the wearer within the machine-loving modernist culture of the space age.

Extensive written signifiers appear in the March 1966 issue. Titled 'See Paris,' the nine-page fashion layout photographed by James Moore contains three full pages of written signifiers penned by editor Nancy White. Here the space signifiers function as double entendres: 'Paris is discovering covering and uncovering new areas in space. The part between the shoulders . . . The space . . . between the knee and the hem – four, three, two, one inches? . . . Space as you can see, is as much a topic in Paris as it is in Houston' (170). Space in this case refers to both outer space and the visual space in the fashion forms. Note the metaphoric use of the

Figure 9.3 'Cardin's Rocket Dress,' *Harper's Bazaar*, June 1968: 112.
Photograph by Bill King©; collection of Janet McClellan; courtesy of
Harper's Bazaar.

countdown – four, three, two, one – referring not to a rocket launch, but
to skirt lengths. Additionally Paris, the capital of the fashion world, is
linked to Houston, home of Cape Canaveral, ground control for all the
United States space missions. Thus, Paris, symbolic of fashion power, is
linked to Houston, symbolic of space age technology and dominance. By
extension, the two sites, Paris and Houston, are conjoined as symbols of
modernity.

Written imagery in the fashion layout is combined with other poetic metaphors such as 'the stretch between armhole and hip is missile straight' and 'the booster rocket – a whole dress of plastic paillettes.' The coats, dresses and hats (Figure 9.1.d) are linked once again to space forms such as missiles and rockets; described in terms of their appropriateness for the space age. For example, 'coats so straight . . . all clutter removed . . . precise enough to walk in space and rendezvous' and 'Baby dresses are set for a soft landing on the moon' (170–3). The fashion editors, drawing from the world of fashion exploration, directly followed astronaut Edward White's first walk in space in 1965. These expressions of modernity may be construed as an 'attempt to reconcile the reality of a fissured culture with the fantasy of utopia' (Wilson 1985: 245–7).

The 'See Paris' fashion layout utilizes only written signifiers to transfer space age meaning to the fashion. In fact, written imagery appeared in 97 per cent of all the 460 space age units documented in *Harper's Bazaar* from 1957 to 1972. Fifty-eight per cent used *only* written signifiers. This finding underscores the importance of written language in transferring meaning from the cultural world to the fashion object.

Only 3 per cent of the space age imagery relied solely on visual signifiers to transfer space age meaning to the fashion. The clearest example is from an October 1966 advertisement for fabrics and fashions made from Celanese acetate (Figure 9.4). It is part of a multi-page advertisement, each page showing a model with her mode of transportation. There is a jeweled car, a motorcycle, a boat, a unicycle and a snow-mobile. The night setting of a city street features the title caption 'The Great Arrival.' The model emerges from a space capsule covered in jewels. The fashionable space age woman has arrived at the opera in her new mode of transportation – the chicly jeweled space capsule. The capsule is on a smaller scale than an actual space capsule but its signification is clear: this is the space age!

By the time this ad appeared in 1966, both print and broadcast media had depicted numerous *actual* space capsules. The Mercury and Gemini space missions, including the splashdowns of the breakaway capsules, had been shown over and over across the world in locations ranging from elementary schools to homes and businesses. America tuned in no matter what time of day to live coverage and watched the astronauts emerge from their silver wombs bobbing in the ocean to be scooped up by the NASA rescue crew. The capsule and the astronauts functioned as icons of the space age; moreover, they pointed toward the excellence of modern American technology, becoming stand-alone *symbols* of the space age. By 1966 the modern space age woman had learned the code and shared in the symbolic terrain based in technology and reinforced through the media.

Figure 9.4 'The Great Arrival' jewelled in space capsule, *Harper's Bazaar*, October 1966: 74. Permission by Celanese Acetate LLC, courtesy of *Harper's Bazaar*.

The featured fashion in 'The Great Arrival' is a red crepe shift with an asymmetric yoke by Kasper for Joan Leslie. The style is not particularly 'space age' aside from being clean and spare, stripped of superfluous decoration. It is the capsule that evokes the space age connotation. By contrast, the cover of the May 1966 issue features a space age look that is also described as space age: 'A twenty-first century, knee-stopped jumpsuit of supple quilted vinyl that cleverly molds the body missile. The head: helmeted geometrically – All ready, with a bold-faced watch that runs on tomorrow's time to sail into the future or on the Seven Seas.' In addition to the white and geometric design and the helmet hat, the jumpsuit appears over and over as a 'space age fashion' suggesting a theme of *encapsulation*.

Encapsulating forms appeared many times. Recall the 'Moonshot' spread previously discussed. Other examples include the jumpsuited 'Galactic Girl,' photographed by Avedon, from April 1965 who has a clear plastic bubble over her head. The cover of the same issue shows model Jean Shrimpton wearing a 'nouveau pink helmet' by Mr John (Figure 9.1.c) described as being 'first in space.' The helmet hat itself is an encapsulating form, and it is repeatedly described as space age or placed in a space age context.

The concept of encapsulation relates to modernism. Modernist design holds 'individuation' as one of its ideals. Encapsulating forms function to individuate, creating a kind of symbolic protection from the hostile, fast-changing environment of the space age. Kurt Back (1985: 12) posited that the influence of modernism has helped individuals accept and adapt to modern technology. He further alleged that fashion trends keep pace with the modernist realities of change and technology by using technical advances in fabric and design, accentuating the individual and flaunting the details of fashion construction. André Courrèges, whose fashions were featured in the April 1965 issue of *Harper's Bazaar*, best exemplifies the 'flaunting of construction' with his use of welt seams and bias edging. Courrèges is often identified as a 'space age designer.'

The December 1969 issue shows an encapsulating cape accompanied by the following copy: 'Lacquer grape space-age cape sweeps the sand as if it were moon dust' (147). The glossy nylon ciré cape is worn with a matching helmet-like hat (Figure 9.1.b). The photograph, cropped into a circle, makes the model appear as if viewed through a hole or scope. The circular shapes and spherical forms echo orbital movement.

Copy in a September 1967 advertisement for Estée Lauder skin care uses words to transfer space age meaning to the fashion product: 'a new collection of six space-age treatment essentials so fast acting they make long complicated beauty rituals obsolete'(46–7). Further, the association with space age meaning connotes modernity. Using the new space age products would spare one from 'obsolete' beauty rituals and therefore would bring one in line with modernity.

Labeling a fashion 'space age' transfers space age meaning directly to the fashion object. Further, specific fashion forms repeatedly signified as space age became space age *fashion symbols* on their own. Fashion symbolic of the space age includes silver metallic fabric, make-up and jewelry; the head-encapsulating form of the helmet hat and the jumpsuit; the color white; overtly geometric and functional designs. A pattern of stylistic signifiers repeated over time solidifies a space age fashion code, a *lexicon* of specific fashion symbols.

By reading *Harper's Bazaar* during the 1960s, the modern woman of fashion could learn the facts about the early space age world, become familiar with its symbolic terrain and consume the signs of the space age because she learned the space age code – a code which looked to modernist design and ideology for its underlying structure, and which was reiterated visually and verbally.

Space Age Imagery Over Time

The amount of space age imagery in *Harper's Bazaar* changed over time as seen in Figure 9.5. During the earliest years of the space age, from 1957 to 1960, a few space age images began to appear in *Harper's Bazaar*. Some of these were advertisements for 'rocket-powered' automobiles or 'space-age appliances.' However, their use declined in 1961 and 1962, almost disappearing in 1963.

The fluctuation in appearance of space age imagery in *Harper's Bazaar* may have been due to uncertainty over the value of space age imagery as a tool to promote fashion. In the early years of the space race the United States was viewed as a laggard playing catch-up with the Soviet Union. Political debates questioned the purpose of the space program in 1963 and 1964 after Kennedy's assassination (McDougall 1985).

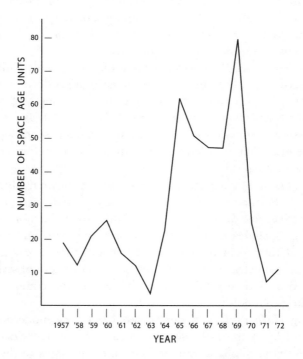

Figure 9.5 Number of space age units over time.

These early years were marked by an increasing visibility of space age objects and concepts; the first manned American space flights with Mercury astronauts such as Alan Shepard, John Glenn and Vigil Grissom took place at this time. The June 1961 *Harper's Bazaar* hailed the men as 'Heroes.' Within a few years, space age imagery appeared in the context of fashion.

The largest amount of space age imagery in the magazine coincided with the most widely publicized and greatest achievements in US space exploration which occurred between 1965 and 1969. Of the years under consideration, 1965 and 1966 had the most manned US space missions. The technological breakthroughs of the Gemini program (which would lead to the success of the Apollo missions) included the first spacewalks, the first space rendezvous, and the first docking of two vehicles in space – all highly publicized evidence that the idea of space exploration was no longer science fiction but grounded in reality.

More space age imagery appeared in *Harper's Bazaar* in 1969 than in any other year. The Apollo lunar landing in 1969, during the Nixon administration, marked the apex of the space age. Use of space age imagery specifically related to the moon was common at this time and both editors and advertisers drew upon the climactic and evocative pictures of the events to promote fashion and modernity. When astronaut Neil Armstrong, the first man to walk on the moon, declared 'one small step for man, one giant leap for mankind,' he drew a circle around all of mankind, not just Americans. The reality of the achievements of space exploration culminated in the planting of the American flag on the lunar surface, which became a symbol of American modernity: a source of pride and a sign of American *power*.

A substantial drop in the use of space imagery occurred during the final years of the space age from 1970 to 1972. Although subsequent Apollo lunar landing projects contributed to our knowledge about the moon, the earth and the solar system, these years were a reorganization period for NASA. National priorities were reassessed in light of financial constraints and unmet needs in the social services sector. Interest in space exploration phenomena declined after the climax of the lunar landing. Also, changing socio-cultural values impacted the ideology of modernity itself.

In 1970, after the lunar landing, the quantity of space age imagery in *Harper's Bazaar* dropped by 66 per cent from the high in 1969 and continued to drop in 1971 and 1972. Further, examples of space age imagery were increasingly non-fashion in nature. Small ads in the back of the magazine featured the stuffed comic character Snoopy dressed as an astronaut (June 1969: 181) and a watch depicting a lunar module (May

1970: 193). Many examples were retrospectives or editorial commentaries that looked back at the 1960s and used written space age imagery only.

The most meaningful fashion editorial during this late period was shown in October 1972. Hiro photographed a model wearing a helmet-hat like one from December 1969 (Figure 9.1.b). The woman is called an 'American Space Age Siren' (87). In the close-up headshot she gazes into space – upward and to the *left*. In the background a fire-powered rocket moves *from right to left* in a window-like frame. No longer luring us, the siren appears to be watching an age gone by . . . bidding adieu . . . the space age had passed. During the final years of the space age, i.e. 1970–72, – space age meaning was no longer a useful vehicle to express modernity in fashion.

Space age imagery became an ineffective vehicle to transfer the ideology of modernity to fashion because the space age itself had become passé. The success of the lunar landing reduced public excitement and press copy. Further, during the late 1960s and the early 1970s the value of space technology was questioned. Enormous social and cultural changes occurred during the 1960s, which were manifested in the civil rights movements, the 'Black Power' movement, the peace movement, the new religion movements, ecological awareness, and the rise of the drug culture (Haskins and Benson 1988). Although 'winning' the space race may have signified pride in United States technology, to those involved in the growing counterculture it increasingly signified all that was wrong with the world. It could be argued that the increasing use of technology in the consumer culture augmented the potential for manipulative use of the mass media by those in power and could stifle political dissent (Ash 1999: 131). To the counterculture, the space race signified an elitism and a hunger for power that de-emphasized humanist values. The focus on the individual eclipsed the value of community.

In the wake of the space age, values shifted away from modernism toward a *new* modernity. Attention shifted to the 'return to nature' and concerns about the earth. Interest rose in alternative lifestyles, such as communal living, and in alternative religions. These religions referenced Eastern philosophy and used meditation techniques to focus on inner space as opposed to outer space.

New softer, more romantic styles began to appear. Peasant and ethnic looks gained importance by the early 1970s. These styles did not exhibit the functional modernist qualities of sleekness, rationalism, geometry and austerity. Instead they displayed a mélange of decoration – flounces, ruffles, layers, patches, beads, embroidery and textured patterned fabrics, often appearing simultaneously. The new post-space age *zeitgeist* based in anti-modernism was underway, and the new fashion forms reflected the changing postmodern ideology.

Conclusion

The United States' space exploration program supplied new signs of modernity to the world in general, and to the world of fashion. These signs took shape as ideas, materials, images, new vocabulary and new uses of old words. New phenomena contributed to the definition of the modern space age world in the 1960s. Editors, photographers and art directors of *Harper's Bazaar* disseminated space age meaning by using basic icons, indicators and complex symbols. These space age signs included visual imagery, but written imagery was overwhelmingly used to structure a codified symbolic terrain which could be widely understood and which signified American power.

When the space age began with the Soviet launch of sputnik in 1957, the ideas and images associated with outer space were either in the realm of science fiction or specialized knowledge. However, with each successive achievement in space technology came new ways of looking at the world – a new modernity.

The concept of modernity may best be viewed in the guise of its temporal meaning and form. In 1965 modernity was cloaked in the values of modernist technology and love of the machine. Space age fashion symbols included helmet-hats, silver, and Courrèges-style dresses. In 1972 modernity reflected the antithesis of modernism. Old-fashioned values of naturalism, romanticism and humanism took the form of earth shoes and feathers, peasant blouses and granny dresses.

Today, modernity takes shape – transforming and redefining itself – from the myriad of ideas, words, materials and processes which present themselves all around us. We may not be able to view the current modernity or its late-postmodern whole until we gain historical perspective. But we grasp pieces of its nebulous form: a collection of disjointed meanings – icons, indices and symbols – of the modern world of now.

Notes

1. Space age imagery was quantified by counting pertinent *signs* – word or image – on each page in the magazine from 1957 to 1972. If space age imagery appeared in any form or combination of forms on a page, the page was counted as one *unit*.

2. Of the 38,138 pages examined, 460 (1.21 per cent) contained space age units. Editorial use accounted for 72 per cent, while advertising made up the remaining 28 per cent (Baldaia 1993).

References

Ash, J. (1999), 'The Aesthetics of Absence: Clothes Without People in Paintings,' in A. de la Haye and E. Wilson (eds), *Defining Dress: Dress as Object, Meaning and Identity*, Manchester: Manchester University.

Back, K. (1985), 'Modernism and Fashion: A Social Psychological Interpretation,' in M. Solomon (ed.), *The Psychology of Fashion*, Lexington, MA: D.C. Heath.

Baldaia, S. (1993), 'Modernity in Space Age Fashion: A Semiotic and Historical Analysis of Meaning Transfer,' Unpublished master's thesis, University of Rhode Island.

Barthes, R. (1977), 'Rhetoric of the Image' in *Image, Music, Text*, Trans. S. Heath, New York: Hill and Wang.

—— (1983) [1967], *The Fashion System*, Trans. M. Ward and R. Howard, New York: Hill and Wang.

Berman, M. (1988), 'The Experience of Modernity,' in J. Thackara (ed.), *Design After Modernism*, London: Thames and Hudson.

Blumer, H. (1969), 'Fashion: From Class Differentiation to Collective Selection,' *The Sociological Quarterly* 10(3): 327–40.

Bullock, A. and O. Stallybrass (eds) (1977), *The Harper Dictionary of Modern Thought*, New York: Harper & Row Publishers.

Eco, U. (1976), *A Theory of Semiotic*, Bloomington: Indiana University Press.

Fuller, P. (1988), 'The Search for a Postmodern Aesthetic,' in J. Thackara (ed.), *Design After Modernism*, London: Thames and Hudson.

Guy, A., E. Green and M. Banim (eds) (2001), 'Introduction,' *Through the Wardrobe: Women's Relationships With Their Clothes*, Oxford: Berg.

Harper's Bazaar, January 1957–December 1972.

Haskins, J. and K. Benson (1988), *The '60s Reader*, New York: Viking Press.

Jakobson, R. (1985), 'Closing Statement: Linguistics and Poetics,' in R. Innis (ed.), *Semiotics: An Introductory Anthology*, Bloomington: Indiana University Press.

Lauer, J. and R. Lauer (1981), *Fashion Power: The Meaning of Fashion in American Society*, Upper Saddle River, NJ: Prentice-Hall.

Marcus, S. (1982), *His and Hers: The Fantasy World of the Neiman-Marcus Catalog*, New York: Viking Press.

Mathews, J. (1991) 'Falling In and Out of Love – With Space Missions,' *Providence Journal Bulletin*, January 5, Sec. A: 13.

McCracken, G. (1988), *Culture and Consumption*, Bloomington: Indiana University Press.

McDougall, W. (1985), *The Heavens and the Earth*, New York: Basic Books Inc.

Morehead, P. (1985), *The New American Roget's College Thesaurus in Dictionary Form*, New York: Signet.

Peirce, C.S. (1985 [1893–1903]), 'Logic as Semiotic: The Theory of Signs,' in R. Innis (ed.) *Semiotics: An Introductory Anthology*, Bloomington: Indiana University Press.

Saussure, F. (1985 [1959]) 'The Linguistic Sign', in R. Innis (ed.), *Semiotics: An Introductory Anthology*, Bloomington: Indiana University Press.

Wilson, E. (1985), *Adorned in Dreams: Fashion and Modernity*, London: Virago. Repr. Berkeley: University of California Press, 1987.

10

Dressing for Success: The Re-Suiting of Corporate America in the 1970s

Patricia A. Cunningham

Editors' Introduction: Although America placed a man on the moon in 1969, it was not able to see the end of fighting in Vietnam until 1973. Fashion during the early years of the 1970s therefore still focused on a protest/hippie look: peasant styles of long skirts worn with shawls and Indian gauze blouses, as well as jeans. Any natural fiber would do. Japanese designers Kenzo, Issey Miyake and others made news on the fashion front while English designers Zandra Rhodes and Vivienne Westwood challenged Paris with avant-garde styles. Yet, by the mid 1970s few young Americans were paying attention. They were focusing on getting and keeping a job. The era, named the 'me generation,' was just beginning to see the efforts of the feminists and environmentalists come to fruition. Young protesters and returning Vietnam veterans competed for scarce jobs. Looking good became important for success. However, the decade had seen a revival of polyester fabrics for men's fashion. There was so much garish and bright, textured polyester used in men's suits, that by mid-decade some authorities began to argue for a return to the classics for menswear suiting. Business consultant and author John T. Molloy presented his case in two 'dress for success' books, one for men in 1975 and one for women in 1977. Americans in the workplace took notice. Women, in particular, adopted the skirted-suit look as they struggled to be taken seriously in male-oriented businesses.

John T. Molloy's best-selling advice books, *Dress for Success* (1975) for men and *The Women's Dress for Success Book* (1977), helped establish new dress codes for American businesses. By the early 1970s American men had already experienced increased interest in men's fashion with the 'peacock revolution,' and were now being regaled with a wide assortment of casual looks, most notably the leisure suit that came in a confusing array of styles, colors and fabrics that ultimately led to its demise. The hippie and other counter culture movements of the 1960s and 1970s left a whole generation of young people with a wardrobe of jeans and second-hand clothing, but little knowledge of appropriate business attire. Sportswear had gained a greater share of the men's wear industry than ever before. Sales of traditional suits were down. As former hippies and other young people grew older they realized that there were alternative ways to 'change the world,' and they sought to enter the established workforce. At the time, however, jobs were scarce. And to make things worse, the many options in clothing caused confusion about appropriate attire for business. In order to be taken seriously, it became clear that former hippies and wearers of the leisure suit needed to learn how to dress appropriately. As noted in *Forbes*, 'a young guy can't go looking for a job in jeans and a Levi jacket and relate to the guy sitting across the desk from him' ('Good-bye, Love Beads' 1976: 20). Appearance had become a factor in competition and advancement up the corporate ladder. John Molloy came to the rescue with *Dress for Success*.

It was not just men who needed advice. When more college-educated women entered the workforce in management positions, and needed sartorial advice to compete with men, Molloy published *The Women's Dress for Success Book*. Molloy's books, based on his research with executives, changed the look of corporate America (1975: 20–31). These small, but influential, books breathed new life into the men's suit industry. They not only aided many established retailers/manufacturers like Brooks Brothers, but they spawned a host of new companies that specialized in business attire for women such as Liz Claiborne and Jones of New York.

This essay examines a number of cultural phenomena that made 'dressing right' so crucial to success for both men and women in the American workplace in the last half of the 1970s. During the preceding decades changing demographics, economics, politics, media, music and arts had an effect on the mindset of young adults who expressed themselves through anti-fashion. The impact of the women's movement in changing ideas about 'women's place' in American culture was crucial. This social phenomenon led to women's acceptance in higher education, their entry into law and medicine, and a corresponding rise of new businesses catering to the 'new woman' in the workplace. It will be argued that the re-suiting of America was not simply a marketing plan, and that it occurred through a complex amalgam of events.

Men's Clothing: A Brief History

During the twentieth century until just after the Second World War menswear included formal traditional suits (single or double-breasted, the former usually worn with a vest), and casual dress for a variety of informal activities and school. Casual dressing for non-work occasions had increased during the pre-war years especially during the 1930s, when casual trousers worn with sweaters, tweed jackets and blazers became the prescribed look for many (Craik 1994: 190–5). Despite an increased desire for casual dress following the Second World War, the mindset of the 1950s became one of conformity symbolized best perhaps by the men's gray flannel suit. However, Americans were beginning to question post-war values. Some began to protest the strict conformity and gendered expectations as seen in the behavior of the Beats (as discussed in Chapter 8) as well as in films of the 1950s that depicted rebellious, restless, and tormented young men wearing blue jeans worn with T-shirts and leather jackets. The best-known were James Dean and Marlon Brando in the films that made their names house-hold words – *Rebel Without a Cause* (1955), *On the Waterfront* (1954), and *The Wild One* (1953). This rebel look also was seen on Elvis Presley who had become a heart-throb in the mid 1950s. From then on, the growing number of middle-class youth in America set in motion a number of new trends. They expressed themselves and their beliefs through their dress.

Disenchantment with the status quo and rebelliousness took different paths. One led to the growing subversion of dress codes by work clothes, expressed best through denim jeans; another route sent young men on a trip toward mass consumption and a renewed interest in fashion. The latter group was aided on its journey by magazines like *Playboy* and *GQ*, and advertisements that promoted the pleasure of consumption and the virtues of living and dressing well. There was a lightening up of the work ethic. The new morality of the times embraced the virtues of pleasure (Conekin 2000: 447–55). At the same time, menswear manufacturers in Europe and America were gearing up to provide suits and sportswear that reflected this new young man with an appetite for clothes (Craik 1994: 192).

The Peacock Revolution in Menswear: 1950s and 1960s

Farid Chenoune stresses the importance of Italy in creating a distinctive new style that became the passion of the growing number of consumer-oriented youth. Italy had many tailors who created elegant, tasteful casual suits. Goods in Italy were desirable because they were abundant, inexpensive and made by experienced crafts people. The suits had narrow pants, copied no doubt from the narrow look of American jeans and chinos. The jackets were short, single-breasted with three buttons, and had sloping shoulders. They became the standard look for young men (Chenoune 1993: 245–6). By 1956 the Italian style became known as the 'Continental look' in the United States, and gained ground as a serious rival to the 'Ivy League look,' the standard gray flannel suit. The latter was Brooks Brothers' 'Number One [selling] Sack Suit' (Chenoune 1993: 250).

Clothiers in France and England began to make inexpensive copies of the Italian style for their youthful customers. The French also emulated American styles and English styles. In England the Italian look became the style of the 'mods,' or modernists, a group of working-class youth. Best known of the new breed of clothiers was John Stephens, who arrived at the new fashion center in Carnaby Street in 1958. Stephens was so successful with his clothing business that he became known as the 'King of Carnaby Street' and the 'Mod millionaire' (Chenoune 1993: 257). Stephens' businesses, and similar shops, offered inexpensive ready-to-wear garments adapted from the Italian and American styles that were right on the mark style-wise, and unlike traditional, conservative Savile Row tailored garments, they did not have to last.

In the 1960s the dress of the mods became the style of the Beatles. The style worn by the Beatles actually had origins not in Italian menswear, but in a suit designed by Paris couturier Pierre Cardin, who in 1960 launched a new 'youthful' style of men's jacket made of corduroy with no tails or collar. The next year, a ready-to-wear Cardin line of menswear became available. It marked the beginning of a system for ready-made menswear with an attached designer label, and strengthened the move toward more fashion shows for menswear (Chenoune 1993: 276–7). By the mid 1960s Pierre Cardin's ready-to-wear label promoted a long, slightly frock-coated silhouette. By this time it was clear that there were many new men's styles being introduced. The proliferation of these styles and new colors is what is called the 'Peacock Revolution' in men's dress.

These new styles did not appeal to everyone. In the 1960s stores like Brooks Brothers and J. Press in New York and Boston offered typical Ivy League casual clothing and conservative suits and furnishings. Tweed jackets, gray flannel trousers, chinos, Oxford cloth button-down shirts and rep ties were still being worn. Stores and their customers no doubt still considered these styles to be more appropriate than the new mod styles. By the mid 1960s many young people were moving away from questions of fashion to express their sentiments about the expanding Vietnam War, nuclear power, and the endangered environment.

Following in the footsteps of the Beats, young people in California began not only to voice the same sentiments, but to create a lifestyle based on them. Many were students, or former students, who rejected anything that suggested authority or tradition. They expressed their discontent through their dress. These young people were at the forefront of the hippie movement, whose adoption of anti-fashion, non-traditional clothing was one phenomenon of many that led to the decline in the traditional menswear market.

The Hippies

The 1960s started out on a high note with the election of John F. Kennedy to the presidency. However, the decade quickly became immersed in national trauma with the assassinations of John and Ted Kennedy and Martin Luther King, riots over civil rights, and other perceived failures in society. The hippies came into being in the midst of these crises. They finally emerged as a definitive subculture in the Haight Ashbury section of San Francisco, but they had sympathizers throughout the country who easily caught the drift of their cause through the popular music of the times. In their discontent, hippies sought self-knowledge through drugs, sex and spiritual advice. Their new manner of dressing distinguished them from the mainstream culture. Hippie clothing is often described as anti-fashion, created from patched clothing mixed together with cast-offs, second-hand clothing, and flamboyant accessories (Polhemus and Procter 1978). It might include a mixture of rumpled past styles and ethnic clothing. The movement generated many merchants selling clothing from Africa, India, Afghanistan and the like. Hippies disdained new clothing and anything made of synthetic fibers, such as polyester and nylon, or with wrinkle-free finishes. In fact, they liked wrinkles. And they especially liked worn denim that by the end of the decade became the uniform of all disillusioned youth (Polhemus and Procter 1978: 260–2). One aspect that was particularly appealing about the hippie clothing was that it offered a great deal of comfort.

When the hippie movement expanded, its clothing began to infiltrate fashion. Young Americans outside of the hippie culture dressed in second-hand clothing that reflected a sense of romanticism that was connected to hippie style. Even though second-hand was not really old, it was old enough to be new. It was symbolic of the rejection of the larger world of consumerism. The hippie American style was copied abroad. It was so pervasive in England that by 1966 the mod look of the peacock generation

was out; in its place Mr. Fish, a London menswear shop, offered a sophisticated version of male hippie fashion (Polhemus and Procter 1978: 262).
Fish preferred self-expression in dress to conformity to any set style,
including mod or hippie. He offered beautiful fabrics in unusual colors and
shirts made of the same.

Leisure Suits

While the adoption of hippie styles and the new mod styles deflated the
traditional menswear industry, they were not the only looks available to
men. Another type of menswear had been making inroads since the early
1950s. This was the leisure suit, that is, a suit to be worn for leisure activities. It was far less formal than even the casual tweed jacket but was not
for sports. It was unstructured, with a jacket more like a shirt, and worn
largely for comfort. While many Americans associate the 'leisure suit' with
pastel polyester textured fabrics and bell-bottom trousers, these were actually fairly late bloomers in the leisure suit stable.

John Molloy provided a history of the leisure suit, noting that it derived
from the British officer's battle jacket worn during the desert campaigns.
On returning home the officers continued to wear it as a status symbol, but
only in casual settings. However, the jacket became popular with big-game
hunters for its comfort and ruggedness. Hemingway adopted the style. In
1975 Molloy stated that this safari style remained a legitimate style for
gentlemen to wear in appropriate leisure settings, not at work (1975: 172).
The *Chicago Tribune* advertised soft shirt-based suits as 'leisure suits' in
the 1950s. These were suggested casual garments for older men, not young
men.

While these were early examples of clothing for leisure, it is quite likely
that the leisure suit worn by men in the early 1970s evolved from styles
promoted in Europe where there was a strong effort to create more
comfortable clothing for men. As an alternative to the closer fitting
Continental styled suits, some French designers offered soft comfortable
leisure suits for men. In the late 1960s a new line by the French menswear
designer Ted Lapidus, who called himself a 'suit engineer,' offered soft
unstructured suits, and later safari jackets, for celebrities such as Roman
Polanski, Jean-Paul Belmondo, John Lennon, and other members of the
Beatles. Lapidus had been dressing the Beatles since the early 1960s
(Chenoune 1993: 277–8). Lapidus, Cardin, and others promoted luxury
men's ready-to-wear manufacturing in France that included leisure wear
and formal wear. The idea of more comfortable menswear gained support

from Yves St. Laurent, who in 1969 began to promote styles that would 'free men from their shackles.' His safari jackets with Russian belts and sailor tunics were offered for both men and women in his Rive Gauche store. Similar styles were promoted in *Esquire* magazine in March 1972. Comfort had been a concern even with the new suit styles of the Peacock Revolution. Gilbert Féruch, who had created a suit with a Mao collar, also called the Nehru, Oriental, Lenin, and Zhivago collar, saw this suit as a reform garment. The prime virtue of the collar was that it eliminated the need for a tie and did not reveal a shirt collar, thus offering comfort to the wearer. The designer Michel Schreiber radically challenged the constraints of the man's suit by eliminating linings, and interlinings, doing away with shoulder pads and waistbands, and banning mock buttonholes on sleeves and lapels. He used sturdy fabrics (denim, wool and corduroy). He also included patch pockets, double seams and metal buttons. The new designs were a big leap for many manufacturers, and at first had little impact on the suit industry. Another designer, Ruben Torres, who promoted tight pants and tunics with side zippers, actually gained the backing of Hart, Schaffner & Marx in 1969 (Chenoune 1993: 284). While at first their influence did not appear significant, when these designers switched from woven fabrics to knits they took off. Their styles were fashionable, and in some respects might be viewed simply as a casual version of the mod and Continental styles associated with the Peacock Revolution in menswear.

As has been suggested, leisure suits were worn by entertainers and celebrities, and they were being produced by well-known menswear designers. These factors lent the leisure suit a certain amount of cachet, which led to its being copied for the ready-to-wear mass market. Unlike tailored jackets, the leisure suit was relatively easy to produce, and thus would be less expensive than a classic suit. At the manufacturing end, producers always sought ways to cut costs by eliminating many of the traditional construction details of suits. In seeking out knits for this purpose, they discovered polyester, which had been used extensively in the mod clothing of the 1960s. In switching from wovens to knits, they were able to further reduce their costs. Thus, between 1968 and 1973 manufacturers successfully produced soft, wrinkle-free suits with no linings.

Polyester, however, was new to the leisure suit market. Previous fabrics for leisure suits were denim, corduroy and other sturdy fabrics, not traditional wool suiting materials. The makers of textured polyester fibers and polyester wovens and knits apparently sought to create colorful materials that would appeal to the young. However, the overproduction of polyester led to a drop in price that immediately allowed the lower end of the market to produce polyester suits in great numbers in colors that were far from traditional. Not only was the style more casual, but leisure suits – in mint green, baby blue, oranges and yellows – also represented a departure from typical menswear colors. Instead of appealing to the young, its low cost, and wrinkle-free qualities allowed the leisure suit to become a favorite of retirees (especially in warm climates), but also of the working class. A Du Pont executive informed me that only salesmen wore the leisure suit, and if a sales manager wore one, he never wore it in the main office.

The effect of these lower-priced casual styles was to undermine the suit industry, for the leisure style began to dominate men's fashion and the market place, replacing the traditional suit (Figure 10.1). The adoption of the leisure suit by so many American males is a clear example of the diffusion of fashion, and a clear indicator that not only is there such a thing as men's fashion, but it can sometimes go awry (Craik 1994: 176–80). Owing in part, no doubt, to its unusual colors and connection with the working class, the polyester leisure suit lost any fashionable cachet that it once had, and instead became the brunt of jokes, jokes that soon crossed over to anything made of polyester. It did not take long before the suit went out of favor, and along with it the miracle fiber, polyester.

Many new ideas were introduced by French menswear designers during the 1960s, and some of them became elements of 1970s' menswear, especially the unstructured leisure suits, but also the bell-bottom trousers that have equal association with the decade. A tailor by the name of Marina, on rue Vernier in Paris, first cut bell-bottom trousers in 1962. He named them *marinettes* for their similarity to wide-bottomed Navy pants. The

Figure 10.1 Leisure suits worn on the University of Rhode Island campus, 1977–8. Polyester suits were priced right and could be found in many styles and colors. Courtesy of Special Collections, University of Rhode Island Library.

tailor and garment manufacturer Simon Cressy picked up on the idea with the encouragement of his two fashionable sons (Chenoune 1993: 267).

Acceptance of the leisure style came at the end of the hippie movement and the Peacock Revolution in menswear. The leisure suit, or shirt suit as it was sometimes called, was immensely popular in the early 1970s, but when it began to lose its trendiness, and became the brunt of jokes, men became perplexed about where they could wear it. Also occurring at this time was a movement toward more casual dress in the workplace. With so many options, men no doubt were simply confused regarding the etiquette of dress. It can be argued that the introduction of these new styles in America led to uncertainty about appropriate dress for the workplace. The apparent doubt encouraged John Molloy to publish an advice book for men on how to dress.

The Return of the Classic Suit

It appears that before John Molloy wrote his now famous books, there had been rumblings that a change was in order. As noted by *Forbes* magazine in 1974, the men's fashion industry was organized to the extent that there were regular conventions twice a year for manufacturers to show their wares to the 8,000 menswear 'buyers for the nation's 20,000 men's clothing stores.' At the Dallas Convention Center in 1974, the middle-of-the-market buyers (60 per cent of the market) were shunning the more contemporary shantung jumpsuits and patchwork jackets, and heading for the safer classics – blue blazers, gray slacks, and button-down shirts ('Year of the Dress' 1974: 29). The trend away from high styles to the classics may have been a further motivation for Molloy to write his book. *Forbes* reported that suit sales jumped 4.4 per cent in 1976. They observed that the more stylish Continental suits by designers Lanvin, St. Laurent and Cardin were being bought by young men, but that classic suits also were being purchased by 'the guy who never bought a suit in his life' ('Good-bye, Love Beads' 1976: 19–20). They noted that even the vested suit was making a comeback.

Dress for Success, the Book

Prior to writing *Dress for Success*, John T. Molloy had been an image consultant to major corporations, advising them on problems of dress. He wrote a column on business dress in the *Los Angeles Times*. He published many articles in business magazines and was a contributor to *Success* magazine. He was on radio and television shows, and lectured extensively throughout the United States, especially on college campuses, on the subject of dressing for success. His campaign reached across America; he was not elitist, yet his model for success was the business dress of the elite.

One of the topics covered in his book for men is 'who not to ask for advice.' The list included wives, salesmen, and fashion designers. Molloy stressed the importance of his advice, which he said was based on his own research (11–19). He experimented with situational research, testing company employees' reactions to clothing in 'real' business situations. In one test he discovered that the upper-middle-class beige raincoat received more positive responses than the lower-middle-class black raincoat. Thus he advised men to purchase the beige coat (24–36).

Molloy stated that the suit was the most important garment in a man's wardrobe. He stressed this point because his research revealed that suits were authority symbols. He offered advice on how to buy a suit, noting that the fabric, pattern, fit, color and style must be appropriate to the job and the person (37–56). He advised against the high style of Cardin for just anyone. Shirts, he felt, were a way to maximize power. That meant all cotton, or cotton-poly, plain or striped fabrics (no fancies), and long sleeves. Ties he believed were a great status symbol and should be selected with care. He discussed the importance of accessories, and went into detail on correct dress for different sports and casual wear. Molloy also offered suggestions for lawyers on how to dress for a judge, for executives on how to create a corporate image, and for job seekers on how to dress for an interview. Finally he offered suggestions on how men should dress for women (176–85).

Although he recognized that men might not want to shop, he encouraged them not only to 'cross shop' in order to compare prices, but to shop during the sales for the best value. He recognized that his readers came from different areas of business, so he advised men to dress for their product and for their customers. They should consider age, ethnicity, and occupation. He also noted that there were regional differences in business dress that needed to be considered (128–35).

He had no use for the rainbow-colored so-called 'leisure suit' that manufacturers pressed on unsuspecting men. Molloy found the myriad of colors and fabrics offensive. However, Molloy did not wholly blame the manufacturers. His understanding was that 'the general public insists that its basically lower-middle-class clothing prejudice be catered to, and each fashion designer pushes further and further out to stay ahead of his competitor' (172–3).

Several magazines reviewed Molloy's *Dress for Success*. *Nations Business* (1977) carried an article titled 'Dress to Succeed' that discussed

John Molloy's advice to business leaders. The article focused on Molloy's observation that successful men and women wear conservative clothing, and that this clothing demands respect. The writer attended a lecture given by Molloy in Kansas City, and thus offered readers a few of Molloy's quips from that talk: 'Never wear a shirt that looks like a pajama top.' 'Wear a bow tie and no one will take you seriously,' and 'If you have a bright plaid suit, give it to a horse' (64).

John Molloy's book may have generated more interest in conservative dress by high-end men's clothing stores. In 1979, *Gentlemen's Quarterly* (*GQ*) featured six exclusive men's shops. According to *GQ*, they were the best men's stores in America. Most of the stores were situated in major cities and thus had a clientele that desired the latest fashions in menswear, yet the owner of Wilkes Bashford's in San Francisco noted that there was a trend toward more conservative dressing. Men wanted to know if a certain shirt or suit was going to remain in style the next year. Customers wanted to be wise investors in their clothing. Another store, Britches in Georgetown, noted that they were carrying fewer designer lines and focusing on a more conservative look, for instance, suits made of darker fabrics to be worn with white shirts (Hamilton 1979: 72–8).

That correct dress was now seen as important for men is apparent in the metamorphosis of Jerry Rubin, who gave up his radical hippie style for conservative suits (Schulman 2001: 242–3). Rubin, a radical in the 1960s, helped to mastermind the disturbances at the 1968 Democratic Convention in Chicago and threw dollar bills on the floor of the New York Stock Exchange (Hertzberg 1988: 100–9). The ex-hippie, war protestor, and founder of the Students of a Democratic Society, Tom Hayden, also adopted a suit and vest for his run for the US Senate: 'But it didn't help. He lost to incumbent Sen. John Tunney ('Good-bye, Love Beads' 1976: 20).

No one had written etiquette rules that addressed when to wear the new styles until John Molloy wrote *Dress for Success*. The book came out at a time when the economy was failing and the unemployment rate was high. These factors only validated Molloy's advice, for after 1975 it was clear that in competing for a job, clothes made a difference (Figure 10.2).

Women Dressing for Success

Young women, of course, were active participants in the various social movements of the 1960s and 1970s. They were involved with counter-culture movements, dressed as hippies, and adopted the dress of their

Figure 10.2 Students at the University of Rhode Island dressed for interviews on campus wearing suits as prescribed by John T. Molloy, 1980. Courtesy of Special Collections, University of Rhode Island Library.

favorite music groups. The fashion industry also provided them with the look, often copying clothing styles seen on the streets. The 1970s started out with the introduction of a long, narrow skirt, the midi, which was not well received. In 1971, hot pants were introduced but they did not last long. Finally by mid-decade the skirt settled to just below the knee, but not before women had adopted pants as a comfortable alternative to the skirt. However, it was the colorful, natural, and ethnic styles of the hippies that influenced many designers, who referred to them as nostalgic or folkloric. Certainly Yves St. Laurent set a standard for the look with his colorful Russian peasant styles, inspired perhaps by the exhibition, 'In the Russian Style,' at the Metropolitan Museum of Art in New York City. A longing for homemade-looking knits, the most natural of items, put Paris designer Sonia Rykiel in the forefront of fashion (Lehnert 2000: 72–9).

The introduction of leisurewear saw more women wearing sweat suits, and breaking the rules for appropriate dress for evening wear – almost any long skirt was acceptable – and traditional evening gowns all but disappeared. While pant suits for women came in velvet, corduroy, tweed, georgette or silk, the introduction of pant suits made of polyester knits carried reactions similar to those regarding the leisure suit for men. The proliferation of these casual trousered garments and folkloric styles no doubt left some questions in the minds of women about what was appropriate in the workplace, and opened the door for Molloy to provide an answer. Women had seen the book for men, and wanted Molloy to do the same for them (Klemesrud 1978: 44). The need for rules was there.

Yet, perhaps even more important to the introduction of rules for women's dress in the workplace was the increase in the number of women entering businesses and professions. That women adopted pants was a sign that they no longer desired to be considered 'hot house flowers' and placed on a pedestal. The women's movement had been instrumental in improving the position of women in society and in raising their sights. Women now wanted to 'do their own thing' and began to reject the dictates of fashion. Many Women's Studies programs were beginning to be established in universities across the country. Although the Equal Rights Amendment did not pass in every state, gains were made in other ways. Improved birth control methods allowed women control and flexibility in starting families. The law was increasingly on their side as well: abortion rights were upheld in the *Roe* v. *Wade* case; Title IX was passed, ensuring funds for young women to have equal opportunity to engage in sports in schools; and the 32-million-dollar case lost by General Electric served notice to anyone who chose to ignore the 1964 Civil Rights Act that prohibited sex discrimination. By 1978 'women comprised 41 percent of the work force, and 1 out of 6 were in a profession' ('In the Professions' 1978: 59–60). While issues of equal pay remained problematic, young women continued to enter the marketplace, and knowing how to dress for their new jobs or professions was critical, for now they were competing for jobs formerly held by men.

The influence of women in the workplace and their new professional clothing soon was apparent to the fashion industry. Women were engaging in investment dressing. The designer Geoffrey Beene noted the change, saying that he did not dress *poupées* (dolls) – but rather 'Tilly the Toiler.' 'Career clothes are hot,' he observed, 'from J.C. Penney to Bloomingdales, today's woman shapes her image on Katherine Hepburn and Carole Lombard, who played lady executives in the films of the thirties and forties' ('Year of the Dress' 1974: 29–30). In 1972, before Molloy's book came out, one of the more conservative looks for women was a conservative shirtwaist dress. Profits from the sale of 2.5 million of Halston's 'ultra suede' version of the shirtdress helped boost his sales to 15 million dollars in 1973 ('Year of the Dress' 1974: 32).

The Women's Dress for Success Book (1977)

In his women's version of *Dress for Success*, Molloy stressed the need for women to have an appearance of authority. Molloy argued that the jacket filled that need. Yet the *U.S. News and World Report* suggested that there was more to it ('In the Professions' 1978: 60). The perception of women in the workplace was essential to their being treated on an equal footing with men. Women needed to strike a balance between appearing too masculine in a suit and seeming too feminine and lady-like which could lead to conde-scension.

Serious clothing, women believed, would lead to an atmosphere of equality in the workplace. Certainly John Molloy's *The Women's Dress for Success Book* supported the same standards and methods used in his book for men. That is, it was thought that women should dress as if they were already powerful and successful. Molloy provided women with an answer to their questions regarding how to dress for the job. He offered a uniform. As Anne Hollander pointed out, Molloy argued that women needed to 'learn not to dress . . . in the recognized mode of female sexual achievers': no high heels, see-through blouses, and so on. She observed that they would have to give up their new trouser outfits and return to wearing skirts. Yet, as she suggested, the skirt denotes straight-forward femaleness, and was no longer associated with sexual bondage or a sexual threat (1977: 27). The skirt provided balance for the woman's business suit. The skirt made it clear. *This* suit was a female garment.

Women will do best on the job, Molloy stated, 'if their uniform consists of a conservative skirted suit, preferably blue, with light colored blouse, preferably white.' They must wear plain pumps, never boots, and they should accessorize their look with an expensive gold pen, and leather attaché case. He emphasized that polyester pant suits should never be worn (Klemesrud 1978: 44). Molloy offered professional women a reprieve from wearing a skirted suit and plain pumps. He referred to women working in the media, fashion, and art, or in offices where men did not wear suits. They could wear clothing that was considered more fashionable and perhaps 'artsy' as long as it conformed to their business dress code.

The Women's Dress for Success Book is organized along the lines of the book for men. Molloy starts with a list of mistakes that women make (15–32) and then describes the uniform for women (33–48), offering sketches of 'doing it right' and 'doing it wrong' (Figure 10.3). He discusses color, pattern, and cut, goes into detail on individual clothing items, from dresses to wallets, and even considers women's use of liquor (62–107). He offers advice for job interviews and on dressing for different professions –

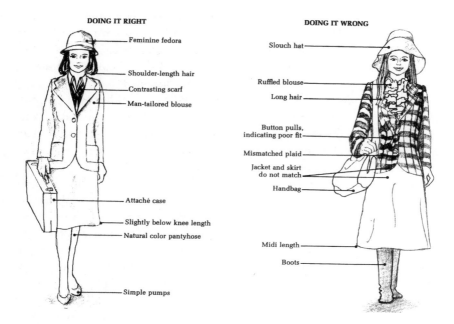

DOING IT RIGHT

Feminine fedora

Shoulder-length hair

Contrasting scarf

Man-tailored blouse

Attaché case

Slightly below knee length

Natural color pantyhose

Simple pumps

DOING IT WRONG

Slouch hat

Ruffled blouse

Long hair

Button pulls, indicating poor fit

Mismatched plaid

Jacket and skirt do not match

Handbag

Midi length

Boots

Figure 10.3 Molloy's *The Women's Dress for Success Book* presented 'do's and don'ts' for women to have instant clothing power. New York: Warner Books, 1977: 38–9.

accountants, reporters, doctors, lawyers, scientists, engineers and those within the glamour industries – and goes into great detail on dressing for sales (108–46). And just as he advised men on how to dress for women, Molloy provides recommendations for women on how to attract men (147–66). In addition, he suggests appropriate dress for the company spouse, including the Executive Wife (177–86). Although Molloy bases his proposed women's uniform on menswear there is no question about the relationship between the two. As noted by Grant McCracken (1985), business dress for women can be viewed as an example of the trickle-down theory at work in modern times. In this instance the men are the elite, and women are the aspirants.

The Rise of a Career Clothing Market

Molloy's books were not the only source for information on how to dress in the workplace. Other books that offered advice to men in the 1970s were: John Weitz, *Man in Charge: The Executive's Guide to Style* (1974),

James Wagenward (ed.), *The Man's Book: A Complete Manual of Style* (1978), Peter Carlsen, *Manstyle: The GQ Guide to Fashion, Fitness, and Grooming* (1977), Egon von Furstenberg, *The Power Look* (1978), Michael L. Speer, *Put Your Best Foot Forward* (1977), William Thourlby, *You are What You Wear: The Key to Business Success* (1978).

Books that came out in the 1980s continued to stress the importance of dress in the workplace, especially for those on the executive track. New terms evolved. Some preferred to use the term 'power dressing' rather than 'dress for success.' Books in the 1980s included: Mortimer Levitt, *The Executive Look: How to Get It – How to Keep It* (1981), Alan J. Flusser, *Clothes and the Man: The Principles of Fine Men's Dress* (1985), Lois Fenton, *Dress for Excellence* (1986), Paul Keers, *A Gentleman's Wardrobe: Classic Clothes and the Modern Man* (1987). Not to be outdone by his imitators, Molloy published *New Dress for Success* in 1988, which was for men, and *The New Women's Dress for Success Book* in 1996. Dress codes in the workplace have changed considerably since those first books appeared. In the new editions, Molloy discusses casual dress in the workplace.

In many respects, Molloy and other advice givers aided the existing men's and women's suit industry and the established menswear market. They also provided guidance for manufacturers and retailers entering the career clothing market for the first time. Many stores created 'career clothing' departments, and offered special assistance to women in selecting wardrobes for work. A number of new manufacturers appeared on the scene: Liz Claiborne started in the mid 1970s with sportswear, but soon adjusted its offerings to meet the needs of career women, and Jones of New York and Evan Picone remain successful by providing career clothing to women. New specialty chain stores such as Ann Taylor, and many other smaller shops in major cities began to specialize in career clothes. Custom shirt makers shifted their product lines and advertised to women. Traditional clothiers such as Brooks Brothers expanded their small women's departments to meet the needs of the career women. Career clothing continues to sell well, even with the steady drift toward more casual dress in the workplace. In some respects casual dress has become career dress. In 1996 an article titled 'Dressing Down for Success' appeared in *New York Magazine*. The author noted that knowing what to wear for dressing down was just as important as knowing how to dress up. Both caused stress, a sure sign of peoples' insecurities regarding appropriate dress and the apparent importance they place on dress in achieving goals ('Dressing Down for Success' 40).

Molloy's books continue to resonate in workplace culture. Perhaps it is particularly the steady movement toward casual dress in American culture that fuels the clothing debates. Certainly 'dress-down Fridays' that started in the 1970s have been replaced by 'dress-down everyday' in some segments of the business world, especially in the high-tech fields. While financial institutions do retain their conservative dress codes, even they allow some dress-down days. Popular literature in 2004 suggested that the suit is coming back. This could just be hype, or it could be a reflection of a swing in the fashion pendulum or competition for scarce jobs. The interest, time, and money spent on sorting out dress codes by both employers and employees certainly validate the basic tenet of Molloy's books: dress is important in communicating authority, prestige, power, and position. This has not altered. The significance of the words 'dress for success,' is clearly understood by all.

References

Chenoune, F. (1993), *A History of Men's Fashion*, trans. By Deke Dusinberre, Paris: Flammarion.

Conekin, B. (2000), 'Fashioning the Playboy: Messages of Style and Masculinity in the Pages of *Playboy* Magazine, 1953–1963,' *Fashion Theory*, 4: 447–66.

Costantino, M. (1997), *Men's Fashion in the Twentieth Century, from Frock Coats to Intelligent Fibres*, New York: Costume and Fashion Press.

Craik, J. (1994), *The Face of Fashion*, London: Routledge.

'Dress to Succeed' (1977), *Nation's Business*, August: 63–6.

'Dressing Down for Success' (1996), *New York Magazine* 29(23): 40.

Ehrenreich, B. (1983), *The Heart's of Men, American Dreams and the Flight from Commitment*, New York: Anchor Press/Doubleday.

Farber, D. (1988), *Chicago '68*, Chicago: University of Chicago Press.

Flusser, A. (1985), *Clothes and the Man, the Principles of Fine Men's Dress*, New York: Villard Books.

'Good-bye, Love Beads. Hello, Watch Chain' (1976), *Forbes*, July 1: 19–20.

Hamilton, R. (1979), 'The Stores Behind the Man,' *Esquire*, October: 68–78.

Handley, S. (1999), *Nylon, the Story of a Fashion Revolution*, Baltimore, MD: Johns Hopkins University Press.

Hertzberg, H. (1988), 'The Short Happy Life of the American Yuppie,' *Esquire*, February: 100–9.

Hollander, A. (1977), 'Anne Hollander on Fashion, The Issue of Skirting,' *The New Republic* 117: 27–8.

'In the Professions, Women are Moving Up' (1978), *U.S. News and World Report*, September 4: 59–60.

Klemesrud, J. (1978), 'John T. Molloy,' *New York Times Book Review* 83: 44.

Lehnert, G. (2000), *A History of Fashion in the 20th Century*, Könemann: Cologne, Germany.

McCracken, G.D. (1985) 'The Trickle-Down Theory Rehabilitated,' in M.R. Soloman (ed.), *The Psychology of Fashion*, Lexington, MA: D.C. Heath.

Molloy, J.T. (1975), *Dress for Success*, New York: Warner Books.

—— (1977), *The Women's Dress for Success Book*, New York: Warner Books.

Polhemus, T. and L. Procter (1978), *Fashion and Antifashion: An Anthropology of Clothing and Adornment*, London: Thames and Hudson.

Schulman, B.J. (2001), *The Seventies*, New York: Free Press.

'Two Up on Francis Macomber' (1972), *Esquire* 77, March: 149–50.

'The Year of the Dress?' (1974), *Forbes,* March 15: 28–32.

11

Television and Fashion in the 1980s

Patricia A. Cunningham, Heather Mangine and Andrew Reilly

Editors' Introduction: The 1980s continued to be influenced by the importance of dressing for success. In fact, the cult of success was seen in the increased consumption of luxury goods by Americans. The Reagan years in America were indeed bountiful. Clothing became ostentatious and worn as a badge of achievement. A coterie of American designers – Donna Karan, Ralph Lauren, and Liz Claiborne – offered women padded shoulders and broad lapels to express their new-found position and commercial power. Women purchased fur coats for themselves, and wore expensive jewelry and silk blouses to add panache to the look. Television aided Americans in their quest for symbols of achievement, for by the 1980s, American television had become a powerful force in American life. Although television entered most American homes during the 1950s, the clothes worn on TV did not influence fashion until the 1980s. In this chapter Patricia Cunningham, Heather Mangine and Andrew Reilly discuss the success of cable and network TV in offering the public numerous fashion ideas. Music television (MTV) appeared in 1981, showing American youth how their favorite musicians dressed. The advent of a new genre, the evening soap opera, showed the world how the fictitious Ewings in Dallas and the Carringtons in Dynasty lived and dressed. These chic TV families symbolized the wealth of cattle ranchers and oilmen of the American West during the Reagan era. The 1980s also saw the popularity of detective shows, particularly the stylish Miami Vice. Miami's newly renovated hotels in the South Beach district helped popularize pastel art deco colors. Don Johnson and Philip Michael Thomas, who wore the latest in Italian menswear by Armani and Versace, introduced a 'no socks' look and pastel T-shirts worn under sports coats to men who never looked at Gentlemen's Quarterly or Esquire.

If commercial television can be considered an integral part of the modern shopping world, then certainly 1980s programming offered consumers a cornucopia of styles. Stylish detective shows such as *Miami Vice*, new music television channels (MTV) and evening soaps like *Dynasty* allowed television to reach not only the expected adult female consumer, but also teenagers and men. Some American programs, *Dynasty* among them, had captive viewers worldwide. The influence of these programs on audiences went beyond the commercials; the persuasive impact flowed from the visual effect of the style and ambience of the fantasy world created by the producers. The effect of these shows on fashions worn by women, men and teenagers in the 1980s was significant. The attempt of the networks to appeal to these specific groups was not an afterthought, but rather a deliberate effort to broaden their audience through an appeal to niche markets. That these programs would actually influence fashion, however, may not have been a goal, at least not initially.

Certainly, influencing audiences to make purchases has been the goal in the film and television industries since their inception. As Andrew Ross noted, 'the purpose of network TV is to deliver an audience to an advertising sponsor' (1987: 321). The early filmmakers were well aware of the promotional capabilities of the moving image, and its potential to create desire. Indeed, Sam Goldwyn of MGM stated that Hollywood could easily replace Paris as the center of fashion. In fact, a number of leading French designers worked for Hollywood studios. During the Golden Years of Hollywood, in the 1930s, there were many opportunities for 'tie-ins.' Garment manufacturers produced fashions seen in the movies, and made them available to department and specialty stores throughout the country. The pattern industry likewise provided Hollywood styles for 'star struck' fans (Emery 2001).

Television, however, is more dependent on ratings and numbers of viewers in making judgments of a show's success. The advertisers want to ensure that viewers are exposed to their products. Thus from the start, television was dependent on the consumer/viewer, but only from the standpoint of advertisements. Of course, the number of viewers increases when a program becomes more successful in the ratings. While the fashions that are seen in television programs are not necessarily crucial to the plot or music, like costumes in a movie or play, they exhibit cachet and certainly lend support to a successful show, some more so than others. What is obvious is that viewers do not passively allow themselves to be entertained, and producers expect viewers to become actively involved in both the programs and advertisements that they deliver.

While television programs often portray individual characters with style, it was not until the 1980s that flamboyant current fashion appeared on television. Hence it can be argued that television moved from costuming characters, to fashioning contemporary style. *Miami Vice* offered a 'new look' for men with the clothing styles worn by the two male leads, Don Johnson and Philip Michael Thomas. MTV first appeared on cable in 1981. It catered to a teenage audience from the start, especially to girls. Since music and fashion have had a long-standing connection, MTV's influence on what these young people wore comes as no surprise. In the early 1980s, the evening soaps, *Dynasty* and its rival *Dallas*, were popular with audiences. Yet, unlike *Dallas*, *Dynasty* had great potential to influence fashion, in part, because the show appealed most to women. The show also had its own designer, Nolan Miller.

Miami Vice

Miami Vice was one of the ground-breaking police programs of the 1980s, along with *Hill Street Blues* and *Cagney and Lacey*. *Miami Vice* aired from September 1984 until July 1989. The elements that made it popular were the look of its main characters, the music, and the setting, the city of Miami, Florida. There is no denying that its 'tropical' lighting, Miami locations, set design, and figure framing camera angles served as a formal force more extravagant than previous crime shows. The use of style, rock music, and the sights, sounds, and colors of the city amplified the emotional content of the series. The effect was similar to film noir (Buxton 1990: 140).

The focus of the crime series was the Miami Metro-Dade police 'vice' department and its continued battle against illicit drugs, prostitution and illegal firearms in the crime underworld of the city of Miami. The main characters were James 'Sonny' Crockett, played by Don Johnson, and Ricardo 'Rico' Tubbs, played by Philip Michael Thomas. They were supported by Edward James Olmos as their tough lieutenant and Michael Talbott, John Diehl, Saundra Santiago, and Olivia Brown as their colleagues on the squad. While the program narratives included these characters, most of the episodes centered on Johnson and Thomas, and clearly they received most of the press, especially Don Johnson who was by far the most flamboyant character in the cast.

The two leads, Johnson and Thomas, were cast as opposites. Tubbs was a street-smart cop from New York and Crockett was a tough guy from the South. Tubbs was rock and roll while Crockett was country, although he dressed more like a drug dealer heavily into the Miami scene (Buxton 1990: 143). Crockett was white, divorced and an ex-alcoholic beach bum who lived on a boathouse with a pet alligator and drove a Ferrari Daytona. Tubbs, his partner and buddy, was a charmer of mixed black–Hispanic descent, with a diamond in his ear. He was romantic, sensitive, and intellectual. He was a recent refugee from New York where his brother had been killed in a gangland murder. He represented New York sophistication. Crockett, on the other hand, was tough and down to earth, a Vietnam vet and ex-football star. He represented the regular guy with small-town values (Buxton 1990: 143).

In keeping with the extravagance of the Reagan presidency, *Miami Vice* began by celebrating consumer wealth and style, but in later episodes, as the nation's economy suffered, the series focused on a premise that economic and moral decline are intrinsically linked (Buxton 1990: 158–9). As a medium of popular culture, television has had great potential to regulate and negotiate public desire. The producers of the show aimed to create desire on the part of the audience through the elements of style – the clothing, colors, setting and cinematography – through the sex appeal of Crockett and Tubbs, and through the use of music (Ross 1987: 324–5; Danbrot 1986).

Music

One of the outstanding features of *Miami Vice* was the soundtrack by composer Jan Hammer. Hammer's music was an essential ingredient during all four years of production. Rock music sequences that interrupted the narrative established the series' aesthetic affinity to MTV. According to Buxton, the use of music clips, and other aesthetic devices such as unnatural color schemes and mood music, filled out the story and avoided the use of irrelevant plot complications. Buxton views the rock video sequences, which often accompanied incidental action, as simply time-wasting devices that did not enhance the narrative (1990: 145). The incorporation of elements of music video – not only the songs and hi-tech musical arrangements, but also the agile, fast-cut cinematography and innovative camera angles that took their cue from rock video – was new to a crime series. Others might give credit to cinema's film noir as a source for the cinematography in *Miami Vice*. The style was similar to the visual dynamics of *Double Indemnity* (1944). Yet, the inclusion of music video was viewed by some as less aesthetic than simply an attempt to win back 'the potential high-level consumer MTV audience' (Ross 1987: 324). Rock stars even appeared as guests on the show. Moreover, the show was so popular that Johnson and Thomas received the attention often reserved for rock stars.

Color

Colors for the sets and clothing reflected the art deco modern architecture unique to Miami, especially the newly renovated South Beach area. The decision to use these colors came from Michael Mann, the executive producer of the series. His motto was 'no earth tones'; 'sienna, ochre, red and brown were eliminated in favor of rose, lime, lemon, aquamarine, turquoise and peach, the sensual feel of pastel and fluorescent colors' (Buxton 1990: 140). Clearly Mann wanted nothing to do with the tired 'earth tones' of the 1970s. In *Miami Vice*, the city was a character in its own right. Each week the audience was treated to visual sights and sounds of the city: Miami cityscapes effused in pastel colors, beach scenes and nightlife.

Fashion

Men's fashion was strongly influenced by the two leads in *Miami Vice*. Crockett always dressed in casual trousers and T-shirts in pastel shades of turquoise, pink or lavender while Tubbs dressed in the more traditional dark suits and neckties that would be approved by John Molloy (Figure 11.1). While Crockett's penchant for wearing no socks with his loafers became a fashion statement, his preference for casual clothes and soft colors soon caught on with men's fashion, especially the Versace invention of wearing a T-shirt in place of a collared dress shirt and tie with a jacket (Lehnert 2000: 90).

In October 1985, the *Toronto Star* included a brief note, 'Real Vice Men Try Modeling,' about an article that had appeared in *Gentlemen's Quarterly*. They noted that the magazine was exploiting the success of the show by using real cops as models to promote expensive clothing such as that worn by the characters Crockett and Tubbs. The clothing and lifestyle of the two lead characters had great appeal, as did the Ferrari driven by Crockett. However, as Buxton observed, the producers felt that the most obvious element of conspicuous consumption, Crockett's Ferrari, needed to be explained during an episode. Ownership of a Ferrari went beyond what might be necessary for an undercover cop. The storyline had Crockett purchasing the car from the police impound lot with a monetary gift, a reward he received for saving a wealthy industrialist's daughter (Buxton 1990: 145).

Sex Appeal

A new masculine type seemed to be in the making with this series. Neither Crockett nor Tubbs fit the stereotype of the ideal male for the era. But then, the show aired at a time of great ambiguity and acceptance of individuality. Both Tubbs and Crockett had sex appeal, and it is clear that sex was an element of desire in *Miami Vice*. Don Johnson was dubbed 'the sexiest man on television' during the run of the show. The seductive power of Crockett and Tubbs was not only inscribed in their sartorial flourishes but was obvious in the superiority of their good looks. Also, in the first year of *Miami Vice*, at a time when male nakedness was more permissible on TV

Figure 11.1 *Miami Vice* stars Don Johnson and Philip Michael Thomas. Courtesy of Universal Studios Licensing, LLLD.

than female nakedness, there was widespread incidence of male flesh in the program. Bedroom scenes where the male was almost naked and the woman fully clothed seemed to prevail (Ross 1987: 322).

In the show's last season, NBC sought to invigorate the low ratings by staging a significant event in the life of one of the leads. It was decided that Sonny Crockett would be married. In keeping with the music theme, he married a real-life rock star, Sheena Easton. For the event Crockett wore a double-breasted tux, a Versace shirt and, in honor of the special occasion, he wore socks by Perry Ellis. The wedding gown was by Eddie Castro. Asked about her scenes with Crockett, Easton noted that he had an innate sensuality and a smile and sense of humor that were very sexy (Sanders 1988).

In the end, *Miami Vice* had an impact on the city of Miami, on television, and on men's fashion. The show revitalized Miami's image and allowed it to become a hub for the entertainment industry. The show marked a turning point in the growth and diversification of the city. For fashion, the *Miami Vice* style was successful in finding a receptive audience (Rutsky 1988). Fashion aficionados, who stayed glued to the television set during the run of the show, did not view the *Miami Vice* style as a form of deceit; they saw it as power. They embraced the new men's style that had been so carefully crafted by the costume designers, Milena Canonero and Richard Shissler. In fact, the show provided a new and enduring casual look for men. In 2005 men continued to wear a crew neck T-shirt or a polo shirt with a sports coat when 'dressing up' for informal occasions. The T-shirt might cost $100 dollars at Saks Fifth Avenue. The pastels are still around. Lavender is a popular dress shirt color for men, easily purchased at Brooks Brothers. *Miami Vice* also was a milestone in that it confirmed for the networks the potential of fashion and music in appealing to an audience. The truth of this lies in television since the 1980s.

MTV

By the time *Miami Vice* took off, MTV had become the emblematic innovation of the decade. Spearheaded by its founder, Robert W. Pittman, MTV began on August 1, 1981 as a twenty-four-hour cable channel with no programs, just rock and roll music geared toward viewers aged between twelve and thirty-four. In essence it was a new way to reach the teenage market. As M. Williams observed in the *Washington Post* (December 13, 1989), MTV influenced not only the music industry and television, but theatre, film, advertising, marketing, fashion, and almost every aspect of

American culture during the 1980s. MTV immediately captured the attention of the younger baby boom generation, perhaps the richest consumer group in the history of the world. 'By marrying rock and roll to the pervasive power of television,' Williams observed, MTV transformed the 'music that had questioned authority into one more facet of consumer culture.' In a *New York Times* article (December 27, 1985) M. Gross included comments made by Judy McGrath, MTV's creative director, in which she expressed her opinion that rock and roll had become mass culture, and MTV was an 'ongoing, almost subliminal fashion show.' Gross also quoted Mick Rock, a video photographer of the 1970s, who observed that the visual image hit before anything else. 'Without fashion,' he noted, 'there is no video.' He believed that David Bowie's persona was solely dependent on his costumes. In the same article Gross noted that in the mid-1970s Malcolm McLaren and fashion designer Vivienne Westwood clearly understood the fashion-music connection when they formed the Sex Pistols 'as musical models for their styles.' Gross also revealed that John Taylor, bassist for Duran Duran, believed that band members were selected as much for their hairstyles as they were for their musical abilities, and that while some people worried about chords, he worried about his clothes. In an earlier *New York Times* article (March 10, 1985), S.B. Smith observed that some bands were successful because of their looks, not their music. Their images sold clothes; thus the calculated disarray of rock performers became the look of the 1980s.

Rock fashion became big business (Hilfiger 1999). Young girls desired to dress like Madonna (Figure 11.2) and Cyndi Lauper, two of the early female musicians on MTV with 'girl' appeal. It did not take manufacturers and retailers long to discover that the carefully cultivated images of rock stars created consumer desire. The shopping mall and department store were sites for female leisure culture. And without question, it was in these sites that the text of the videos and the teenage female consumer coalesced. The look of 'Madonna is everywhere,' one observer proclaimed. One mall in California took on the moniker 'Madonna Mall' because so many girls who shopped there tried to look like the singer (Lewis 1990: 100–1).

Cyndi Lauper's style proved to be an inspiration for the ready-to-wear manufacturers and retailers. *Seventeen* magazine carried information about Lauper-influenced fashion accessories: black leather bracelets (12 for $4), rhinestone bracelets ($9) and gunmetal and rhinestone bracelets ($30). Yet, it was Madonna whose persona and 'look' inspired the greatest fandom.

The Associated Department Stores recommend that its member stores open FTV (fashion television) departments. With rock videos blaring, Macy's opened in-store boutiques with a Madonna connection, 'Madonnaland' and 'Girls Just Want to Have Fun,' where they sold 'cropped sweaters ($30) and

Figure 11.2 'Mini-Madonna.' Courtesy of the University of Texas Erwin Center.

cropped pants ($21).' When they opened one of these boutiques just before one of Madonna's New York concerts, they sold out of Madonna-licensed and inspired clothing and jewelry in two days (Lewis 1990: 100–1). Lest sales were to wane, Macy's sponsored a Madonna look-a-like contest, and to promote it ran a full-page ad in the *Village Voice* that echoed the title of a Madonna film, *Desperately Seeking Susan*:

> JRS!
> DESPERATELY SEEKING MADONNA LOOK-ALIKES
> Join our Madonna Day contest, Thurs, June 6 in Madonnaland
> on 4, Macy's Herald Square. If you're a brassy material girl, get
> into the groove and prove it . . .

MTV and ABC Evening News both featured the event on camera where the Madonna look-a-likes gushed about how they wanted to be 'looked at' like their idol, Madonna (Lewis 1990: 100–2).

The appearance of music video displays in junior departments in shopping malls and department stores across the country serves as testament to the conversion of teenagers into MTV junkies. Fashion is always quick to respond to whatever is new. And the 'consumer girl' is always ready. She is poised to subvert the old and grasp the new in her quest to distinguish herself and gain support from her peers. Therein lies the pleasure and power in consumer girl culture.

Licensing the Look

In 1984, a clothing manufacturer calling itself '1045 Park Avenue' shipped $5 million worth of MTV-inspired clothes to stores such as The Limited, Bloomingdale's, and Lord & Taylor. They constructed the clothing with fake leather and zippers, included large shoulder pads, and then added silver gloves, replicating the fashion seen in Michael Jackson videos. But the items did not sell well. Apparently Jackson did not have the dynamic of Madonna. Through her music and ever changing persona, Madonna offered her fans a whole new way of dressing that was in total contrast to the current look of junior fashion. Each new video, based on a hit song, carried a new look. Macy's fashion director at the time observed that she had never seen anything like the excitement created by Madonna. She questioned if Madonna would have such an impact without MTV (Lewis 1990: 100–2).

Madonna came out with a new line designed by Marlene Stewart of Wazoo in August of 1985. She had a jewelry line out in the spring of 1986 that included 'Boy Toy and Love belt bracelets, stretch ID bracelets, ankh and peace symbols, happy faces, rubber heart and cross earrings' that sold from $3 to $15, which was well within the range of adoring adolescent girls. According to the jewelry designer, Marie Paule Fauque, there was no guarantee that these teenagers would purchase the line (Lewis 1990: 100–2). Indeed, there never is a guarantee; consumers are fickle. And, as E. Sporkin observed in the *New York Times* (December 21, 1989), rock fans are hard to please; even Madonna and Jackson-licensed products did not always sell.

Critics of MTV

Since MTV's inception, its provocative nature has brought much criticism to the cable network. Some critics have taken the position that the images and music have the potential to adversely affect the young by provoking violence and sexism. This criticism has appeared in academic literature as well as the mass media. As noted by M. Williams in the *Washington Post*, supporters of MTV believe that it was always meant to 'alienate a lot of people,' except those consumers who were its target, the baby boomers. Of course, viewers could choose not to watch it. Robert Pittman noted that many videos seen on MTV actually spoofed sexism. Indeed, supporters of early MTV note its 'weird dispassion' to 'defy the audience to take it seriously.' And it is possible to view MTV as an art form with a 'permanent smirk' . . . a jokey medium that was more ironic than serious (*Washington Post*, December 13, 1989).

In the case of Madonna 'wannabes,' her anti-mainstream look became the adolescents' tool to achieve power in an environment of conservative codes for young girls. By choosing to copy Madonna's on-screen fantasy wardrobe girls could alter their appearance, so they did not meet their parents' expectations, or those of society. These were rebellious acts, typical of teenagers who are finding their way. Lisa Lewis sees these acts as appropriating activities and spaces reserved for male adolescents. 'Girls Just Want to Have Fun' and 'Borderline' both deal with girls taking over the street. It is an example of female subversion of a traditional male gender role. It is not surprising to learn that as teenagers Madonna and her best friend dressed up 'trashy' like prostitutes to create a sexual persona that was sure to alienate their parents, and thus subvert the power that their parents held over them. In turn they created some of their own (Lewis 1990: 92–5).

Fashion and MTV

There was a bond between fashion designers and rock stars. Writing about fashion and rock music in the *New York Times* (December 27, 1985), M. Gross observed that the designer Betsy Johnson had proclaimed that rock and fashion are one and the same. She was referring to the inspiration that she got from watching rock performances. Clearly fashions inspired or worn by rock stars had a natural market among rock fans. Stephen Sprouse, a designer to rock stars, built a business on rock-based clothing before he burned out. Fashion designers, photographers and editors frequent rock shows to pick up on the latest styles of influential rock stars. The connection between television and fashion was so strong in the 1980s that MTV, Ray Ban and *Miami Vice* won awards from the Council for the Fashion Designers of America for their contributions to fashion. The Council was so taken with videos that they also gave an award to fashion designer Norma Kamali for her use of rock-style videos to promote her lines (*New York Times*, December 27, 1985).

Seeing the links between MTV and fashion inspired MTV producers to create a series of half-hour segments called 'House of Style.' As noted by J. Hatfield in the *Boston Globe* (August 12, 1989), 'House of Style' drew on a fast-paced format of singers, music, and rap to show fashions meant to appeal to teenagers and young adults. They used fashion model Cindy Crawford as host and rap artists Salt-n-Pepa as models to show their first spring line of designs by Betsy Johnson and Katherine Hammett, a British designer. A segment that aired on August 26, 1989 looked at how rock stars pioneered fashion trends again using the rock stars as models.

MTV also decided to promote itself using its own clothing line. In the December 21, 1989 issue of *USA Today* E. Sporkin predicted that by spring 1990 MTV would be putting its own 'spin' on fashion by offering trendy MTV logo clothing and accessories to surf shops, boutiques and department stores. MTV teamed up with a California company, Vision Street Wear, to produce clothing that reflected MTV's edge and mentality, with colorful graphics. They were working on jeans, bicycle pants, print shirts, motorcycle jackets and shorts. Another company, License Works, developed a line of accessories for MTV: fanny packs, baseball caps, sports bags, and other accessories aimed at the eighteen to twenty-four-year-old viewer. While these products have been successful, this sort of promotion pales in comparison to other means of self-promotion by MTV. They are better known for their MTV Awards Show, rock tours, and MTV Museum of Unnatural History that toured shopping malls in the late 1980s.

Beyond Promotion: Music is Fashion

Another aspect of the connection between MTV and fashion (or simply television and fashion) is the importance of music in forecasting new trends. Betsy Johnson alluded to this connection with her comments. No self-respecting fashion forecaster would fail to attend rock concerts or watch MTV, nor would fashion photographers, designers and magazine editors. The influence of music on fashion was enormous in the 1980s and music continues to influence designers and manufacturers. As rock music has moved from early rap, to grunge and hip-hop, we have seen rock stars going beyond the success of earlier groups like the Rolling Stones, who in 1989 produced their own line of clothes, including a leather motorcycle jacket with studded epaulets for $450.00 and bandanas for $5.00 (*Newsweek* August 28, 1989). In the twenty-first century the trend has taken off; rock stars have made clothing a big business by moving to main-stream mass fashion. Their lines are in many large department stores; they have moved beyond the concert venue (Blackwell and Stephan 2004).

Dynasty, a Prime-Time Soap Opera

While MTV was appealing to adolescents, *Dynasty* captured the attention of their parents, especially their mothers. ABC came up with *Dynasty* in response to the success of *Dallas*. Millions of viewers were tuning in to CBS to watch *Dallas*, and ABC wanted to cash in on a similar show. The network assigned producer Aaron Spelling the job of finding an equivalent show. When Ester and Richard Shapiro offered him their script about the problems of rich people and family intrigue he knew he had it. The pilot premiered January 12, 1981. The show followed the life of the wealthy oil magnate Blake Carrington, played by John Forsythe, his new bride, Krystle, played by Linda Evans, and his family, acquaintances, and business associates. With low ratings in its first season, producers soon added a female version of the manipulative, evil sort of character embodied by *Dallas'* J.R. Ewing: Alexis Carrington, Blake Carrington's ex-wife and the mother of his children (Shephard 2001).

Alexis Morell Carrington Colby Dexter Rowan, played by black-haired Joan Collins, was a sophisticated, classy, beautiful and sexy mother to four children, who by the end of the show had four ex-husbands, one of whom had tried to kill her. Alexis was known as a ruthless, powerful tycoon. She took over and ran Blake's biggest oil competitor and became his arch rival. She caused pain and suffering to most of the show's other characters as she plotted and schemed. Viewers either loved her or hated her. Alexis hated Krystle, and continually schemed to break up her marriage to Blake (Shephard 2001).

Krystle and Alexis represented a dichotomy of good and evil. Blonde Krystle Grant Jennings Carrington had been a secretary to Blake Carrington before they married. She was the exact opposite of the devilish Alexis. Krystle was sweet, caring, kind, and helpful to everyone except Alexis. Bad things always happened to her including being raped, having a miscarriage after falling off a horse, and being harassed by many men. She ran away, suffered from depression, her baby was kidnapped, she had a brain tumor, and was even in a coma (Press 1990).

One of the most significant aspects of both characters was that they personified beauty beyond youth, a relatively new idea to Americans. Evans joined the cast in her late thirties, while Collins was in her forties and each was sophisticated and beautiful. According to Collins, *Dynasty* showed viewers that women could be vital, sexual, and powerful past the age of thirty-five. Louise Farr, fashion editor for *Women's Wear Daily* and *W*, believed that the reason for the show's popularity was that female viewers could identify with these two main characters (Shephard 2001).

Patricia A. Cunningham et al.

Dynasty Fashion

Soaps usually have their own unique fashion, often including designer labels and Harry Winston jewels. However, according to Stella Blum, *Dynasty* was trying to outdo other shows (Nonkin 1984: 280–4). Spelling and the other producers believed that when trying to create a fantasy world about the rich and famous they needed to be authentic; viewers would be able to spot anything that was not real (Shephard 2001). No detail was overlooked, especially when it came to the clothing. One of the central characteristics of the show, of course, was its 'look.' The look of *Dynasty* was based on fashions created by Nolan Miller, who had his big break with this show. Miller had designed costumes for previous shows including *Charlie's Angels*, *Matt Houston*, *Hotel* and *The Love Boat* (Champlin 1983: 66–8). Miller said he was given almost carte blanche to create the fashions. Producers did not want to see the same clothes worn twice. They wanted the characters' clothing to fit an idealized picture of the rich and famous. For each show Miller was given a clothing budget somewhere between $15,000 and $50,000 (Maychick 1985)). For special episodes like the royal wedding, he spent $100,000 (Danbrot 1986). He even spent $18,000 on one dress for Krystle (Shephard 2001). He not only decided what the characters would wear by choosing a Calvin Klein blouse for Krystle, or a Jonathan Hitchcock gown for Alexis, but he also designed much of the clothing himself (Nonkin 1984).

Publicity pictures shot for the show, scenes from original footage that can be seen on websites dedicated to the show as well as images in numerous magazines, including *TV Guide*, *People*, *Vogue*, *Harper's Bazaar*, *Mademoiselle*, and *Soap Opera Weekly*, reveal the clothing worn by the characters. The clothing can best be characterized in a single word: glamorous. *Dynasty* has been described as an hour-long commercial for clothes (Leerhsen 1984). It emphasized a kind of out-of-date glamour with ornate clothing in bold colors and glitter. Alexis embodied the outrageous 'look' of the show (Leerhsen 1984). According to Miller, clothes designed for Alexis made the statement that she was rich and ruthless (Danbrot 1986). Alexis's clothes were dramatic with the use of bold colors like purple and black to suggest her power and evilness (Champlin 1983). In her first appearance on the show, Alexis was seen in a well-cut black and white suit, with a large hat and a black veil over her face (Shephard 2001). She was often seen in suits in bright colors like red or in simple black and white statements. She often donned her trademark hats, either large brimmed or pillbox, usually with a black veil. This sophisticated look was often completed with matching gloves, beautiful

222

precious jewels and fur trim, or at the very least, a fur wrap (Shephard 2001).

Evening gowns worn by Alexis certainly gave audiences what they wanted. Her gowns were of luxurious fabrics in reds and golds. One of the most important parts of the entire ensemble was the jewelry. Ninety-nine per cent of the time, Alexis was draped in lavish jewelry that would be considered gaudy a decade later. Necklaces, bracelets, and earrings were large and made of diamonds and other precious stones. With the help of her attire, in 1984, Collins was voted the most beautiful woman on television (Shephard 2001).

Although different, Krystle's clothes were no less extravagant. In 1984, Krystle was voted the third most beautiful woman on television (*TV Guide*). Miller designed her clothes to reflect her character. He tried to keep the clothes soft in order to show her kindness and understanding. Fashions for Krystle were also influenced by Linda Evans' body. On top she wore a size twelve; on bottom a six. Miller found it best to accentuate her top while keeping the bottom slim. Consequently, Krystle was rarely seen in full skirts. Her daywear often consisted of matching well-fitting trousers and long-sleeved silk blouses with broad shoulders. The necklines were either v-neck or high collars with bows around the neck. For Evans's character, subtle pastels were used to demonstrate her softness (Champlin 1983). Often she was adorned in white to signify her purity (Nonkin 1984). Her gowns had long sheath silhouettes, with deep v-necks and long sleeves. Embellishments were often full beading of the entire dress. The most significant detail of her eveningwear and her daywear was the shoulders. The shoulder pads were uncharacteristically large even for the time period, and gave Evans' silhouette a beautiful triangle, according to Nolan Miller (Champlin 1983). Krystle was also adorned in extravagant jewelry. Aside from the expensive jewels, the look of Krystle could not be complete without Linda Evans' characteristic hair. Her platinum blond hair was cut in a long straight bob with bangs feathered back from her face. In most scenes it was worn down, but sometimes it could be seen in an upsweep puffing out from the sides of her face. As the show went on, her hair seemed to get bigger and bigger. For those obsessed with *Dynasty*, this big hair was a perfect example of a 1980s must have ('From Hair to Eternity' 2002).

Dynasty and 1980s Fashion

The look and style of *Dynasty* were so extreme that some thought the characters were simply laughable. They no doubt thought, 'who would really want to look like that?' On the other hand, viewers who enjoyed the show would say the opposite, 'who wouldn't want to look like that?' (Geraghty 1991). A common way to identify with a favored celebrity is to imitate their dress (Lewis 1990). Since Collins and Evans were among the most liked actresses of the 1980s, many women adopted this style. Some women admitted they watched the show just for the clothes (Nonkin 1984). *Dynasty* was seen as a fashion authority, like *Vogue*, where women got new fashion ideas and learned ways to dress. One admirer commented that her father called her 'Linda' because she dressed like Linda Evans. She said that *Dynasty* was her favorite show and revealed, 'I wanted to look like her so badly' (Laufer 2003).

The show's costume designer, Nolan Miller, knew that *Dynasty* had an impact on the fashion of the 1980s. In his opinion, Evans popularized the large shoulder pads characteristic of the 1980s and Collins brought hats back into vogue. The shows creator and writer, Ester Shapiro, claimed that before *Dynasty*, no one wore hats anymore. Once Alexis appeared on the show in her elegant hats, Neiman Marcus and Saks increased their hat offerings by over 200 per cent. The influence *Dynasty* had on fashion was made clear to Miller when he saw a young girl at an airport dressed in a white suit with a black and white hat with a black veil over her face, 'and you knew she thought she was Alexis' (Shephard 2001).

According to Louise Farr, the effect of *Dynasty* on fashion was astounding (Shephard 2001). People would call or write and ask the show where they could get *Dynasty* fashions (Leerhsen 1984). Nolan Miller received over 5,000 letters each month asking for sketches of his designs (Shephard 2001). It did not take long for Twentieth Century Fox to try to cash in on the popularity and license merchandise inspired by *Dynasty* (Leerhsen 1984). According to Shephard, this merchandise was the first of the television-licensed products that targeted upper-middle-class adults. Nolan Miller at one time had his name on eight different product lines (Figure 11.3). December 1983 brought the Carrington's Christmas clothing line to Marshall Fields. The fashions displayed on mannequins were made to look like *Dynasty*'s characters (Shephard 2001). The *Toronto Star* (December 5, 1985) carried an article by E. Bot, who commented that Miller also created *Dynasty* patterns for the McCall Pattern Company. He created over forty patterns of actual styles worn on the show. While Miller noted that more than 90 per cent were easy to make, some styles included extravagant details – draped sleeves, tiny tucks, and coordinating capes.

Available in stores in 1984 was 'The *Dynasty* Collection.' This collection consisted of reasonably priced fashions similar to those seen on the show. When the line was launched in fall of 1984 at a special event at Bloomingdales in New York City, cast members were there to promote the

Figure 11.3 *Dynasty* star Linda Evans modeling a suit by Nolan Miller. American Museum of the Moving Image.

new collection and over 20,000 shoppers showed up. According to Michael Nader, who played the role of Dex Dexter, the store was so crowded that no one could move. Stores across the United States had already ordered the merchandise in excess of $200 million in wholesale prices. The licensed clothing had the same glamorous feel as that seen on the show. It was meant to be sexy with fitted waists and soft skirts. Details of the clothing included décolletage, feathers, and fur (Leerhsen 1984).

In Beverly Hills, Krystle-type outfits sold the best and her namesake perfume, 'Forever Krystle,' was continually sold out in department stores across the United States. Lingerie inspired by Alexis was also popular. Another hot seller was costume jewelry that was Carrington-esque. For example, a zirconium copy of a ring Krystle pawned was a popular item that sold for $560. Other products in various lines of *Dynasty* merchandise included necklaces, towels, pantyhose, dolls, rugs, children's clothes and more (Leerhsen 1984).

By comparing the fashions seen in *Vogue* with the fashions seen on *Dynasty*, it becomes apparent that *Dynasty* reflected some of the fashions of the 1980s but also introduced and popularized others. For example, white was not popular in the mainstream until Krystle began wearing it. Although shoulder pads were worn in the beginning of the decade, *Dynasty* helped to popularize them, as well as the inverted-triangle silhouette, mostly due to Linda Evans' body shape. *Dynasty*-inspired body-skimming columnar evening gowns became a hit with women of the decade. Also, tailored suits, as depicted by Alexis, gained popularity and became the women's power suit of the period. Prior to the 1980s women's fashions were leaning toward androgyny. However, after *Dynasty* women's wear took on a more feminine look. For example, hats, gloves, jewels, large ruffled sleeves, soft and sensuous fabrics, and expansive décolletages were seen in 1980s fashion. *Dynasty* fashions were adopted largely by middle-aged women. It was this group that identified with Linda Evans and Joan Collins, who exemplified beauty beyond youth.

Conclusion

Miami Vice, MTV and *Dynasty* provide clear examples of how television influenced fashion in the 1980s. Male consumers quickly adopted the 'new look' of casual dress put forward by the producers of *Miami Vice*. The fashion industry was quick to pick up on the fashion and television connections, and very quickly manufactured clothing to appeal to the teenage viewers of MTV. As a product of the wealth and excess of the 1980s, *Dynasty* showed female viewers a fantasy world of the wealthy. In seeking to identify with this ideal, women tried to incorporate aspects of the fashions shown into their lives. Consequently, it can be said that television reflects and impacts popular culture more than is realized; and, in the 1980s, it was indeed fashioning contemporary style.

References

'Behind *Dynasty*'s Breakdown and Recovery' (1986), *TV Guide*, May 17.

Benedik, E. (1985), 'Inside Miami Vice, Sex and Drugs and Rock & Roll Ambush Prime-time TV,' *Rollingstone*, March 28: 56–62, 125.

Blackwell, R. and T. Stephan (2004), *Brands that Rock: What Business Leaders Can Learn from the World of Rock and Roll*, Hoboken, NJ: John Wiley & Sons.

Butler, J.G. (1985), 'Miami Vice, the Legacy of Film Noir,' *Journal of Popular Film and Television*, Fall: 127–38.

Buxton, D. (1990), *From The Avengers to Miami Vice: Form and Ideology in*

Television Series, Manchester: Manchester University Press.

Champlin, S. (1983), 'Nolan Miller Woos and Wins *Dynasty*'s Women with his Razzle-Dazzle Fashions Every Week,' *People Weekly*, December 19: 66–8.

Clerk, C. (2002), *Madonnastyle*, London: Omnibus.

Conrad, P. (1982), *Television: The Medium and its Manners*, London: Routledge.

Danbrot, M. (1986), 'An Exclusive Look Behind the Dressing-Room Door,' *Ladies Home Journal*, January: 102–5.

'Don Johnson' (2000), *Biography*, 4(11): 67.

Emery, J.S. (2001), 'Dress Like a Star, Hollywood and the Pattern Industry,' *Dress*, 28: 92–9.

Evans, L. (2000) Interview in *Hello*, November 21.

'From Hair to Eternity' (2002), *TV Guide*, May 8.

Geraghty, C. (1991), *Women and Soap Opera: A Study of Prime Time Soaps*, Cambridge, UK: Polity Press.

Gripsrud, J. (1995), *The Dynasty Years: Hollywood Television and Critical Media Studies*, London: Routledge.

Hilfiger, T. (1999), *Rock Style: How Fashion Moves to Music*, New York: Universe.

Kielwasser, A.P. and M.A. Wolfe (1989), 'The Appeal of Soap Opera: An Analysis of Process and Quality in Dramatic Serial Gratifications,' *Journal of Popular Culture* 23: 111–24.

Laufer, A. (2003), Interview, November 28.

Leerhsen, C. (1984), 'Putting on the Glitz,' *Newsweek*, December 3: 95–7.

Lehnert, G. (2000), *A History of Fashion in the 20th Century*, Cologne, Germany: Könemann.

Lewis, L.A. (1990) 'Consumer Girl Culture: How Music Video Appeals to Girls,' in M. E. Brown (ed.), *Television and Women's Culture: The Politics of the Popular*, London: Sage Publications.

Maychick, D. (1985), 'Wearing Pants in Prime Time,' *Mademoiselle*, November 18.

Musto, M. (1984), 'Interview with Joan Collins,' *Issue*, September 7.

Nonkin, L. (1984), 'Prime Time Style,' *Vogue*, May: 280.

Pollen, M. (1985), 'The Vice Look,' *Channels*, July/August: 24–8.

Press, A.L. (1990), 'Class, Gender and the Female Viewer: Women's Responses to Dynasty,' in M.E. Brown (ed.), *Television and Women's Culture: The Politics of the Popular*, London: Sage Publications.

Price, S. (1986), 'Vice Guys Finish First: A Rare Interview with Don Johnson Television's Sexiest New Star,' *Ladies Home Journal*, May.

Ross, A. (1987), 'Miami Vice: Selling In,' *Communication*, 9: 305–34.

Rutsky, R.L. (1988), 'Visible sins, Vicarious Pleasures: Style and Vice in Miami Vice,' *SubStance: A Review of Theory and Literary Criticism*, 35: 77–82.

Sanders (1988), 'A Wedding Belle Gives Miami Spice,' *People Magazine*: 133–7.

Schwichtenberg, C. (1986), 'Sensual Surfaces and Stylistic Excess: the Pleasure and Politics of Miami Vice,' *Journal of Communication Inquiry*, 10(3): 45–65.

'Sexy and Rich: The New Look this Fall from Paris' (1985), *Harpers Bazaar*, October: 240–9.

Shaw, E.T. (1982), 'Joan Collins Takes Over . . . and How!,' *TV Guide*, October 23.

Shephard, E. (2001), Dynasty: *The E! True Hollywood Story*, Los Angeles: E! Entertainment Television.

Weiner, E. (1992), *The TV Guide TV Book,* New York: News America Publications.

12

Flava in Ya Gear: Transgressive Politics and the Influence of Hip-Hop on Contemporary Fashion

Robin M. Chandler and Nuri Chandler-Smith

Editors' Introduction: In creating a distinctive style, youth in the 1990s rejected the power look of the 1980s as well as the hippie look of their parents. Yet, revivals that had been so abundant in the 1980s continued to abound. Influences seemed to come from everywhere. Multiple cultures and various historical periods offered a barrage of ideas for presenting oneself to the world. Casual dress and the mixing of styles, called 'bricolage,' had reached new heights. Labels, especially for jeans, proliferated. The retro look was balanced by the rise of minimalist fashion made of high-tech fibers and fabrics. Lycra spandex began to appear in many garments. By now some business dress codes allowed casual dress to be worn in the workplace. Of significance in pulling away from formality during this decade was the influence of youth and music on dress. American youth formulated a look that had its roots in music. This pairing of youth style and music first appeared with the rise of jazz music and quickly moved into rock and roll, punk, and, in the early 1990s, grunge. As noted in Chapter 11, since the 1980s MTV has bolstered the phenomenon by making music styles accessible to television viewers worldwide. In addition to the grunge look, the 1990s saw the rise of the musical form called rap and the hip-hop culture that developed around it.

According to Tasha Lewis (2004), rap was the original music of the hip-hop culture. It initially emerged among both the Latino and African American gangs from the Bronx as early as the 1950s and 1960s. It took root and flourished among the gangs of the city and eventually spread

229

downtown and to Brooklyn. The first popular rap song, 'Rappers Delight' by the Sugar Hill Gang was released in 1979. Lewis notes that hip-hop fashion is not just one style, but a mixture of influences from both the street and high fashion designer labels. At first preppy labels, such as Tommy Hilfiger and Polo, were popular with hip-hop followers. Hip-hop style can include brand name baggy clothes, baseball caps, sneakers, sports jackets and jerseys and other sport clothes such as hooded tracksuits, and puffer vests. To this mix of masculine styles female rappers added 'door knocker' earrings. By the 1990s the female stars had switched to a sexually provocative bombshell look of Lycra-tight and revealing clothing, stilettos and high fashion hair. Branded merchandise was such an important aspect of hip-hop that rap stars soon created their own successful brands of clothing. Sean Jean, Phat Farm, Baby Phat and Rocawear are just four of the brands that have been money makers. Female stars Jennifer Lopez, Beyonce Knowles, Eve, and Lil'Kim have become 'fashionistas' by adopting and promoting couture and by creating their own fashion lines as well.

In Chapter 12 Robin Chandler and Nuri Chandler-Smith discuss the influence of hip-hop culture. They note that the subculture of hip-hop resonated first with American youth across racial lines, then with youth around the world. They view hip-hop as a multifaceted cultural phenomenon that manifested itself in the clothing styles of the hip-hop generation.

(You got me shook up shook down shook out on your loving)
(On your loving)
I want a girl with extensions in her hair
Bamboo earrings
At least two pair
A Fendi bag and a bad attitude
That's all I need to get me in a good mood
She can walk with a switch and talk with street slang
I love it when a woman ain't scared to do her thing
Standing at the bus stop sucking on a lollipop
Once she gets pumping its hard to make the hottie stop
She likes to dance to the rap jam
She sweet as brown sugar with the candied yams
Honey coated complexion
Using Camay
Let's hear it for the girl she's from around the way

LL Cool J lyric, 'Around the Way Girl,' *Mama Said Knock You Out*, 1990.

In this global age of multiple identities, the 'American' body and its adorn-ment have become a religious enterprise, an intersection of cultural nation-alisms, a science of passion and desire. The Africanization of American style as seen in hip-hop fashion is relentless and carries with it a code of dressing. In his admiration for the female body, LL Cool J voices the twenty-first century sentiments of his hip-hop generation in a call and response to Langston Hughes' poem 'When Sue Wears Red' written as part of the Harlem Renaissance a century earlier:

When Susanna Jones wears red
A queen from some time-dead Egyptian night
Walks once again.

Blow trumpets, Jesus!

And the beauty of Susanna Jones in red
Burns in my heart a love-fire sharp like pain.
Sweet silver trumpets, Jesus!

At the dawn of the twentieth century, Harlem's Langston Hughes reified Susanna as a memorial to female beauty with 'jive' poetic exclamations of the male passion and erotic desire of a smitten young man. Not only does Hughes' gaze frame his *inamorata*, his object of desire, strutting in a parade of liquid lyricism clothed in the 'power color,' but he notes the exaggerated public profiling and vogue-ing that have come to be associated with black paralinguistic representation. It's not only what you rock but how you rock it. At the twilight of that century LL Cool J describes a hip-hop girl 'dressed to the nines.'

American fashion permits imaginative indulgence in the mythologies of its own time by creating an aesthetic space in which artifice and ambiguity emerge from the world of the street, popular taste and the fashion industry. Hip-hop style, as an extension of American 'black' fashion, gives form to another generation's fantasies and identities of choice by experimenting and appropriating from preceding systems of American, African and Latino taste to create new mythologies. Immersed in the identity formation typical of the young, hip-hop folk (hip-hop heads) are defined by their gear. Gear confers a look that is 'official' 'dope,' and personalized, and makes the jewelry-laden bling-blinger 'rock with ice.'

As a product of a digital and wireless generation equipped with cell phones, pagers, and MP3 players, hip-hop fashion of the twenty-first century screams high-tech. In keeping with 'a fierce aesthetic' (Nunley

1987) – a black aesthetic – hip-hoppers are generationally, demographically, and spiritually predisposed to hyper-linkages or networking. Hip-hoppers transmit information on what is 'cool' in fashion across national and international boundaries creating a hot and relentless buzz. Rapidly moving information on trends in fashion, rap poetics, and social activism, or b-boying/girling, downloading music, and the para-linguistics of body movement seems to be culturally rooted. In black fashion, the apple doesn't fall far from the tree. In *Race: The Floating Signifier* (1996) Stuart Hall notes that all that can be said about race has not yet been said, and given the fluidity of black style popularized among so many cultural groups, its future is bright. There is something ineffably spiritual in the capacity to sink cultural information into style codes which generate new social trends, an aesthetic that transcends the politics of the race. The relevance of hip-hop as a global movement, its nascent cultural principles which seem to instantly syncretize with cultural forms in Turkey, Japan, South Africa, Cuba, Germany and varied cultural sites, points to its resiliency and power as a hypertext of embodiment and empowerment. From an intergenerational perspective this may be difficult to appreciate. However, this chapter intends to unravel these style codes of hip-hop. As a hypermodern phenomenon, hip-hop fashion is the global black hypertext of this era, one more visual, more readable, more unrivalled in its imitations than any other fashion trend in recent history.

Hip-hop's global dress code is in its second wind. While old school hip-hop fashion may have been nurtured within poverty, recent hip-hop promotes high-end acquisition: the most expensive sneaker, twenty-four-karat jewelry, vintage clothes from previous fashion eras, and hair adornment. As with much traditional Afro-Latino apparel, the artist, whether on the stage or street, thrives on the praise of the spectator. Masking, masquerading, and processional as early forms of social organization and socialization reproduce themselves generations later in the culture of hip-hop. The concept of being both feared and respected through group behavior and adornment is also a mimesis of West African cultural practices in which 'play, threat, and histrionic behavior are based on the participants' ability to recognize signals as signals and map-territory relationships' (Nunley 1987: 190). Youth cultures in the Americas continue to engage police restrictions on public 'masked devil' parades that bear resemblance to the perception of a menacing, or nihilistic 'ghettocentricity.' In many parts of the Afro-Latino diaspora, public parades, processionals, masking celebrations, and rituals were banned during, and long after, slavery by reactionary white government officials, even in such remote areas as Bermuda with its Gombey dancers. Applying Nunley's fancy/fierce model to hip-hop highlights historical links between hip-hop and West African Sierra Leonean cultural societies whose political and social organization practices were reflected in their apparel. However, the fancy/fierce aesthetic opposition is also a gender dichotomy between maleness and femaleness.

Nunley writes that the 'attraction of sparkling and bright materials constitute what is called in Freetown fancy dress' (1987: 103). The 'fine dress, stylish music, and dancing of youth groups' derived from Egungun, Gelede, Arishola, and Ambas Geda societies in Sierra Leone relate to what hip-hop *fashonistas* would call 'bling-blinging.' 'Bling-blinging,' the hip-hop version of conspicuous consumption, is black commodity fetishism at its most profound. The style of Jelly Roll Morton, Fats Domino, and Isaac Hayes is reproduced in this strategy of hyper-adornment which legitimizes the use of gaudy baubles for men. Bling-blinging erased the ambiguous gender taboo by which jewelry signified femininity or homosexuality and was epitomized in Morton's gold and diamond-embedded tooth, then in Domino's signature star diamond watch and ring, and later in Hayes' chain mail torso and designer eyewear. Two features distinguish this accessorizing trend launched by black men; first, although Elvis Presley, Liberace, and Elton John may have appropriated bling-blinging in their stage attire from black style setters, the trend was clearly launched within the matrix of black notions of mythical style; and second, generally white fans did not adopt the stage attire of prominent white performance artists nearly as enthusiastically as did black audiences. Ceremonial practices are contained in the fierceness of 'gangster style' or the fanciness of 'mackin style.' With the media industries' love affair with the poor-boy-to-rich-boy selective promotion of 'bad boys,' thug life, and the criminal underground as the sole authenticity indicator, the conceptualization of hip-hop style tends to reduce hip-hop fashion to a formulaic stereotype, an urban metaphor, but it also constitutes identity formation. The same political organization which prompts much of West African political partisanship permeates the volatile ancestral forces pushing groups toward bonding or combat. What cap you wear in the hood defines your gang affiliation, but such ethnic-based gear, colors, or patterns are common among ethnic groups in every nation.

In the mid 1980s, with the popularity of Public Enemy, a wave of black nationalism unearthed the radical gear of the 1960s. African leather medallions, T-shirts reading 'it's a Black thing, you wouldn't understand,' Kente cloth, 'X' caps (for Malcolm X), and African-inspired apparel revived the red–black–green revolutionary colors of the previous generation. African idiomatic style maintains cultural continuities through the black fashion imagination. It has bred hip-hop traditions in dress dating from the South Bronx of the 1970s, one of many contexts that produced clothes for function – Sunday clothes, work clothes, school clothes, and party attire.

Unraveling the Code

From black and Latino precursors hip-hop extends and elaborates upon the art of seduction, political resistance, performance and spectatorship, and the interplay of the cultural subject with concentric loyalties to the wider sphere of American fashion. Engaged in ever-circulating rhythms of appropriation and *bricolage* of 'things African,' hip-hop has been a dominant player in keeping American fashion at the center of international fashion language. Roland Barthes' semiological analysis of adornment as a 'sign' to be decoded suggests that *bricolage* – the appropriation and collaging of everyday objects to create new forms and meanings – is, in fact, an invention of class subversion, thus blurring class lines, or what Hall would term counter-hegemonic resistance. Whatever is 'American' in US fashion is, however, itself derivative of European tastes. The amalgamation of culturally-based fashion trends in the United States conforms to the tendency on the part of (white) fashion systems to make style primitive, exotic, or ghetto, in effect, 'to plunder "exotic" techniques and codes from "other" looks' (Craik 1994: 17). The hip-hop movement, as a set of aesthetic practices, reverberates with the reinvention of style which has deeply influenced youth cultures around the world, thereby transmitting broader American culture and ideological referents to remote corners of the globe to maximum effect. These expeditions across the borders of the US are themselves a form of plundering.

In 'wearing red,' Susanna Jones fulfills a fantasy of pleasure, evident in Run-D.M.C.'s 'My Adidas' (1985), which continues to resonate with hip-hop stylists and performance artists like Jaheim in his lyrical declaration of seduction 'Tight Jeans' (*Still Ghetto*, 2002) as he blows new millennium trumpets 'killing me softly in those Prada tops and mini skirts.' Jeans remain a staple of youth culture in whatever form they might be manipulated, retaining their 'worker-style' appeal. The status elevation of jeans in the 1970s, from *basse couture* to *haute couture*, was concerned with socioeconomic patterns of consumption, the progressive values of that era of civil resistance and sexual freedom, and broadening to a more androgynous and male-inclusive consumer. As a fashion commodity targeting youth (similar to the running suit), jeans provided a liberating outlet for casual male dressing as much as they allowed young women to liberate themselves from the conventional 'dress' codes of femininity.

The designer jean movement popularized the pant as androgynous attire, both fancy and fierce. Inaugurated by Calvin Klein in the late 1970s, the designer jean refocused the unisex sensual body on the hips and legs, elongating the body's appearance and, at the same time, providing a casual-worker contrast to accompanying adornments. Men could now wear jeans with a jacket and tie and expensive shoes. Women could now wear jeans with halter bikini tops or silk blouses as in white American style. The tighter the jean, the greater the wearers' ability to stimulate desire. Among black hip-hop fashion consumers, the steatopygous *derrière* (enlarged buttocks) could be more easily accentuated and *au courant* as today's 'bootylicious' in jeans that were individualized by the wearer. 'While many young people may tear, rip, appliqué, or tie-dye their jeans, designers produce "sporty formal" denim suitable for more bourgeois lifestyles' (Craik 1994: 195). The personalization of attire among hip-hoppers was, and remains, a way of 'making it your own': 'You had to take something and make it hip-hop. If you had some inexpensive Bugel Boy jeans from Sears you had to take them and make them your own, make it exclusive so that you had the only one. I would paint my jeans and make then RobOne exclusives' (Gibbs 2003).

In four interviews conducted in the Fall of 2003, Rob Gibbs' memories of childhood and the hunger to be in style typify black fashion culture. The act of recreation blurs the line between hip-hoppers and major designers in the fashion world, and Barthes would be the first to caution against a solely black authenticating subjectivity by suggesting 'the better to separate Fashion from its creator gods [so that] it is imputed not to its producers, but to its consumers' (Barthes 1983). In the 100th issue of the *Source*, the reader is asked to 'remember back in the days when ni**as had waves, Cazal shades, and cornbraids?' (McGregor: 91). Three decades after the inception of hip-hop in the South Bronx, it is possible to craft a theory of hip-hop style and a system for embracing its many aesthetic tributaries, both 'fierce' and 'fancy' (Nunley 1987).

In his analysis of fashion systems, Barthes (1983) notes three strategies through which 'Fashion' is rationalized. These strategic modes determine what strata fashion ideas originate from and how these mediate human groups to become 'laws.' Barthes suggests that, by creating 'obligation-filled-futures,' fashion trends prescribe and authenticate their own aesthetic frontiers by: 1. suggesting the 'appearance of a feature as a natural phenomenon'; 2. aiming at a shifting originator (producer or consumer); and 3. noting the 'subject of appearance, an autarchic universe.' Barthes' modes of analysis of fashion magazine hype in *The Fashion System* (1983) can be updated and interpreted, I would argue, in hip-hop as follows: 1. 'black, in any case, your [Armani suit], and of course you'll add the "cold show [of] my rings" and my diamond studs' (McGregor 1998: 92); 2. They love [running suits] 'fresh dipped like a million bucks' (McGregor 1998: 91); and 3. 'This year, [hats] come in three styles-Kangols, baseball caps, and kufis].' This is all toward the end of 'keepin' it real.'

Hip-hop heads salute differentiated internal streams of genre-based musical culture-mackin', party, jazz–bohemian, gangsta, or propaganda. As such, they have established a fashion rhetoric which dismantles the linear temporality of past, present, and future reassembling new forms of identity in which the consolidation of era-based dressing defies appropriateness. Anything goes, with one exception: lack of cleanliness. 'There's an essential importance in being clean, no stains, not looking raggedy, matching, et al that is omnipresent throughout all of black styles. Whether it's grandma dressed to the nines for church in her hot pink suit with matching shoes, purse, and hat with the large feather, or a graff writer who's rockin' Ecko from head to toe with sneakers to match his outfit' (Chandler-Smith). To some degree the cleanliness ethic may derive from the precariousness of life in urban communities of color in which severe dislocations of structural inequality persist and ensemble dressing provides a public platform for defying social and economic deprivation. Looking good is an aesthetic convention, a text, simultaneously of the past, present, and future.

Such a perspective on hip-hop as a fashion system considers the appropriation of style as a normative sign of the passions which 'place fashion outside humanity . . . and constitute it as a malign contingency: Fashion places itself at the crossroads of chance and divine decree: its decision becomes an obvious fact' (Barthes 1983: 271). In hip-hop the fashion rhetoric is as precise as it is elaborate. It is filled with the stylistic laws of 'should' and 'must have.' Fashion choices are charged with the spirit of metaphor and symbol. Hip-hop is now a fashion elder complete with its own vintage apparel, its 'throwbacks.' Rather than 'dogmatically reject' the old school fashion which preceded it (as Barthes would suspect), contemporary hip-hop recirculates its own internal ethnic traditions in a wider black fashion system. This recirculation signifies on its own aesthetic memories from the 1920s to 1970s, thus preserving cultural ways of being. P-Diddy, vogueing on stage in an Armani suit, looks over his shoulder, aesthetically, to Cab Calloway strutting in a zoot suit thus increasing the mileage of the black fashion rhetoric. The bohemian appropriation of jazz-infused hip-hop genres popularized by Erykah Badu's head wraps harks back to the popular use of head wraps by white women in the 1920s, itself an appropriation of African style, which was later re-appropriated by the 'black is beautiful' and black power movements of the 1960s and 1970s. Giving props to history is a mantra of hip-hop culture. In the lushly photographed *Men of Color: Fashion, History, Fundamentals* (1998), Lloyd Boston notes that 'living in the twentieth century garments are considered as valuable as financial portfolios, luxury vehicles, and real estate. Trespassing on the grounds that we've called duds, threads, vines, rags, and even gear is more than an invasion of personal space, it's an assault on the only element of our image that we have fully controlled: our style' (1998: 12). Here, style preserves memory. 'In hip-hugging, thigh-grabbing, double knits, we took on the world, telling our stories. We danced out our lives, felt the sorrow, pain, happiness, and joy of being Black and male and telling the world our story' (Boston 1998: 145). Old school icon Fab 5 Freddy recalls meeting, and later collaborating with, musician Debbie Harry and others in 1981 and taking them to the 'Police Athletic League in the Bronx for this big sort of hip-hop convention . . . to the P.A.L. at 183rd . . . and to this party, which was Mercedes Ladies. I think Cold Crush was there and a couple of other groups' (Fricke and Ahearn 2002: 283). *Yes Yes Y'all* documents the underworld womb of hip-hop, its gang culture origins, and the way in which gang attire signaled affiliation, territoriality, and visibility across the Afro-Latino imaginary spaces, particularly those plagued by urban neglect. The South Bronx matrix of early hip-hop brewed a cross-cultural sensibility in urban social identity.

'Savage Skulls were strictly Puerto Ricans. They were smaller than the Black Spades, but they were the most notorious gang in New York City . . . Me being part of that, going home I had to take my bandana off, my jacket off, because of my parents, but they knew something was going on' (ibid: 6). As 'enthusiastic co-originators of Hip-hop' (Rivera 2002), *Latinidad* (whether west or east coast), *pachuco* or *Boricua cultures*, of Chicano or *Puertorriqueno* sensibilities), together with African Americans and Afro-Latino communities specialized in transgressive politics in lifestyle by using music and fashion to reify and implement new identities; that is, by 'putting on a new skin' (Sanchez-Tranquilino and Tagg 1992: 558).

In a sense, there is no separate language of music, dress, and style in cultural production in the Afro-Latino diaspora. The apparatus through which hip-hop culture speaks so eloquently is the body. Cultural systems are, therefore, interdependent and recirculating tools of social and political resistance. As long as resistance is demanded by the social and economic policies of underdevelopment, black and Latino cultural production and taste will continue to evince an authenticating transgressive politics in dressing which reflects artifice and ambiguity. Generation E.A. (Ethnically

Ambiguous) explores multi-racial themes of chic, exotic, 'left-of-center beauty' (LaFerla 2003) in the presentation of the body and modeling and ad agencies that promote ethnic hype are often criticized for retreating from faces and bodies which reveal African blood.

While the bling-bling factor defines hip-hop, hip-hop did not invent flamboyance. As Boston notes: 'Dizzy Gillespie's chic tam-o'-shanter inspired a nation of White beatniks . . . Hip-hop style setters RUN DMC and LL Cool J brought back the porkpie, breaking it down in the crown to create a halolike effect' (Boston 1998: 157–9). Breakin' down or breakin' in clothing items is an essential operation in black trendsetting.

The microeconomic vision of the hip-hop fashion industry as a discrete sector of the fashion economy suggests that producers and consumers make choices about products using both market and non-market signals for the allocation of goods and resources. So while there may be a distinctly 'black fashion' niche, what drives this niche is the music of hip-hop and the social commentary emerging from its impresarios and performance artists. To portray identity, mediate identity, transform identity, mask identity, and commodify identity (as a nationalizing tool of industry power, cultural power, as well as apparatus of the state), youth magnify the significance of adolescence as a statement of rebellion, commentary and individuality. Aficionados as well as fans of music forms take on the identities of their favorite performance artists by dressing similarly and new trends emerge. Thus, the once-private body becomes a canvas and adornment its expressive platform of language and communication. In the new millennium, 'biting' is a convention in an interdependent fashion industry. The inexpensive, available, affordable, and second-hand were re-contextualized as aesthetic signifiers inside communities of color, and rapidly became *haute couture* in the fashion world. Black fashionistas have appropriated dressy and casual European attire, whether the zoot suit or the running suit, since the early twentieth century. However, it is also true that the African-based fashion text has transmuted the very idea of American fashion from merely clothes to clothes-cum-paralinguistics. Then there is the body language that must accompany the hip-hop 'uniform,' codified gestures and expressive language which are identifiably hip-hop, but which are also indigenously black and Latino. There is – the swagger.

The Branding of Black Culture

Fashion is a multi-billion-dollar construction industry, one which constructs social meaning in tandem with the music industry. Whether with regard to the symbolic importance of hip-hop's baggy pants, the inherent sign of the jean, or the convention of the male trouser for both male and female, ownership and property rights pervade the world of style-setting. Describing the 1980s, George notes the relationship between successive musical genres and fashion in stating that 'rap still rules, but its new jack swing offshoot, together with new wave disco, a/k/a house, is now the cutting edge of black street aesthetics' (George 2001: 119). Hip-hop celebrities remain the focus of this storytelling by assuming the role of the archetypal mannequin, promoting street-inspired styles and endorsing brand names of designers who craft prototypes for market distribution to the middle classes and the knock-off industry. Things have changed since the old school days of hip-hop when the music held greater significance than the 'look,' before hip-hop became a consumption industry. However, whether styles originate in the designer's workspace or on the street, by the time styles make it to the rack, many have already been displaced by new trends. Former-street-hustler-turned-impresario, and owner of Phat Fashions, Russell Simmons suggests that, in the pursuit of 'class,' hip-hop is a major trendsetting machine: 'Hip-hop chooses: Bentleys are hot because Puffy and my wife drive them' (Rozhon 2003: BU9).

The construction and penetration of the 'teen market' by market advertisers in the 1950s suggested that much of the dynamism of American popular culture would come from youth. The first major hip-hop brand, Cross Colors, was soon followed by Karl Kani, later by Mecca, FUBU, Ecko, and subsequently by P-Diddy's Sean Jean label and Jay-Z's Rocawear. Mogul Russell Simmons, the multimillionaire hip-hop entrepreneur, has diversified his clothing-based companies to include banking and philanthropy. From the platform of contemporary fashion, many celebrities of color are attempting to sway urban-inspired fashion dollars away from mainstream (read: white) designers – Hilfiger, Klein, and Lauren. For example, as businessman Russell Simmons negotiates licensing agreements and brokers mega-deals to promote his clothing lines and other commodities in the department store sector. The competition has been a horse race. However, as George reminds us: 'The hip-hop-driven growth of designers like Hilfiger and Lauren . . . did not drive smart African-American companies out of Business' (George 1998: 163). From the hip-hop consumer's perspective the marketing of new styles has rarely had a predictable life cycle. But young buyers remain hypnotized by the celebrity seal of approval:

Grand Puba talking about *Girbaud, Tommy Hilfiger, Nautica* . . . Well, nobody knew who they were, but we went to Filene's basement, saw it, and had to get it just because he was hollerin' about it! Style evolved from breaking your neck to have something that had a label on it. People would go into stores just to steal tags so you could put the label on the knock-off version you could afford. (Gibbs 2003)

The procurement of trendy 'threads' in hip-hop derives from multiple streams of desire. Throwback ensemble pieces or items such as hats or sports shirts suggest the recycling of an old aesthetic, a dip into the nostalgia pool. Meanwhile Bruce Lee's martial arts films spawned not only an interest in the disciplinary techniques of the East, but also the integration of the martial arts uniform into the aesthetic language of the hip-hop generation and athletic wear. E-commerce now displaces the department store, discount outlets, thrift shops, vintage clothing and consignment stores where Blue Marlin and LRG lines are being popularized by Missy Eliot and Roots. In the mode of diversification, Blue Marlin boasts a line of venerable Latino, Negro, and women's baseball league attire with purchase prices in the hundreds of dollars.

American fashion is hyperbolical and aspires to the high life. Why should hip-hop not *bling-bling* us into blinding oblivion? *Haute couture* fashion designers of all ethnic and national backgrounds stand alongside hip-hop designers such as Rocawear, Phat Farm, Lady Enyce, and Sean Jean. In its centering and re-popularization of the black male body, hip-hop has also cast a light on black and Latino designers inspired by urban culture motifs. Diketo and Andre Martin, Sister Bucks, and Damat and Tween, all of Johannesburg (South Africa), feature influences located in the aesthetics of African idioms and street cool. Russell Simmons is less of a style maven than P-Diddy, but every bit the conglomerate ideologue, pushing businesses by licensing to manufacturers and raking in $20 million–$30 million in profits. *Vogue* magazine's André Leon Talley elicited the branding-celebrity correlation from the Sean Jean impresarios thus: 'What Hip-hop endorses becomes popular' (Talley 2002). While the elite buying demographic is arguably smaller than the popular markets to which hip-hop designers appeal, hip-hop as a fashion movement has attracted a 'lifestyles of the rich and famous' reputation in precious gems, high-end motor vehicles and motorcycles, real estate, tourism and resort, spa and beauty, and vacation retreat markets which rely on the very wealthy to patronize and sustain their products. Fast living requires not only fast cars, but customized vehicles which impress envious fans and contribute to the jet-set image so central to conspicuous consumption. Yet while the twenty-first century is the style century, class is not so easily obtained, even with money.

To 'bling' or not to 'bling,' that is the question. The pursuit of recognition and upward mobility through wearing the 'in' fashion, is a reach for a kind of nobility. However, accumulating pricey real estate next door to 'old money' elites, driving a Bentley or Lamborghini, or sipping expensive and rare wines or liqueur, may not guarantee class. Dream merchants tantalize, seduce, and enrapture the consciousness of hip-hop consumers through television fare such as *Cribs* and in the hood of old school hip-hop, the car, fashion, and sex magazines. Why would hip-hop aspire to any other dreams when to be American is to *bling-bling*. In identifying what is classic or can be made classic, we look for permanency, endurance, appeal, elegance. As the Motown era was concerned with creating a charm school where performance artists were taught to address the press, they also were tutored to dress for success. The boy and girl groups of the 1950s, 1960s, and 1970s wore chic suits and gowns, hair was stylized or wigged, stage make-up was theatrically overdone, and jewelry was garish and overstated. The late Celia Cruz performed in four-inch stilettos while James Brown and Little Richard similarly wore over-the-top stylized hair and apparel.

'Ghettocentricity' and Street Credibility

In the twenty-first century, the ingénue 'b-girl' (girl break dancer) described below, far from a catwalk queen, possesses the stylistic flair which announces her regal arrival onto a competitive space in which her clothes become a secondary signifier of her performative virtuosity (Figure 12.1).

Imagine the scenario with applause before, during and after: 'Fashion release, Boston, MA . . .' 120 pounds hip-gliding into line-of-sight, a Kangol in glistening white cocked AC/DC encircling a short raven hair cut, white cropped 'wife-beater' hugging a slender torso, winged tattoo fanning from her navel, white hip-slung pants, bangles, multiply-pierced ears and navel, regulation b-girl kicks. At this Boston 2003 b-boying competition, fly-girl was *'da bomb,'* a poster babe for contemporary hip-hop fashion, the *dernier cri* of a b-girl. More than a fashion plate, the girl could spin. In his essay 'All Part of the Act' (1991), Albert LeBlanc discusses 'making reputation' in the popular culture music industry as a matter of establishing a *persona*. In a holistic theory of 'costuming' he presents the constitutive elements of grooming – hair and facial bearding, make-up, jewelry, eyewear, and tattoos – as integrative in the creation of *persona*. Such a hip-hop system of adornment accommodates both a 'fancy' and 'fierce' aesthetic derivative of both American and European fashion and includes all of the grooming features listed. 'Shades' (or sunglasses) are as integral to looking 'dope' among hip-hop performers as they were crucial to bebop-

Figure 12.1 Boston Floorlords b-girl, Yhinny Matos, in gear. Nuri Chandler-Smith.

pers trying to achieve an aesthetic of 'cool.' 'Ghettocentricity' is a reinterpretation of the fancy/fierce aesthetic of African cultural prototypes which still manifests the art of costuming in performance rituals. Both ghettocentricity and *pachuco* culture 'got into the dress codes of white male status and normality, playing with the images of an Anglo popular culture's own masculine "outsiders" – the Southern dandy, the Western gambler, the *modern* urban gangster . . . and ruptured their structures of Otherness' (Sanchez-Tranquilino and Tagg 1992: 559).

The twenty-first-century music industry continues to promote ghettocentricity most defiantly as pimp culture. By 2003 Nelly's 'Pimp Juice,' 50 Cent's 'P.I.M.P.,' David Banner's 'Like a Pimp' and Jay-Z's 'Big Pimpin' had extended the preoccupation with what many critics consider a social pathology. The fashion message of these hip-hop performance artists, broadcast widely through MTV, presents the visual language of pimp culture through simulated sex choreography and the stylized dressing of 'pimp-as-dandy' and 'ho-as-golddigger.' The gender games, in fact, have another side in this fast-forward to 1988.

> Some older girls take Kim out . . . [she] finds herself at Manhattan's Latin Quarter nightclub in its heyday . . . witnesses the dark extravagances of the drug game. Kim sees cats dressed in thick gold ropes, custom-tailored Louis Vuitton- and Gucci-style leathers made at Dapper Dan's, the infamous clothier of Mike Tyson, LL, and a gener-ation of young capitalists growing rich from the crack trade. (Vibe 2001: 133)

Style, in the service of popular fashion, both emulates pathological and mythological aspects of street culture, and inter-generationally recasts stereotypes in social stone. Manliness and womanliness – theatricalized constructions of femininity and masculinity – determine a limited set of roles for youth audiences and, consequently, deeply influence individual and group behaviors, both internally (within black and Latino communi-ties) and externally (to white audiences and marketers). To be a man, in other words, one must dress like a man for, in the common rubric, 'the clothes make the man.' The inability to discriminate between stage dressing and social/everyday dressing in hip-hop culture, suggests an ambiguity of those structural inequalities that persist in communities of color. Artifice is constructed through fashion and fashion distracts us from the political pragmatism devised, prefigured, and exhibited initially for the stage. The concept of street credibility, so central to the style-minstrelsy game, is a subject of controversy. Internet chat room discussions field such debates as 'How pimp are you?' featuring comments which suggest an ambiguous border between the roles of 'pimp' and 'player,' roles in which Armani and Gucci suits, alligator shoes and custom-designed hats and jewelry signify an 'alternative universe.' Fashion becomes a tool of assimilation and nationalism, affluence and materialism, and finally, cultural transference. As if the economic explanations of urban economic marginality were suffi-cient rationalizations for the recirculation of impermanent social roles, the fashion message of *'pimpalicious'* remains the animus of indiscrete sexu-ality for younger and younger, especially male, groups.

The female counterpart to the pimp – the 'ho' – achieves a role as co-signifier, one accentuated by the reductive attire of voluptuous young girls whose sexuality is defined by the fashion politics of pimping. The 'ho' is a style proxy for the pimp, both in her role as actual sex worker and in the adoption of revealing, figure-defining clothing in the attire of everyday life depicted by the quartet of divas who restaged Lady Marmalade's 'Voulez-vous coucher avec moi.' Both female 'mannequins' are real figurations of 'streetwalking,' of fashion's utility in the 'prostitution' of black female culture. The more progressive genres of hip-hop modify this hard-edge stereotype of dressing with female celebrities whose fashion choices are focused on more 'real' women-centered concepts of fashion. Soulful Jill Scott, Queen Latifah, lyrical genius Lauren Hill, and Erykah Badu prefer feminine statements of style consciousness that do not objectify, but reify, the female body. Not only have America's 'manchild media masters' (George 1998) glorified hip-hop as a domain of misogyny through lyrical obscenity, but the more visibly marketed women's fashion preference circulates 'briefly' between underwear and a beach thong.

Young women do not necessarily read this typecasting as a definition of women's role by a non-negotiable masculinity, but rather play into it or, by inversion, as with Lil' Kim, claim a subversion of masculinity with a dominatrix model of power and gold-digging. Clearly, more vibrant models of self-reflexive hip-hop feminism would ventilate these more juvenile fashion possibilities among hip-hoppers. With so many more women than men in MTV videos which confuse sexuality with love and mistake simulated sex for choreography, black and Latino machismo values transmitted from Superfly to Big Pun ensure that gender relations never evolve beyond old-fashioned concepts of manhood and womanhood. Fashion is the ultimate fantasy tool for legitimizing misogyny and feeding it intravenously to an impressionable youth audience experimenting with identity issues. Outside of the US, props must be given to hip-hop *raperas* in Cuba, as one example, such as Las Kruzas, Atracción, Mónica of Doble Filo and Obsesión, whose performance attire is either politically inspired or Afrocentric. The Cuban female group Instinto, however, 'drew as much applause at the Festival de Rap Cubano for wearing patent-leather hot pants as for their lyrics . . . a playful approach, taunting and teasing men out of their mach armor with a wink and a hip-shake' (Verán, 1998: 138). African-Latino public attire and the art of profiling are elements of social interaction and congregation, ingathering and ceremonializing, celebration and competition. The Africanization, Latinization, and Indigenization of the Americas over the last four centuries have been written in the blood of pan-ethnicities. America as well as the idea of America have transnationalized the exportation of culture.

Strictly underground, the early culture of hip-hop was dominated by the mackin'/partying genre, instituted by the block parties organized by luminaries such as Africa Bambaataa. Old school hip-hop style was characterized by nameplate belts, Sergio Valente jeans, and running suits. This type of *bricolage* in contexts of urban poverty stimulated a sensibility of form and function associated with party culture for audiences and stage 'uniforms' for the early performance artists. Against the backdrop of high inflation and unemployment in the US, the OPEC oil embargo, Lukas' *Star Wars* films, the home computer revolution, Watergate, the Iranian revolution, the Cambodian genocide of 2.5 million people, the creation of UNIX and 'C' language, widespread strikes and industrial unrest in the UK, the end of the Vietnam War and fear of nuclear war, the anomie of the early generation of hip-hoppers and their party imperative seem highly remarkable and constructive contributions to global stability and cultural development. Not unlike the Harlem Renaissance of the 1920s, the early hip-hop movement inside black and Latino communities was a healing, a strengthening, a renewal. The public disgrace of urban blight and renewal underwent a transformation of substance, a process of collective action in which hip-hop artists inaugurated these fashion rites, stimulated audiences, and moved youth culture into a state of grace. Today, the attire of old-school styles might be classified as pre-vintage classic.

The East coast brand of hip-hop apparel was influenced by New York proper, the world's cultural and financial capital during the Harlem Renaissance. Harlem in its heyday had been a center of black style.

Gender, the Unisex and Body Politics

If dressing is a language, then black dressing is a dialectical language, a text. It indicates enthusiasm for a sense of belonging to community, a belief in the possibility of reforming and mythologizing gender. Those who determine points of style and enforce that style are themselves masters of an androgynous subtext. The running suit acknowledges unisex patterns of behavior which transcend gender and a new sexuality manifests blurry lines of the feminine and masculine in black style. As health and fitness became an American obsession, sports and casual wear was popularized and patronized by designers and the fashion industry. Both men and women, consumed with the Utopian body and its public image, began to concern themselves less with the treadmill and the yoga mat than with side-stepping fitness by wearing sports clothes which merely suggest physical fitness. Women, as much or more so than men, whether in or out of professional sports careers, defined fashion as a signifier and indicator of lifestyle. Ironically, few who wear running suits may actually run. In hip-hop, physical fitness may be an overstated goal of a youth market dominated by those who are young and, therefore, in shape. However, the sports paradigm is pre-eminent in hip-hop culture given the culturally programmed sports/entertainment goals of many young black and Hispanic populations.

The demographic influences of race and culture are relentless. They suggest that aspiring wanna-bees can always jump-start public culture with their sports and entertainment loyalties. As more women enter sports, including those sports historically under-representing minorities such as tennis and golf, more young people will want to dress for success imitating Tiger Woods and Serena Williams. What they wear on the court and on the course affects fashion markets. In black and Hispanic culture, moreover, specific gender modalities prevail concerning style. While the 'hoochie mama' style of a Lil' Kim or Foxy Brown – 'the official chickenhead patron saints' (Morgan: 199) – may reflect the prevalence of sexy street attire and the desire for womanly appeal, two realities persist; that much of hip-hop (like rock and roll, hippie, and heavy metal) emerges from the immature vision of a generation that has yet to grow into adulthood; and that the actual patrons of young women's fashion sense lay somewhere in between the 'hoochie mama' and the African goddess. It all begins with a fantasy. 'It all begins with a dress. A hot little thing. A spaghetti-strapped Armani number, with a skintight bodice and a long flowing skirt, in that shade of orange that Black girls do the most justice' (Morgan: 17). When the clock strikes twelve, however, we all turn back into pumpkins, all of us except hip-hop celebrities who believe their own hype.

Such are the dreams of the young and an American consciousness too easily seduced by a culture of sexually-obsessed entitlement. Yet the more popularized media is predatory concerning the 'pimpalicious,' with an unhealthy idolatry of a historical pimp culture that victimizes women and, while predatory itself, reduces men to solicitors who live off the earnings of vulnerable women. Dramatic, in-your-face sex dressing identified with the 'hooking' profession serves to reinforce and, at the same time, make a fantasy of the misfortunes of young women and men whose economic constraints present prostitution as an illegitimate but accepted option for survival. Styles are intersectional, and body swagger is essential language. What you see on the corner may appear on the runway, on Vegas show-girls, or on your daughter. That is, if you have the body for it. Missy Elliott's weight loss has been positive role modeling for an American culture in which youth obesity is a rising health phenomenon. Without betraying generational biases, however, the young are, in every successive generation, explorers of the frontier of the forbidden sexual body and use fashion as a means to express flowering womanhood and manhood.

Hip-hoppers are increasingly social and political activists through an underground that sometimes sells 'fashion' to a skeptical audience disdainful of being trendy. Yet, even the underground carries out a non-stylistic approach to attire and body presence which is itself style conscious. Jeans, T-shirts, nationalistic or religious jewelry, sports clothes,

Figure 12.2 Hip-hop group Adrenalyn Rush from Cleveland, OH. Courtesy of Charles Reed Jr.

sneakers, construction attire, all items associated with youth or workers, have become a type of proletarian call to arms identifying adherents from continent to continent (Figure 12.2). The '*bad boy family*' (Puff Diddy, Notorious B.I.G., Jay-Z, Lil' Kim) migrated to *haute couture* for the status afforded by their new-found wealth and were welcomed by the catwalks and private salons of American and European designers as big spenders who gave *haute couture* its second wind. In New York, downtown went uptown once again for such revitalization as in the film *Wildstyle* (1983) in which break dancers (b-boys) and graffiti artists are seduced into the chic art galleries of wealthy whites. P-Diddy, wearing Armani suits in the early 1990s, conforms to customary Western male dress; yet suits, despite their adoption by women, still connote corporate maleness and power dressing designed to suppress the feminine body.

Young women in hip-hop opt for diverse genres parallel with hip-hop rap and musical genres. Fashionistas can be identified by their gear and paraphernalia. No matter that these first incursions into the sophisticated world of established fashion involved mispronunciations of the names Versace and Gucci. One may not expect the children of the hood to be polyglots, yet raps' Ebonic–Spanglish–Spanish linguistic structures suggest otherwise. Now that *def* and *phat* are in the eleventh edition of the Merriam-Webster Collegiate Dictionary, the slang of American English has been further Ebonicized by hip-hop. What goes on the black body, the postcolonial body, the 'multicultural' body, is public spectacle. Fashion forecasts new global pluralisms that surface in a geopolitical imagination tempered by chaos. Americans, sampling from the cultural memory of the indigenous, the enslaved, the refugee, the indentured, and the immigrant, exploit the *barrios*, the ghettos, the townships, the *favelas*, and the reservations creating a reservoir of multiple identities, the deep cache of underground aesthetic moorings out of which hip-hop and other cultural ways of expressing angst emerge.

With a generation reviving and recycling styles, culture, blood, and fashion can be profoundly democratized. While only mixing can make blood democratic, style can make culture both political and transgressive. When blood mixes we do not always get even loyalties to one or the other culture. But we do get even. Genetics allows us to recreate new lineages which demand erotic notice and it is through style, fashion, and ceremonial dress that we submit ourselves to the rule of desire. What goes on or covers the body must, in the twenty-first century, be expressive of what the previous two centuries forbade – the pleasure of the body as public text. If critics attack the gangsta aesthetic, then perhaps hip-hoppers are the Dadaists of their generation.

Crowning Glories and Tattoos

From the pompadour to the Afro, black hairstyling for men and women has been a venture into three-dimensional image-making (Figure 12.3). 'At Kinapes and other Afrocentric barbershops the fade flattop became a sculpture: cuts became lines, lines formed words, words turned into elaborate

Figure 12.3 Nuri Chandler-Smith (right) interviewing Rob Gibbs at Artists for Humanity. Nuri Chandler-Smith.

etchings. Mixed and matched with dreads, braids, and in Atlanta and on the West Coast even curls, the fade (the 'Cameo', the high-low) is the most culturally conscious and comfortably unisex hairstyle since the Afro' (George 2001: 119). The Kente head-wrap, popularized during the Black is Beautiful/Black Power movement of the 1960s, revived by Salt-n-Pepa, was, in turn, reflective of the jazz–bohemian genre for women. With *Baduism*, released in February 1997, Erykah Badu took her 'head-wrapped home girl' look to the charts and with it she brought her sense of style and 'single-handedly injected a much needed shot of refreshing diversity into the hip hop aesthetic.' Her towering head-wraps stood in 'defiant opposition to the swarms of bootylicious R&B kewpie dolls' (Vibe: 104).

Silk head-wraps or doo-rags, with colors indicating not only ensemble coordination but also gang loyalties, donned mostly by men, are in fact, an appropriation from previous generations when men wore stocking caps or head-wraps to smooth down processed or newly pomaded hair. When 'high-top' hairstyles were trendy, the doo-rags were generally abandoned. But still, they persist. In males, they are a counterpoint to the female head-wrap. Underneath the headgear, there may be designer barber cuts. The New York skyline, a fashion or gang logo, any abstraction may appear on the male hip-hop head. The female hip-hop head is color-treated, processed, *au naturel*, or augmented by wigs, weaves, and extensions. When Mary J. and Jennifer Lopez went blonder and blonder, the noted replication of white girls with long, blowin'-in-the-wind tresses gripped the fantasies of many younger (and older) black women searching for another look which exploited the contrasts between 'conventional' darker skin tones and 'conventionally' darker hair.

In communities of color the styling of hair has been chronicled, analyzed, and critiqued after the presence of peoples of African descent in the Americas and histories of hairstyling customs in Africa have been written (Byrd and Tharps 2001; Mercer 1992; Sieber 2000). A clash of beauty standards regarding body type, phenotype, hair texture and length, for both men and women has crossed the borders of the public and the private, the black hair care industry including barbershops and beauty parlors (Byrd and Tharps 2001) as social sites of information and trans-formation. All critiques about hair in these debates can be sheltered under the framework of an understanding of how artifice and ambiguity are embedded in postmodernity.

A subset of hairstyling techniques has emerged since the 1970s including the high-top fade, embellishments of the re-appropriated Afro, advancements in hair weaving, dred locks, Jheri Curls, cornrows, exten-sions, twists, and continued use of the perm processes and hair plaiting, all to achieve even greater versatility. Since the histories of miscegenation have produced differentiation among people of color, sweeping differ-ences in hair texture and attitudes about hair pervade hair culture. The Africanization of the planet has produced mixed ancestries as far afield as Australia and the Middle East, and throughout Central, South and Latin America. In these geographically diverse places identical issues surface regarding hair preferences and prevalent beauty standards. Scholars of fractal mathematics note the multiple appearance of a fractal aesthetic in diverse aspects of African societies, from African settlement architecture, to textile design/weaving, sculpture and household objects, personal adornment, and hair braiding methods in which evidence of fractal patterning can be seen (Eglash 1999). American cornrowing, sustaining African tradition, is also known by its Yoruba name, *ipako elede,* 'which means the nape of the neck of a boar – because the boar's bristles show a nonlinear scaling' and the nonlinear contours of the human head hair are followed in plaiting using abstract spatial transformation (Eglash 1999: 81). Further, Senegalese wigs, braiding on Dan masks, and Cameroonian braiding are examples of the process of iteration making a 'cascade of predetermined transformations' (Eglash 1999: 112), a recursion in hair design through 'coils of coils' and 'braids of braids' techniques. Hairstyling, therefore, among African diaspora stylists constitutes the preservation, transmission, and re-adaptation of Old World-to-New-World retentions in which cultures can breathe dynamic life into ever-circulating practices of holistic grooming and fashion. The same may be said regarding tattooing, particularly in relation to the Bamana fractal scaling on the feet and palms of the hands as well as tattooing among the Maori of the South Pacific. Fractal design may be seen as a compressed code which African slaves transported across the black Atlantic. Given the 300-year duration of this trade and the 12+ million cohort, the reproduction of this design sensibility was an ideal construct within which to preserve vital aspects of the African cultural self into the modern era. Since the tattoo is so popular among hip-hop heads and Gen X, mention of the use of the body as a text must be included in any presentation of how hip-hop culture expands its vocabulary of adornment within the context of its own generational urges.

Every inch of the hip-hop body is fair game – from navels to buttocks, earlobes to ankles (Brain 1979). It is to imagine the late Tupac or 50 Cent as icons of hip-hop in advertising or live performance without the tattoo peripatetically making its way from bicep to belly, buttocks to breast, lip to tongue. Male haircutting techniques, featuring incised abstract or representational forms, were pioneered by urban hip-hop heads. Male and female processing, weaves, and flamboyant time-consuming styling designed to straighten curls, or wave tightly-curled hair are not, in themselves, hip-hop novelties, but staples in communities of color (and others) and among those who entrust their idealized self to the arbiters of taste, barbers and hairdressers. These two community players, more than any stylist, clothes designer, or *fashionista*, constitute the dreammakers of black cultural fantasies regarding how people of color see themselves, idealize themselves, and imitate and innovate trendsetting. Any ethnographic observation of urban street style among hip-hoppers must acknowledge hair and skin color. With an ever-indeterminate authenticity rooted in the 'total look,' the gendered body offers ornamentation as a dynamic plaything of power, transgression, and invention. As a text, the body remains ambiguous. It hovers around artifice. The idea, then, of 'things African' in the hands of an immodest Western materialism, makes the US the perfect cross-cultural playground for tag-teaming styles back and forth making what was once *fierce*, now *fancy*, then *fierce* once again in an 800 billion dollar design economy.

In the final analysis hip-hop fashion, in its virtuosity, inventiveness, and pursuit of pleasure will remain the stuff of legends for future pop culture historians. Within a music-centered lifestyle of combative and aggressive politics reflecting the structural inequalities of urban life, the construction of a culturally-specific approach to fashion by young hip-hoppers is a statement. It is a collage of experimentation, appropriation, innovation, resistance, and *bricolage* in which the aesthetics of 'cool' and 'hip' and 'down' are now 'Word!' In other words, *is your thang, your style flowin'*? If not, get some flava in ya gear.

References

Barthes, R. (1975). *The Pleasure of the Text*. Trans. by Richard Miller, New York: Noonday Press.

—— (1983), *The Fashion System*. Trans. by M. Ward and R. Howard, Berkeley: University of California Press.

Beat Street (1984), VHS, Orion, Prod. Belafonte H. and Picker, D. Color.

Bordo, S. (1997). 'Bringing body to theory,' *Twilight Zones-The Hidden Life of Cultural Images from Plato to O.J.*, Berkeley: University of California Press: 173–91.

Boston, L. (1998), *Men of Color – Fashion, History, Fundamentals*, New York: Artisan.

Brain, R. (1979), *The Decorated Body*, New York: Harper and Row.

Branch, S. (1993), 'How hip-hop fashion won over mainstream America,' *Black Enterprise* 23, June.

Byrd, A. and L. Tharps (2001), *Hair Story-Untangling the Roots of Black Hair in America*, New York: St. Martin's Press.

Chandler-Smith, N. (2003) Interviews, September–December.

Craik, J. (1994), *The Face of Fashion – Cultural Studies in Fashion*, New York: Routledge.

Daniels, D.H. (2002), 'Los Angeles zoot: race "riot," the pachuco, and black music culture,' *The Journal of African American History*.

Delgado, F. (1998), 'Chicano ideology revisited: rap music and the (re)articulation of Chicanismo,' *Western Journal of Communication* 62(2): 95–113.

Deyhle, D. (1998), 'From break dancing to heavy metal – Navajo youth, resistance, and identity,' *Youth & Society* 30(1): 3–31.

Eglash, R. (1999). *African Fractals – Modern Computing and Indigenous Design*, New Brunswick: Rutgers University Press.

Flores, J. (2000), *From Bomba to Hip-Hop: Puerto Rican Culture and Latino Identity*, New York: Columbia University Press.

Frick, J. and C. Ahearn (2002), *Yes Yes Y'All: The Experience Music Project Oral History of Hip-hop's First Decade,* New York, Da Capo Press.

George, N. (1998), *Hip Hop America,* New York: Viking.

—— (2001), *Buppies, B.Boys, Baps, & Bohos – Notes on Post Soul Black Culture,* New York: Da Capo Press.

Gibbs, R. (2003). Interview by Nuri Chandler-Smith. September 29 and December 4.

Graffiti Rock-and Other Hip-hop Delights (2002), DVD, MTH Prod., Color.

Guerrero, E. (1993), *Framing Blackness – The African American Image in Film,* Philadelphia: Temple University Press.

Heroes of Latin Hip-hop (2002), DVD, Fred Sherman. Chronic Media and Digital Downloand Inc. Color. 85 min.

Hughes, L. (1974), *Selected Poems: Langton Hughes,* New York: Vintage.

Kincaid, J. (1988), *A Small Place,* Plume/Penguin.

La Ferla, R. (2003), 'Generation E.A.: Ethnically Ambiguous,' *New York Times,* December 28, <http://www.nytimes.com/2003/12/28/fashion/>.

Le Blanc, A. (1991), 'All Part of the Act: A Hundred Years of Costume in Anglo-American Music,' *Dress in Popular Culture,* edited by P.A. Cunningham and S.V. Lab, Bowling Green, OH: Bowling Green State University Popular Press, pp. 61–73.

Lewis, T. (2004), 'From fabulous to glamorous: fashion change in hip hop culture,' paper presented at Popular Culture Association Conference, San Antonio, TX, March.

Light, Alan (ed.) (1999), *The Vibe History of Hip Hop,* New York: Three Rivers Press.

McGregor, T. (1998), *The Source,* January.

Mendes, V. and A. De La Haye (1999), *20th Century Fashion,* London: Thames and Hudson.

Mercer, K. (1990), 'Black Hair/Style Politics,' *Out There: Marginalization and Contemporary Cultures,* Cambridge: MIT Press and New York: The New Museum of Contemporary Art.

Mitchell, T. (ed.) (2001), *Global Noise: Rap and Hip-Hop Outside the USA,* Middletown, CT: Wesleyan University Press.

Morgan, J. (1999), *When Chickenheads Come Home to Roost,* New York: Touchstone.

Negron-Muntaner, F. (2002), 'Barbie's hair – selling out Puerto Rican identity in the global market,' *Latino Popular Culture,* edited by M. Habell-Pallán and M. Romero, New York: New York University Press: 38–60.

Norment, L. (1990), 'Black beauty is in: from beauty queens to fashion magazines, women of color reign supreme,' *Ebony* 45, September.

Nunley, J.W. (1987), *Moving with the Face of the Devil – Art and Politics in Urban West Africa,* Urbana and Chicago: University of Illinois Press.

Paniccioli, E. (2001), *Back in the Days,* New York: PowerHouse Books.

Rivera, R. (2002), 'Hip hop and New York Puerto Ricans,' *Latino – A Popular*

Culture, edited by M. Habell-Pallán and M. Romero, New York: New York University Press: 127–43.

Rose, T. (1994), *Black Noise Rap Music and Black Culture in Contemporary America,* Middletown, CT: Wesleyan University Press.

Rozhon, T. (2003), 'Can Urban Fashion Be Def in Des Moines,' *New York Times,* August 24.

Rubenstein, R. (2001), *Dress Codes – Meaning and Messages in American Culture*, Westview Press.

Sanchez-Tranquilino, M. and J. Tagg, (1992), 'The pachuco's flayed hide: mobility, identity, and buenas garras,' *Cultural Studies*, edited by L. Grossberg, C. Nelson and P. Treichler, New York: Routledge: 556–70.

Talley, A.L. (2002), 'In the house,' *Vogue*, November: 176–96.

The Freshest Kids – A History of the b-boy (2002), DVD, QD3 Entertainment, Color.

Through the Years of Hip-hop, Vol. 1 – Graffiti (2001), DVD, Rap Entertainment Prod. Karunaratne, M. Color.

Verán, C. (1998), *Source* January.

Vibe Hip Hop Divas (2001), New York: Three Rivers Press.

Wildstyle (1997), VHS, Los Angeles: Rhino Home Video, Color.

Yee, L. and F. Sirmans (2001), *One Planet under a Groove: Hip Hop and Contemporary Art* (exhibition catalog), The Bronx Museum of the Arts.